GETTING STARTED WITH
Lionel® Trains
Your Introduction to Model Railroading Fun

by Allan W. Miller

LIONEL SINCE 1900

Published by

krause
publications

700 East State Street • Iola, WI 54990-0001
715/445-2214 • FAX: 715/445-4087   www.krause.com

Please call or write for our free catalog of publications. To place an order or obtain a free catalog, please call 800-258-0929. Please use our regular business telephone 715-445-2214.

Library of Congress Catalog Number 2001088595
ISBN 0-87349-248-X

Copyright and Trademark Information:
Licensed by Lionel LLC

ACKNOWLEDGMENTS

Thanks to the following individuals and organizations for their assistance and support:

Dick Maddox, John Brady, Julie Laird, Mike Braga, Dawn Magar, Todd Wagner, and Chuck Horan at Lionel LLC assisted with all aspects of the book, ranging from content review of the manuscript to providing product support, photographs, and technical drawings.

Charles Bednarik, and his son, Ryan, constructed the project layout featured in this book. The foundation for the layout was constructed by Tony McAndrew.

Richard Kughn and Cindy Basler, of Kughn Enterprises, provided photographs of Mr. Kughn's spectacular Carail Museum layout.

Dan Veiga, owner of Star Hobby in Arnold, Maryland, provided supplies and technical support.

Jack Sommerfeld and Tom Palmer, of Sommerfeld's Trains in Butler, Wisconsin, assisted with obtaining photographs.

Ruean Holt, and her colleagues at Woodland Scenics, graciously provided a wide variety of scenery materials for the project layout.

Rob Adelman created the computer-generated track diagrams displayed in this book.

Fred Dole, Editor of *O Gauge Railroading* magazine, provided a number of inspirational photographs of Lionel layouts. Thanks to Myron Biggar, Publisher, and Barbara Saslo, Vice President and Chief Operating Officer, for permitting the use of related material from the magazine.

Additional photographs and content for the book were provided by Joe Bolton, Liz and Paul Edgar, Allen Engle, Des Landon, Dave Leonard, John and Kevin Mangan, Walter Rapp, Jim Richardson, Peter H. Riddle, Peter Vollmer, and Craig Wright.

Back cover photo:
With horns blaring, a Lionel SD-90 MAC diesel, in Union Pacific colors, passes the passenger depot on Peter Vollmer's Lionel layout. Produced in 2000 as part of its "Centennial Series," the 20-1/4 inch long SD-90 ranks as the largest diesel-electric locomotive produced by Lionel, to date.
Photo courtesy of Peter Vollmer

TABLE OF CONTENTS

Chapter 1

Why Lionel? ...and other frequently asked questions

No Christmas is truly complete without a Lionel train running beneath the tree, and this is just as true for the Roy Everett family as it is for countless others. This is the "Christmas Division" of Roy's permanent and much larger Little Lakes Line. The Christmas Division is a modular layout measuring 4 feet by 8 feet overall, with the two front corners cut at an angle to provide more floor space and to break away from the usual rectangular appearance. Roy enjoys operating vintage Lionel trains on his Christmas layout, which can handle three trains at the same time. The train on the outer loop is a Lionel set from 1941, and an earlier Lionel "Flying Yankee" passenger train can be seen on the inner loop.

• Why Lionel trains?

Lionel Electric Trains have been an important part of model railroading for more than a century. The name "Lionel" is itself synonymous with "electric trains" in the minds of many, and the trademark is an established and trusted icon in American toy making. Although ownership of Lionel trains has changed hands several times over the years, each new custodian of the trademark has benefited from, and built upon, the experience of his predecessor. The Lionel trains you buy today incorporate more than 100 years of craftsmanship and tradition—a claim that can be made by no other manufacturer of electric trains.

Lionel trains are also a great value, and the range of Lionel trains and accessories is extensive and continually growing. There's truly something for virtually every interest, need, and budget in the Lionel product line, and each item is supported by a nationwide network of authorized Lionel dealers and service stations that is unique to the industry.

• What's the difference between O gauge and O scale?

In both real railroading and model railroading, the term "gauge" refers solely to the distance between the two running rails of track. On prototype railroads in the United States, that measure is exactly four feet, eight-and-one-half inches, when measured from the top inside edge of one rail to the top inside edge of the opposite rail. In O gauge railroading—the track gauge that Lionel trains operate on—this measure is 1-1/4 inches between the two outside running rails.

"Scale" designates the proportional size of a model locomotive or car (or any other modeled item), as compared to its life-size prototype. A true O scale model of a particular locomotive, for example, would be 1/48 the size of the real-life version of that locomotive. This scale size may be designated as a fraction (1/48), or as a proportion (1:48)—both represent the same thing. O scale is one of a number of popular model railroading scales, which, when ranked from smallest to largest, include: Z, N, HO, S, O, Standard Gauge (created by Lionel), and Large Scale.

You'll often hear model railroaders use the term "O gauge" to refer to both the gauge *and* the scale of their trains. Although technically incorrect, as the above definitions clearly demonstrate, this way of describing the trains has come into such common use that it's unlikely to change. Nevertheless, if you want to be correct about describing these trains, you would say that you are operating O scale trains on O gauge track—*if*, in fact, they are O scale! Read on!

• OK! So what's O27 then?

Good question! As noted in the response to the above question, O scale models—those that are truly O scale—are made to exact proportions: 1/48 the size of their prototype. This means that everything—length, width, height, and all parts and appliances, are rendered in that correct 1:48 scale. However, in the three-rail O gauge world, things are often not quite that simple! Although Lionel has made and continues to make true-to-scale models, a number of Lionel trains are made to less-than-scale proportions. This is intentionally done to permit locomotives and cars to negotiate the tighter-radius curves of the most commonly used three-rail track systems.

In real-life railroading, curves are most often very broad, sometimes almost imperceptibly broad if viewed from ground level. To duplicate such curves on an O gauge layout would require vast amounts of space—much more than almost any home could possibly offer. Therefore, toy train track, such as that offered by Lionel, is made with much sharper curved sections. This allows the hobbyist to fit an entire Lionel layout on, say, a standard size sheet of plywood. Train items made to negotiate these tighter curves may themselves be made shorter or smaller than true O scale models in one or more dimensions, and these smaller locomotives and cars are commonly referred to as O27 trains.

O27 is not a scale, *per se*, because it is actually a designation for the smallest radius O gauge track curve (27 inches in diameter), but the umbrella term "O27" has come to be accepted as a way of designating many smaller-than-scale O gauge items. The "selective compression" applied to O27 items has helped to bring Lionel railroading into many thousands of homes that could otherwise not enjoy O gauge railroading if full scale proportions were consistently used.

Photo courtesy of Lionel LLC

A typical Lionel O27 starter set. The Chessie Diesel Freight Set includes everything needed to get up and running with a Lionel layout. All you need supply is the imagination and a bit of fun-filled time.

• Which track should I use? O27 gauge or O gauge?

That decision is really up to you, and one of the first things you should consider is the space that you have available for a Lionel layout. If space in your home is at a premium, and you're going to be restricted to a small layout, perhaps one as small as 4 feet by 6 feet, you might want to stick with O27 track—the type that most likely came with your starter set—and its 27 inch radius curves. The minimum radius of Lionel O gauge track is 31 inches, so that should give you some idea of the difference between the two. If space is not a problem, you may enjoy some of the added features of the O gauge track line, including lighted lamps on switch motor housings and controllers, and wider radius curved sections. Also, if you plan to purchase some of the larger Lionel locomotives and rolling stock in the future, O gauge may be the best way to go.

• Can I mix-and-match O27 and O gauge track?

Yes, you can, although it certainly is easier to simply select one type or the other, and then use that same type of track throughout your layout. Say, for example, that you have a Lionel starter set that was given to you as a holiday gift. It came with an oval of O27 track. Now you decide that you want to use O gauge track for your permanent layout. What to do? Well, one solution might be to set that O27 track aside for use under the tree each year, and to start fresh with a new assortment of O gauge track. The cost of replacing starter set sections with O gauge sections will be minimal, and you won't have to fuss with slightly modifying O27 gauge track sections to mate properly with O gauge sections.

• Why three-rail track? Don't the real railroads have two rails?

Indeed, most prototype railroads, with the exception of some light rail and other commuter lines, operate on a two-rail track system. One advantage the prototype rail lines have over most model railroads is that the power for real-life trains is most often generated within the locomotive. That being the case, they don't have to worry about electric current being passed through the rails. However, in most model railroading scales, current provided through the rails is what actually powers the locomotive's motor.

When two rails are used to provide the electricity, one of those rails is the power rail, and the other provides a return path for the current that passes through the locomotive's motor. Think of the power rail as being filled with little "+" signs as power goes from the transformer or power pack to the locomotive's motor, and think of the return rail as being filled with little "-" signs. As long as the + signs make no contact with the - signs along the path of electrical flow, everything will work just fine. On a simple oval of track, for example, at no point will a + touch or cross over a -. But, if you dismantle that oval and form a loop at one or both ends so the track curves around and rejoins itself at some point, the result will be what is known as a "dead short." That track configuration is called a "reversing loop," and if you're using two-rail track, this arrangement requires special wiring and control features.

Joshua Lionel Cowen, the founder of Lionel trains in 1900, wanted his trains to be as simple to set up and operate as possible, and for that reason three-rail track was chosen to avoid the more complicated electrical wiring associated with two-rail model railroading. With a three-rail system, the only "+" rail is the center rail, and it always remains the center rail no matter how you arrange the track. This being the case, no special wiring is required for reverse loops,

Jim Richardson's Lionel layout is modest in size, measuring 4 feet by 10 feet, but it nevertheless packs plenty of railroading action in the available space. A mountain in the center of a layout is not all that common, but Jim effectively uses that feature to divide the layout into separate and distinct scenes.

crossings, or any other complex track arrangements. Cowen believed that most of his customers would prefer running their trains instead of crawling beneath the layout to connect a maze of wires, and time has proven him right.

• Won't these trains require a whole lot of space if I want to set up a permanent layout?

Not really! You can build a fun-filled Lionel layout in a surprisingly small amount of space. Some layouts measuring no more than 4 feet by 6 feet feature enough trackwork for operating two trains and several operating accessories. A standard sheet (4 feet by 8 feet) of plywood also makes an excellent supporting platform for an attractive layout, and this is how a great many hobbyists get their start in O gauge railroading.

• Should I buy a starter set to begin with, or should I purchase individual components?

A starter set is generally the most economical way to get started in Lionel railroading because the cost of a complete set is usually less than the cost of each component purchased separately. Most Lionel starter sets come complete with a locomotive, freight or passenger cars, enough sections of track to form a simple oval, a transformer, the nec-

essary wires and clips to connect the transformer to the track, and documentation, including an owner's manual and warranty registration. That's really all you need to get started in Lionel railroading! Perhaps you have already been the lucky recipient of a Lionel starter set as a holiday or birthday gift. If so, you're all ready for some railroading action!

On the other hand, if you're preparing to venture into Lionel railroading on your own, your first step should be to see what starter sets are currently available, and then determine if any of these sets will satisfy your needs and interests at this early stage. You'll find starter sets in both freight and passenger configurations, and in a variety of the most popular roadnames and paint schemes. Some are powered by steam locomotives, and others are powered by diesels. The selection is large, and the choice is entirely up to you.

If you know that you want a train representing a certain railroad or particular type of locomotive, and if a model of that railroad's equipment is not available in a starter set, you may want to consider purchasing individual components. That way, you can acquire the specific locomotive and cars that appeal to you, along with enough track sections and perhaps a switch or two to fit the space you have available. You'll also need a transformer, and this would be a good time to consider purchasing one with sufficient output power to allow for future expansion of your rail empire. There's certainly nothing wrong with "custom designing" your first train set, but do be aware that you'll likely pay a bit more for the individual components.

Photo by Fred M. Dole, Editor, O Gauge Railroading magazine

Dick Foster's spectacular layout provides a splendid example of what can be achieved when Lionel trains and accessories are combined with a lot of imagination. Such a layout does not materialize overnight, of course, but with careful planning and a willingness to devote the necessary time, effort, and resources to the hobby, even a small Lionel layout has the potential to expand into a rail empire like the one Dick has created.

• What happens if my train needs to be repaired?

Lionel has a nationwide network of authorized service centers that are qualified to handle a great many of the repairs that might be needed on either new or older Lionel trains. You can locate the authorized service center nearest you by checking the Yellow Pages of your local phone directory; referring to the list of authorized dealers that came with your starter set; or by contacting Lionel LLC either by mail, phone, or on-line via the Lionel Web site on the Internet (www.lionel.com). You'll find the contact addresses and related information in Appendix C of this book (see page 121).

Repairs that can't be handled by an authorized service station are attended to by the Lionel Main Service Department, at the firm's headquarters in Michigan. This facility has state-of-the-art equipment and skilled technicians, supported by a full inventory of components and parts. If you experience a problem with a Lionel product, your best course of action is to take it to an authorized service center in your area, if one is available. If they can't make the repairs there, they'll normally send the item to the Michigan facility.

• I have some old Lionel trains that were given to me. Will these trains work with the newer Lionel trains?

Yes! There has been no planned obsolescence on the Lionel Lines for a great many years. Any of the earlier Lionel O gauge trains that were intended to operate off AC track power will perform just fine with today's Lionel track and transformers. Do be sure to properly clean and lubricate those older items before placing them into service, however, because lubricants tend to dry out, leak, or evaporate over prolonged periods of storage. You'll find more information on this subject in Chapter 12 of this book (see page 110).

• Will locomotives and cars made by other manufacturers work on Lionel track, and mix with Lionel products?

Yes! Any trains made to operate on O or O27 gauge three-rail track will operate properly on Lionel track with power provided by conventional Lionel transformers. Certain sound features on locomotives made by other manufacturers may require a separate activation button, but the trains will operate properly in all other respects.

Photo courtesy of Kughn Enterprises

A stunning amusement park scene on Richard Kughn's breathtaking Carail Museum layout. Kughn was the owner of Lionel Trains, Inc. from 1985 to 1995, and he continues to be one of the principals involved with the current Lionel LLC. The Carail layout features the finest of Lionel's early and more recent Standard Gauge trains, which operate on a track gauge measuring 2-1/8 inches between the running rails.

• How often will I need to lubricate my locomotives?

It's a good idea to clean and lubricate your Lionel trains after every 25 hours or so of operation. This routine operator maintenance—details of which are covered in the owner's manual packaged with each locomotive or set—will assure that your equipment lasts a lifetime. A great many Lionel trains operating today are nearly a century old, and with proper care they will likely perform well into the next century. Cleaning and lubrication requires only a few minutes of your time, and is usually accomplished without any major disassembly, aside from possibly removing the locomotive's shell. The Lionel Lubrication/Maintenance Kit contains the items you'll need. More cleaning and maintenance tips are provided in Chapter 12.

• Why do I often hear O gauge trains referred to as "tinplate"?

For a great many years, Lionel track has been made of steel that is coated with a tin plating to prevent rust. Steel is used rather than brass, aluminum, nickel silver, stainless steel, or some other metal because of its high iron content. Although other manufacturers of track products commonly use these other metals for their track systems, Lionel has stayed with tin-plated steel because the magnetic properties of the high iron content are needed for the Magne-Traction feature of many Lionel locomotives to perform most effectively. Magne-Traction involves magnetized axles fitted on some locomotives to increase the tractive effort. You can tell if a Lionel locomotive has Magne-Traction by simply placing it on a loose section of track, and then lifting the locomotive. If the track sticks to the wheels, you have a Magne-Traction equipped locomotive!

Over time, the term "tinplate" came to be associated not only with the track system, but also with the trains that operate on such track. Indeed, in the early years of Lionel trains, the locomotives and cars themselves were often made of sheet metal that was either painted or lithographed, so the term "tinplate" was very nearly an appropriate description for these items. Today, most toy electric trains are made of die-cast metal, formed brass, or molded plastic, but the "tinplate" designation is nevertheless loosely applied to nearly all trains that operate on three-rail track.

• What is "Hi-rail" model railroading?

Hi-railers are those model railroaders who choose to make their three-rail layouts as realistic as possible, despite the fact that their trains operate on three-rail track. This often involves scale-size or close-to-scale equipment that may be custom decorated or weathered to look more realistic; layout scenery that is as complete and highly detailed as possible; and accessories that are properly scaled and conform to the overall theme of the layout. You'll learn more about "theme" development in Chapter 7. Even the track-

work on a true Hi-rail layout is treated to look as realistic as possible, with the use of a ballasted roadbed embankment, realistic ties, and rails that are painted to look like rust-coated prototype rails.

If "serious" model railroading appeals to you, you may want to explore the world of Hi-rail modeling. You'll find contacts and sources of information in Appendix C.

• The terms "prewar," postwar," and "modern era" are often used in describing Lionel trains. What do these terms mean, and why are they used?

These are the terms most often used by collectors of Lionel trains to describe specific production eras in the long history of Lionel trains.

"Prewar" refers to the period from 1900 to 1942, and the formative era of Lionel production when Lionel trains were produced by the Lionel Manufacturing Company and The Lionel Corporation. There was no train production during the war years, because Lionel was actively involved in producing items for the nation's defense.

The term "Postwar" is applied to the years between 1945 and 1969, when The Lionel Corporation experienced what was, to that time, it's greatest era of growth and prosperity. The Lionel Corporation ceased production of electric trains in 1969, when the train line was acquired by the food giant, General Mills.

The period from 1970 to the present is referred to as the "Modern Era" of Lionel trains. The Lionel trademark changed ownership several times in the Modern Era—first from General Mills and its Model Products Corporation (MPC) and Fundimensions groups; then, in 1985, to the hands of Detroit real estate mogul and avid Lionel enthusiast Richard Kughn (it was called Lionel Trains, Incorporated during this time); and subsequently to the current owners, Wellspring Associates, which produces the trains under the Lionel LLC name. Richard Kughn and rock singer Neil Young, another avid Lionel enthusiast, retain minority interests in Lionel LLC.

Now that Lionel trains are into their second century, it's likely that the collecting community will come up with yet another term now to describe the new millennium of Lionel production.

• Can I run more than one train on the same track?

Sure you can! There are actually a couple of ways that you can operate more than one train on the same track. If you're using conventional Lionel transformers, you can form "blocks" along the line to electrically isolate one section of track from the section ahead of or behind it. One train can be running in one or more of these blocks, and a second train can be operating in blocks not reserved for the first train. The procedure for creating insulated blocks is described in more detail in Chapter 5 (see page 35).

An even easier way to operate two or more trains on the same track is to use the Lionel TrainMaster Command Control system (TMCC) to control all of the action on your layout. TMCC uses electronic signals, carried through the rails, to issue instructions to each locomotive equipped for TMCC control. Each locomotive has its own "address" so you can control its functions independently, regardless of where it is operating on the layout. TMCC is explained in more detail in Chapter 6 (see page 47).

• Where should I buy my Lionel trains?

If there's an authorized Lionel dealer in your area, you're best bet is to purchase your train items at that establishment. There are distinct advantages to supporting a local dealer. For one thing, he or she has a vested interest in making you a satisfied customer, because then you're apt to return to the establishment time and again for items you'll want and need as your layout expands. Also, authorized dealerships are best equipped to service what they sell. If you have questions about product availability, the operation of a particular item, or are having trouble getting something to work properly, these folks can answer your questions and assist you with needed repairs.

Mail ordering Lionel trains is another alternative, particularly if you live in an area where there are no authorized Lionel dealers. You'll find a number of these businesses advertised in hobby periodicals such as *O Gauge Railroading* magazine and *Classic Toy Trains* magazine. Regardless of whether you place your order by phone, fax, e-mail, or letter, make sure that you know exactly what you are ordering, and how much you will be paying. Be sure to verify that the dealer is an authorized Lionel dealer; otherwise the Lionel warranty will not be valid. Also determine, in advance, what the firm's return policy is, and see if there is any restocking fee charged. Remember, too, that most mail order firms do not provide service for the items they sell. If something is amiss, you'll need to rely on a local Authorized Service Center or the Service Department at Lionel LLC.

Other sources for Lionel trains include train shows, auctions (both live and on-line), and individual sellers who may advertise in your local newspaper or in a magazine. Be aware, though, that the Lionel warranty will often not be valid for items purchased through these sources unless the seller is an authorized Lionel dealer. Also, you would be well advised to exercise caution in buying from such places, because once the sale is concluded, you often have little or no recourse if something goes wrong, or if you aren't fully satisfied. If you're new to the hobby, it's a good idea to take along a more experienced hobbyist when you embark on such shopping ventures. You can usually find someone who will be willing to assist you by contacting a local dealer or club. Don't be timid about asking for advice—sharing is a large part of what this hobby is all about!

• Where can I learn more about Lionel trains?

A good place to start is the appendix section of this book! There, you'll find enough printed resources to stock a complete toy train library, along with magazines and periodicals, clubs, relevant web sites, and even a comprehensive listing of after-market suppliers who provide products that will enhance your adventure in Lionel railroading.

Another good place to learn more about Lionel trains is at your local authorized Lionel dealer's shop. In addition to the proprietor and staff at that establishment, you'll likely encounter a few customers—perhaps even neighbors—who are already involved in Lionel model railroading. And, you can learn about any O gauge clubs that may be active in your area. These local groups, along with national associations such as the Lionel Collectors Club of America (LCCA), Lionel Operating Train Society (LOTS), Toy Train Operating Society (TTOS), and the Train Collectors Association (TCA), as well as the Lionel Railroaders Club (LRRC) sponsored by Lionel LLC, are excellent ways to stay informed of developments in the hobby. Most important of all, membership often leads to some lifetime friendships!

Chapter 2

The Lionel legacy

Photo courtesy of Peter H. Riddle, from the book America's Standard Gauge Electric Trains.

A colorful and nostalgia-evoking scene on Richard and Linda Kughn's huge Carail Museum Standard Gauge layout. Richard Kughn is the former owner of Lionel Trains, Inc., and is a partner in the current Lionel LLC. Standard Gauge, the predecessor of O gauge, was the creation of Joshua Lionel Cowen, and was largely responsible for the early acceptance and success of Lionel Electric Trains.

When Joshua Lionel Cowen was once asked why he had named his toy making enterprise "Lionel," he reportedly replied: "Well, I had to name it something." But while the Lionel trademark may have started out as little more than the founder's middle name, treated almost as an afterthought, it has since grown to become the first name in toy electric trains for millions of hobbyists around the world. Today, the mere mention of "toy trains" tends to trigger the image of "Lionel" in the minds of most individuals who know anything at all about the hobby, and even in the minds of many who know nothing at all about toy trains. Indeed, no brand name in American toy making history has ever managed to attain the longevity and continued prominence of that single word: Lionel.

• A century of tradition

There are any number of factors that have led to Lionel becoming dominant in its industry and in the minds of millions of consumers, but perhaps the four most important relate to (1) the lasting quality and value of the Lionel product itself, (2) the marketing savvy of Joshua Lionel Cowen during the first half-century of the firm's existence, (3) the inspired and inspiring consumer catalogs that have never been equaled by any other toy maker, and (4) the inexorable link that Cowen himself established between toy trains and the Christmas holiday celebration.

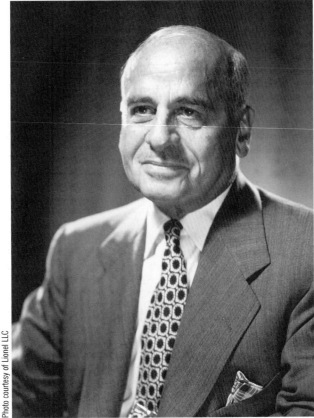

Joshua Lionel Cowen, founder and namesake of the Lionel tradition.

These factors provided the all-important cornerstones for what has since become the continuing Lionel tradition, and as you review the Highlights of Lionel History section presented at the end of this chapter, you'll see how each of

them, combined with the foresight to be innovative and the willingness to change as times in our society have themselves changed, has allowed the Lionel name to endure and prosper as a genuine American icon. That said, it's worthwhile to examine these four cornerstones in a bit more depth because they define not only the Lionel of old, but also the Lionel of today.

Product quality has been a part of the Lionel tradition from the very start. If you were fortunate enough to have the many thousands of dollars that would be needed to acquire one of the few remaining examples of Joshua Lionel Cowen's first "Electric Express" motorized gondolas, you would likely find it still capable of performing just as it did more than 100 years ago in a small New York shop window. By and large, the same can be said for the countless thousands of Lionel trains that have been produced over the intervening years. Lionel trains were built to last, and last they did—so much so that Lionel trains are often passed along from generation to generation, to be enjoyed by the original purchaser's children, grandchildren, great grandchildren, and beyond.

The value of Lionel trains extends beyond the purchase price and their worth as a collectible. Lionel trains also have tremendous educational and play value. These trains "do something," and this provides a valuable learning tool for young and old alike. The trains themselves operate, of course, but the process of setting them up and making them perform as desired teaches fundamental skills in engineering and electricity. If a more permanent layout is erected, basic construction skills are quickly acquired, and the hobbyist is also afforded opportunities to develop artistic and creative skills when adding mountains, tunnels, streams, towns, and a myriad of other scenic details to the railroad empire. If some Lionel operating accessories are added to the layout,

Fun for the entire family! The cover of the 1949 Lionel consumer catalog.

Rail-gripping Magne-Traction was a featured attraction on the cover of the Golden Anniversary Year consumer catalog in 1950.

the trains can actually be used to load and unload freight, and perform a variety of other tasks in an active, participatory environment that simulates real-world activities.

Skillful marketing and promotion efforts in the early years of Lionel history—mostly the result of Joshua Lionel Cowen's astute business sense, his keen ability to keep a finger on the pulse of consumer interests, and his uncanny ability to stay one step ahead of his competitors—led to a brand name that ranked right up there with the likes of Cadillac and Sears in terms of brand name recognition in the early 1950s.

In that period, which is often regarded as the "Golden Era" of Lionel trains, the Lionel product was virtually everywhere, particularly during the Christmas holiday season. Each new issue of the annual Lionel catalog was eagerly awaited by youngsters across the nation, and Lionel ranked at the top of nearly every boy's Santa Claus' list. Enhancing the lure, the trains could be seen in action on display layouts in virtually every major department store, hardware store, and toy shop. Cowen insisted that Lionel trains be properly displayed in stores, and that they be seen operating on these layouts, many of which were constructed by

Everything a young Lionel engineer could wish for! Mighty steam-powered freights and gleaming diesel-powered passenger trains on the cover of the 1951 consumer catalog.

Perhaps the most popular Lionel catalog cover of all time was this colorful and dynamic presentation from 1952.

Lionel and shipped to individual retailers. A manual was also published to instruct salesmen on the best ways to sell Lionel trains.

Lionel also saturated the airwaves with radio advertising and, as television began to appear in living rooms across the United States, the message was spread via that new medium. Even the Sunday comic pages of newspapers carried bold and colorful advertisements proclaiming the advantages of Lionel trains. Similar ads also appeared in national publications such as *Look*, *LIFE*, *Popular Science*, and *Boy's Life*. It can truthfully be said that Lionel visibility was ever-present at this important juncture in the firm's history.

Lionel consumer catalogs merit special "cornerstone" status simply because there has never been anything quite like them in the annals of toy making, and because they inspired dreams that, if not realized in one's youth, would later be fulfilled when boys became men with families of their own. These renowned "wish books" rank as the finest and most successful of all Lionel marketing and promotional tools, with the period of the late 1940s and early 1950s being regarded by many as the finest hour for Lionel in terms of its ability to use skillfully created catalog artwork to spark the active imaginations of countless millions of young boys and girls. In 1950 alone, more than a million Lionel catalogs were printed and distributed to prospective young Lionel engineers.

During this period, the Lionel magic was displayed on the cover and inside pages of every new catalog, where beautifully drawn Lionel trains could be seen performing "real life" work against a variety of backgrounds representing different seasons, different railside environments, and different geographical locations. These catalog images inspired dreams of travel and adventure in many young minds, and when they eventually became older and more settled minds, the dreams were still there and capable of

being realized, at least in part, because Lionel trains were still there, as well.

The catalogs have changed over the years, and for the most part product photography has replaced the meticulous drawings. But the products themselves are still with us— there are even more of them and they are often bigger, better, and equipped with more features than their predecessors. This, in large measure, is what helps to keep the fascination with Lionel trains alive and growing.

Lionel trains became inseparably linked to the Christmas holiday season thanks, once again, to the insightful efforts of Joshua Lionel Cowen. Recognizing that many families adorned the base of their Christmas trees not only with miniature nativity scenes, but often enough with miniature villages, ponds, figures, and such, Cowen saw a splendid opportunity to combine the traditional oval of Lionel track with these made-to-fit surroundings. Starting in the early days, when large Standard Gauge trains carried the banner of the Lionel line, and continuing even to the present, the word was spread that no Christmas tree was truly complete without a Lionel train circling the base. Even commercial establishments recognize this fact, and you continue to see Lionel trains performing their seemingly endless journeys in window displays, in television commercials, in motion pictures, and just about any place where the American Christmas tradition is symbolized. When Joshua Lionel Cowen passed away in September 1965, *The New York Times* made it a point to observe that this man had made Lionel "the third wing of Christmas, along with the evergreen tree and Santa Claus."

• *Trains for the ages, and for all ages*

The mortar that holds these four cornerstones and the remainder of the foundation together is a tradition of Lionel railroading inspired by continued customer loyalty to a brand that endures even to this day. Generations of American families were exposed to, and grew up with, Lionel trains. Today, these trains are preserved and perpetuated in a manner quite unlike most other playthings, which are generally used and then discarded, sold in a garage sale, or even given away. Not so with Lionel! Because consumers perceived these trains as quality items when they were initially purchased or received, and because often they were subsequently treated as valued family heirlooms, the trains were more carefully protected than most toys, and they were cared for lovingly. Even if they were forgotten for a few years as youngsters went off to college and then started careers and families of their own, it was usually only a matter of time before those older Lionel trains were discovered in attics or closets, and given new life by a whole new generation of enthusiasts.

At the same time, these earlier products tended to stimulate the market for newer Lionel items. The need for a few additional track sections or the search to replace a missing Lockon would often enough lead to a local hobby shop. Once there, this new generation member of the extended Lionel family was apt to spot those familiar orange-and-blue Lionel boxes. "Gee! I didn't realize that they still made those trains!" is an exclamation heard by many hobby store proprietors over the years. Once these surprised customers saw the current array of trains and accessories, it was likely they would leave the store with a crisp, new orange-and-blue boxed treasure in hand. Thus, the hobby has continued to grow, backed by a trademark that has come to be associated with quality, durability, longevity, and value.

Although they were originally intended as a plaything for young boys, Lionel trains have always transcended both gender and generations. Even in the earliest days of the firm's history, Lionel trains were enjoyed as much by fathers as by sons, and the resources to buy the trains frequently came only with mom's blessing. Early Lionel advertising, which was directed primarily at boys, gradually gave way to ads that emphasized the bonding between father and son

The 1953 Lionel catalog cover depicted four of the most renowned steam and diesel locomotives of the postwar era.

Photo courtesy of Lionel LLC

The cover of the 1954 consumer catalog featured a father and his son—the traditional Lionel "team"—and a head-on view of four of the greatest Lionel locomotives of that year.

that their Lionel relationship made possible. The truth be told, Lionel worked an effective "guilt trip" on fathers across the nation, making them feel that by failing to provide their son with a Lionel train, they were also neglecting their parental responsibility to form a nurturing and lasting friendship with their boy.

Over time, moms and daughters were also introduced into the promotional campaigns, with mother and little sister first appearing on the consumer catalog cover in 1949. Thereafter, mom and sis made regular appearances in Lionel posters, catalogs, and other advertising material. An attempt was even made to create a special train for little girls in 1957—a Girl's Train headed by a pink locomotive pulling

Diesels galore in '54! An array of Lionel diesel locomotives was displayed inside that year's catalog.

pastel freight cars, and controlled by a white transformer—but it was a resounding flop because Lionel learned too late that little girls preferred to play with the same trains that appealed to little boys. Nevertheless, Lionel executives eventually recognized that Lionel railroading is a rewarding hobby for *every* member of the family, and it remains that way to this day.

A great many of the early Lionel enthusiasts, or the sons and daughters of these early fans, have also gone on to become collectors of Lionel trains, and this, too, has helped to perpetuate interest in these toys. There have always been collectors of Lionel trains, dating back to before the midpoint of the twentieth century, but the real boom in toy train collecting coincided most closely with the life cycle of post-World War II "baby boomers." These were the folks—vast in number—who played with Lionel trains in their youth, and these were the folks who, years later, would seek to relive a part of those innocent and happy days. Nostalgia plays a very important part in the continuing Lionel trains saga. A longing to recapture childhood memories, coupled with a desire to acquire the objects that may have proved to be elusive during that childhood, is what largely drives the passion for collecting. Lionel has long been regarded as one

of the preeminent collectible toys, and today many thousands of collectors around the world conduct exhaustive searches for that "one more item" that will make their collection complete.

But regardless of one's age, and regardless of whether one intends to buy a Lionel train to place around the Christmas tree, operate on a beautifully constructed and highly detailed layout, or add to a colorful wall display of prized collectibles, there's something for everyone in the Lionel line—past, present, and future. Of course, that's something *you* already know, because you have elected to read a book about this very subject!

We've only managed to touch on a few of the more significant highlights of the Lionel legacy in this chapter, and in the "Highlights in a Century of Lionel Trains" sidebar that follows. Entire *sets* of books could be written on the subject of Lionel and its product line. Indeed, more than a few such books have been written. In fact, more than 100 published references, guides, and manuals are available to those seeking more detailed information about virtually any aspect of this history-making toy maker and its products. You'll find many of them listed in Appendix A (see page 116).

Santa Fe — the red streak of the golden prairies

Bigger than life! The always-popular Santa Fe F3 is depicted streaking through a realistic environment in the 1954 catalog.

The following timeline recounts 100 years of Lionel history, in an admittedly abbreviated form. The list is by no means complete, but it nevertheless highlights some of the most significant dates and events in the long, colorful, and successful tenure of a fascinating American enterprise that has brought countless hours of joy to many millions of lives.

HIGHLIGHTS IN A CENTURY OF LIONEL TRAINS
PREWAR LIONEL

1900

Twenty-two-year-old Joshua Lionel Cowen receives a U.S. Navy contract to develop an explosives detonator, and launches a business known as the Lionel Manufacturing Company in a second-story loft at 24-26 Murray St., in New York City. He subsequently tries his hand at manufacturing electric fans, but this enterprise meets with little success because fans are such a seasonal item.

1901

Cowen seeks an alternative use for his electric fan motor, and develops a motorized gondola that runs on two-rail track for New York toy and novelty shop owner Robert Ingersoll. In concept, the ever-circling gondola is supposed to attract attention to the window display and help to sell more goods. However, the idea backfires because customers want to buy the track-mounted motorized gondola, and not the other merchandise. Cowen soon finds himself in the toy train business, and the No. 200 "Electric Express," running on 2-7/8 inch track, becomes the first Lionel Electric Train.

1902

The first Lionel catalog to feature trains makes its debut, and the product line expands to include the "City Hall Park" trolley, along with the firm's first accessory: A bridge. Battery power drives all of the early Lionel trains.

1903

Lionel introduces its first locomotive—a model of a B&O electric-outline locomotive. A crane car that children can actually use to lift objects is also introduced, and Cowen quickly realizes that youngsters are attracted to action cars and accessories. From this point on, cars and accessories that "do something" become an important staple in the Lionel lineup.

1906

Lionel introduces "Standard Gauge" trains, which run on three-rail track with the outer rails spaced 2-1/8 inches apart. Cowen elects to use three rails because this greatly simplifies wiring a train layout. The trains are called "Standard" simply because Cowen *said* they were standard! It was a shrewd marketing tactic that works very well, and consumers and competitors alike buy into the scheme. The new Lionel trains are now powered by an electric transformer, replacing battery power.

1912

Lionel introduces the Multi-Volt transformer, equipped with a rheostat to control locomotive speed.

1915

Lionel introduces its first O gauge locomotive—a model based on a New York Central electric-outline prototype. Three-rail O gauge track also makes its debut.

1917

When the U.S. enters World War I, Lionel produces equipment for the U.S. Navy and Signal Corps. An armored military toy train is also produced. Lionel moves its manufacturing plant to Irvington, New Jersey.

1918

The Lionel Manufacturing Company becomes The Lionel Corporation, with Joshua Lionel Cowen as its president.

1920

Lionel begins is extensive advertising blitz in newspapers, magazines, and the Sunday comics section, and annual sales exceed $1 million for the first time.

1925

Sales top $2 million in the silver anniversary year.

1927

Lionel opens its renowned New York City Showroom—a magnet for Lionel train enthusiasts for years to come.

1928

Lionel joins with American Flyer and Dorfan to purchase a primary competitor—The IVES Manufacturing Company—for the sum of $73,000.

1929

Lionel buys-out American Flyer's interest in IVES, thereby given Lionel sole access to the coveted (and patented) sequential reversing unit for toy trains that Cowen had long wanted. The start of the Great Depression dashes hopes for the best holiday sales ever.

1934

A Mickey Mouse wind-up handcar, costing just $1, helps Lionel to survive the impact of the Great Depression. Some 253,000 of the handcars are sold, providing Lionel with a much-needed infusion of cash. Additional credit for saving Lionel from disaster also goes to the firm's model of the Union Pacific M-10000 streamliner, which gains much consumer acceptance and acclaim.

1935

Lionel introduces a remotely activated air whistle, mounted in the steam locomotive's tender. The whistle responds to a brief pulse of DC current sent through the rails. The longest-lived operating accessory in the Lionel line is also introduced: The Automatic Gateman, which is still cataloged to the present day.

1937

Lionel introduces the 700E Hudson locomotive—the first true-to-scale model ever produced by the firm, and the first to be mass-produced O scale model.

1939

Production of Lionel Standard Gauge trains ceases.

1942

Lionel stops production of toy trains and assists the U.S. war effort during World War II. The firm once again produces instruments for the Navy, just as it had done during World War I. No Lionel catalog is published in 1943 and 1944, and only the hard-to-assemble Lionel Paper Train is available to satisfy consumer demand.

1944

Although no new toy trains are being produced, Lionel perfects the magnetic knuckle-coupler, and prepares to outfit all of its postwar trains with this item. Lionel trains made more than half a century later will all couple reliably with trains equipped with this earliest knuckle-coupler.

POSTWAR LIONEL

1945

Lionel resumes production of electric trains, on a limited and rushed basis, just in time for the 1945 Christmas holiday season.

1946

Postwar production begins in full. Smoke is added to Lionel steamers. A paper shortage forces Lionel to print its 1946 catalog as a 16-page ad insert in *Liberty* magazine. Everything in the product line sells very well.

1947

Lionel introduces a model of the Pennsylvania Railroad's distinctive GG1 electric-outline locomotive. The model can actually operate off overhead catenary lines, just like the prototype. The most famous Lionel operating car, the Operating Milk Car, also enters the market this year.

1948

Working with the full cooperation of General Motors, Lionel introduces the striking F3 diesel locomotive. The Santa Fe version of this locomotive will go on to become the best-selling Lionel locomotive of all time. Lionel also introduces its now-famous ZW Transformer, which can control up to four trains with 250 (and ultimately 275) watts of power.

1950

The Golden Anniversary of Lionel trains. Magne-Traction, which enhances tractive effort, pulling power, and rail grip at high speeds by magnetizing the axles and wheels of locomotives, is introduced. More than one million Lionel catalogs are scooped-up by eager consumers.

1953

The best sales year for Lionel in its 53-year history—$32.9 million—help to make Lionel the world's number one toy maker.

1954

Lionel introduces the #50 Gang Car—the first in its long line of small and very popular motorized units.

1957

The last profitable year for the original Lionel Corporation. Lionel introduces a pastel-colored Girl's Train, led by a pink locomotive. It is an immediate flop, because girls prefer the same trains that boys have. The Girl's Train later becomes a prized and valuable collectible. Lionel announces an HO scale line of trains, which enters the marketplace too late to effectively compete with more established brands in that scale.

1958

Lionel, along with the United States and the Soviet Union, enters the space race following the Soviet launch of Sputnik by creating the first items in what will be an extensive line of space and military locomotives, cars, and accessories. Joshua Lionel Cowen retires, and his son, Lawrence, assumes control of Lionel.

1959

Joshua Lionel Cowen and son Lawrence sell their shares of Lionel stock to an investment group headed by McCarthy-era figure Roy Cohn. This marks the end of Cowen family involvement in Lionel.

1960s

Train sales continue to plummet, as television and other leisure-time distractions divert attention from toy electric trains. Lionel tries its hand at alternative product lines such as science kits and slot cars, but nothing seems to work.

1965

Joshua Lionel Cowen dies at his Palm Beach, Florida, home at the age of 88. He is buried in a New York cemetery, within view of the tracks of the Long Island Railroad.

1967

For the first time since the war years, Lionel offers no new catalog. Lionel acquires the failing American Flyer line of trains manufactured by the A.C. Gilbert Company. Subsequently, Lionel files for bankruptcy protection.

1969

The Lionel Corporation sells its toy train line to cereal giant General Mills, which continues to manufacture and sell Lionel trains under its Model Products Corporation (MPC) and Fundimensions banners.

MODERN-ERA LIONEL

1970

General Mills establishes the Lionel train production facility in Mt. Clemens, Michigan.

1982

Lionel begins to use simple and reliable can motors in some of its locomotives, replacing the long-standing open-frame motors. Train production is relocated to a factory in Mexico; then quickly moved back to Mt. Clemens when quality control becomes an issue.

1985

Real estate developer and avid Lionel collector Richard Kughn buys Lionel from General Mills, and immediately begins innovative product improvements. Kughn later reintroduces Standard Gauge trains to the Lionel product lineup. The new firm is named Lionel Trains, Incorporated.

1989

Lionel RailSounds is introduced, marking a significant improvement in locomotive sound systems for toy trains. A scale model of the Reading Railroad T-1-class 4-8-4 Northern locomotive is released. Using all-new tooling, this is largest Lionel steam locomotive produced as of this date.

1994

Lionel forms a partnership with LionTech, founded by rock singer and Lionel enthusiast Neil Young, and introduces TrainMaster Command Control—a high-tech wireless command control system which affords full operator control of trains away from a stationary transformer or control panel.

1995

Richard Kughn sells Lionel Trains Inc. to the Wellspring Associates investment group, and the firm's name becomes Lionel LLC.

1997

Lionel LLC initiates the Century Club to commemorate the brand's first 100 years. Five of the most popular Lionel locomotives from the postwar period are reissued for sale to club members.

1999

Lionel enhances its presence in cyberspace, as its flashy *www.lionel.com* Web site is launched.

2000

Lionel celebrates its 100th year as a continuing enterprise by introducing its largest and most detailed steam locomotive ever—a model of the Union Pacific 4-6-6-4 Challenger.

Chapter 3

Today's Lionel

Photo courtesy of Lionel LLC

A Lionel Shay locomotive—the first geared-type locomotive ever offered by Lionel—hauls its load of log cars through a beautifully executed scenic setting. The Shay, along with other types of geared locomotives, was used extensively in logging and mining operations throughout the early years of the twentieth century due to its ability to negotiate tight curves and steep grades.

To paraphrase a well-known car manufacturer's slogan: These are not your father's, grandfather's, or even great grandfather's Lionel trains! Today's Lionel trains benefit from all of the improvements in manufacturing and technology that have shaken and reshaped nearly every industry and business enterprise in recent years. You'll find Lionel trains made today that emulate the real thing in just about every respect, short of blackening your ceiling with coal dust or filling the train room with the aroma of diesel fuel.

Innovation, action, color, reliability, and durability are key words that describe the ever-expanding Lionel lineup of trains and accessories. Priced to fit virtually every budget, many of today's Lionel trains also come with features that could only be dreamed of relatively few years ago, such as glowing fireboxes on steamers, Odyssey System speed control, true-to-life digitally mastered locomotive sounds, CrewTalk and TowerCom announcements, and engineer and fireman figures in the cabs, and others.

• Motive power

In the realm of toy and model trains, there's little disputing that locomotives retain "most favored" status in the eyes of the majority of operators and collectors. Although a locomotive by itself does not constitute a train, no train can be complete without a locomotive, and these are, after all, the items that bring our passenger and freight trains to life. So it's probably understandable that locomotives attract and hold the attention of the greatest number of hobbyists as they eagerly await the next new model to add to their railroad's growing roster. The truth be known, a good many model railroaders actually have more locomotives in their inventory than they do freight and passenger cars—a situation opposite of what exists on the real railroads.

Given their popularity and overall importance in the eyes of most hobbyists, it's worth discussing today's Lionel locomotives in some detail to explain what's currently avail-

The Chief Engineer at today's Lionel LLC is President and Chief Operating Office, Richard N. Maddox (left). Other principals with the firm are recording artist Neil Young (center), whose LionTech firm developed the innovative TrainMaster Control System, and Richard Kughn (right), former owner of Lionel Trains, Inc.

able, and to address the questions and concerns that some-one new to the hobby may have when they are buying their first locomotive, regardless of whether it is part of a set or a separate purchase item.

To start, there are three general types of prototype loco-motive models to choose from, as determined by the source of power used to drive the locomotive's wheels. Lionel offers examples of all three types: Steam, diesel-electric, and electric-outline.

Steam locomotives, which continue to rank as favorites among a majority of hobbyists even though very few full-size steamers are seen these days, are powered by burning wood, coal, or oil to heat water, which, in turn, boils to gen-erate steam. In recent years, Lionel has produced models of each of these types of steam locomotives, ranging from the diminutive 4-4-0 American-type wood-burning locomotives most often associated with the Old West and the Civil War era, through a large variety of coal-fired locomotives, and even a few oil burners, such as the Southern Pacific 4-4-2 Atlantic and 2-8-0 Consolidation locomotives.

Diesel-electrics are the type of locomotives most com-monly seen on today's railroads. Although generally referred to simply as "diesels," they are indeed diesel-electrics because diesel motors are used to turn generators that pro-vide the current needed to drive electric traction motors, which actually power the wheels. Lionel has produced a wide variety of diesel-electrics, including early NW-2 switchers, the Fairbanks-Morse Trainmaster, the renowned F3 streamlined units, the massive SD-90 MAC powerhouses of today's rail lines, and virtually everything in between.

This New York Central RS-11 diesel locomotive provides a fine example of the level of accurate detail seen on today's Lionel motive power. The RS-11 features the Odyssey System for speed control, and is equipped with the TrainMaster Command Control System and the RailSounds sound system.

This colorful and nicely detailed 4-6-4 Atlantic Coast Line steamer is capable of operating on O27 curves.

A set of Rio Grande F3 diesels, with one powered unit and one non-powered unit. These larger diesels are designed for operation on Lionel O gauge (O31 or wider) curves.

Electric-outline locomotives derive current for their electric traction motors directly from overhead wires or a "live" outside third-rail. Units in this category can range from small trolleys, interurban cars, and industrial switchers, to large and powerful road units such as the EF-57 Rectifier, EP-5 "Little Joe," and the best-known electric-outline locomotive of them all: The Pennsylvania Railroad's distinctive GG1.

The ever-popular GG1 locomotive of the Pennsylvania Railroad first joined the Lionel roster in 1947, and it has been offered a number of times over the intervening years.

The Virginian Rectifier locomotive provides a colorful example of heavy-duty electric-outline motive power. This Lionel model, which can negotiate O27 curves, can also be modified to operate off an overhead catenary system.

Every Lionel layout needs a trolley for Lionelville's public transportation needs. These units are self-reversing, so all that's needed for continuous operation is a stretch of track with a bumper at each end.

Lionel has also offered a good many small motorized units over the years. Some are locomotives capable of hauling a few cars, such as the Great Northern and Rio Grande Snowplows, while others, such as the various Trolleys, Handcars, and the Track Inspection Car, are self-propelled units designed for solo operations.

The #53 Rio Grande Snowplow is typical of the wide assortment of small motorized units made by Lionel over the past fifty years. The original #53 was released in 1957, and this current model is a faithful duplicate released as part of the Lionel "Postwar Celebration Series."

There truly is a locomotive for every virtually need and interest in the Lionel line. If you don't find what you're looking for among current catalog offerings, it's usually easy enough to find the item from among the offerings produced at some earlier point in the long history of Lionel trains. If you're searching for a particular item, you can often find what you're looking for by joining one of the national clubs or associations (listed in Appendix C, page 121), many of which publish buy/sell/trade/wanted lists for their membership. Another source of previously issued Lionel trains might be train shows that are held regularly in nearly all areas of the country. You can also locate many Lionel items on-line, via Internet auction sites and hobby retailer sites on the World Wide Web. Just be sure to exercise appropriate caution in any on-line transactions. Some useful tips in that regard are provided in Chapter 4 (see page 29).

The gold-plated 100th Anniversary Hudson locomotive—a fitting tribute to the most popular Lionel steam locomotive of all time, produced in commemoration of the 100th anniversary of Lionel trains.

Speaking of tips, here are a few others that you might want to consider before making that all-important, and often expensive, locomotive purchase:

➤ Although you should always feel free to acquire any locomotive that appeals to you, it makes good sense in the early stages of your hobby involvement to focus on models that best support the planned theme for your model railroad layout (see Chapter 7, page 59). You might, for example, ask yourself if steam, diesel, or electric power is most appropriate for the era you intend to model. If you choose to model U.S. prototype railroading through the 1930s, steam is a logical choice in most instances, although electric power was also seen in the later years of that period. If the period from about 1940 through the mid-1950s most appeals to you, you can select from a good variety of late steam, electric, and early diesel power. And, if you choose to model a more contemporary period in American railroading, you'll likely want to focus on the powerful diesel-electrics seen operating today.

➤ Select locomotives that will both look right and perform properly on your layout. The primary consideration in this regard involves the switches and curved areas on your layout. Smaller and shorter Lionel locomotives will operate fine on O27 *and* O gauge track, switches, and curves. Some larger locomotives (and cars, as well) require broader curves and a greater side clearance, and you may need to go with O gauge track components to handle these items. Current Lionel catalogs list the minimum curve radius required for the various locomotives and cars, so be sure to study the descriptive information before going forward with your purchase.

➤ If you are buying your locomotive from a local source, ask the dealer to test-run the locomotive for you before it leaves the store; this will ensure that everything is operating properly. Your dealer will also be able to demonstrate the various features of the locomotive, such as smoke and sounds, and show you how to use them. Ask the dealer to show you how to lubricate your locomotive, as well. Most will be happy to perform the simple pre-operation lubrication procedure that many model locomotives require.

• Rolling stock

When it comes to rolling stock for your trains, Lionel again has something for just about every type and era of American railroading. From nineteenth century wood-side passenger coaches, refrigerator cars, and cabooses, to contemporary Hi-Cube boxcars and Maxi-Stack well cars, you're sure to find rolling stock items that will meet your personal railroading needs.

There are freight cars available in the Lionel line for virtually every type of industry and commodity.

➤ Boxcars, which are by far the most common type of freight car, can be used to haul virtually any type of freight that needs to be protected from exposure to the elements.

➤ Hoppers, gondolas, and ore cars can be used to transport coal, iron ore, gravel, grain, scrap metal, trash, and many similar loads.

➤ Refrigerator cars, which are essentially insulated boxcars fitted with cooling units, transport dairy products, produce, meat, and anything else that needs to be kept at a consistently cool temperature.

➤ Tank cars are available to handle liquids and gases of all types.

➤ Stock cars will safely transport your cattle, pigs, chickens, sheep, and other animals to market.

➤ Flat cars carry loads of steel pipes and beams, lumber, containers, trucks and other vehicles, and a wide variety of oversize loads, such as large generators and other machinery.

➤ Of course, we can't forget the caboose—a special type of rolling stock that lives on in the hearts of railroaders, even though very few real-life versions are seen on the prototype roads today. Lionel has made models of virtually every type of caboose, including early cupola, center-cupola, bay window, extended-vision, Pennsy N5C-type, Southern Pacific-type, bobber, transfer, work, and maintenance cabooses.

Chances are good that if you see a particular type of rolling stock operating on a railroad that runs through your hometown, or have seen an interesting freight or passenger car in a railroading book or magazine that you've been reading, you'll be able to find a similar O gauge example of that car in one of the Lionel catalogs published over the years.

A striking red, white, and blue Norfolk & Western hopper car.

Short ore cars are perfect for smaller layouts.

A Delaware & Hudson gondola car, complete with scrap load.

Tank cars are a favorite with both operators and collectors of Lionel trains. Many tank cars, such as this Ethyl single-dome tanker, are adorned with colorful graphics.

No self-respecting train is really complete without a caboose, even though the prototype railroads seldom use them anymore. Cabooses are also a very popular item with Lionel collectors.

Lionel passenger cars come in three sizes: O27 cars for smaller layouts with tighter curves; longer and larger O gauge cars that are designed for O31 and wider radius curves; and O scale cars that are true-to-length replicas of real passenger cars. Classified by car types, the assortment includes heavyweight (Madison) steel-side cars from the pre-streamliner days of railroading, and both smooth- and fluted-side streamline cars from the more contemporary era. Depending on the specific type of car offered, you'll find coaches, Pullman cars, baggage cars, combines, diners,

dome cars, and observation cars—all made in a wide variety of roadnames and markings. A series of nineteenth century passenger coaches and baggage cars is also offered to complement the various "General" (4-4-0 American-type) locomotives that Lionel has produced over the years.

Most Lionel passenger cars, regardless of size or type, feature interior illumination. Many also feature passenger silhouettes in the windows. There's no doubt that when the inhabitants of Lionelville need to travel for business or pleasure, there will always be space available aboard a sturdy and reliable Lionel-built passenger car!

• Operating Cars

Joshua Lionel Cowen was a firm believer that electric trains should do far more than just run around in circles. It's not certain that he ever claimed credit for creating the term "play value," but he certainly would have been entitled to make that claim. Not satisfied to simply equip a train with a variety of colorful cars, Cowen wanted these cars to *do* something, and he, along with the creative inventors at Lionel, regularly dreamed-up new ways to give freight cars, in particular, a genuine purpose on a model railroad. Today, thanks to their efforts, and to the efforts of those who foster that line of thinking, a wide array of Lionel cars can load and unload goods of all types at the touch of a button. Here are just a few examples of some of the action-packed items in the long line of Lionel operating cars:

➤ A diligent worker loads milk cans onto a trackside platform from the Operating Milk Car—the most famous of all Lionel operating cars.

➤ Cattle and horses are given a chance to stretch their legs by exiting their respective Operating Cattle or Horse Cars; circling through a trackside corral; and then re-entering the car to continue on their journey.

➤ Coal can be unloaded from Lionel Operating Coal Cars in two ways: One type of car features a tilting bed that dumps coal into a trackside bin or hopper, while another type of hopper car unloads coal through doors that open on the bottom of the car.

➤ Logs and lumber loads are dumped alongside the track from Operating Dump Cars, which work in a manner similar to the tilting coal cars.

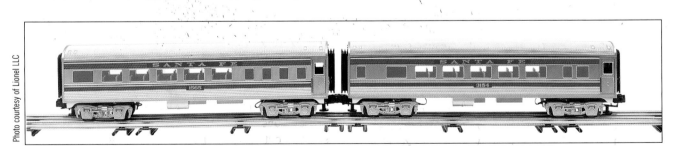

These Santa Fe streamlined passenger cars will handle O27 curves. They are sold in "2-Pack" sets, so you can quickly expand your passenger car fleet.

➤ Railway post office clerks toss their bags of mail onto the station platform from the door of a Lionel Operating Mail Car.

➤ Cops chase the bad guys and hobos around the deck of the fun-to-watch Cop & Hobo and Sheriff & Outlaw Cars (a number of popular cartoon figures engage in the same activity aboard other specialty cars of the same basic design).

➤ Military cars of all types protect Lionelville with Missile Launching Cars, Helicopter Launching Cars, Canon Boxcars, Searchlight Cars, and a variety of other military-theme rolling stock. Similar items have been produced in a line of Space Cars.

These are just a few examples of the great variety of Lionel operating cars produced over the years. Ducking giraffe cars, aquarium cars, radioactive waste cars . . . the list goes on and on! It's a sure bet that at some point you'll want to partake of some of this action.

Welcome to Lionelville!

This Alaska RR Operating Log Car doesn't just transport logs; it dumps them right at the doorstep of your lumber mill. A remote control track, sold separately, is required for operation.

The Operating Barrel Car has been a favorite item of Lionel rolling stock since the 1950s, and has been released in several different colors and roadnames. A remote control track, sold separately, is required to operate the car.

In all of model railroading, there has never been a more active and thriving metropolis than Lionelville—that mythical and magical metropolis born in the creative genius of Lionel inventors and engineers, and constructed with the imagination of millions of Lionel enthusiasts! The accessory line developed for Lionelville and its environs includes more than enough items to fill several large volumes (which, in fact, it already has), and the assortment just keeps getting bigger and better. From small highway signs to grand and glorious operating accessories of all types, Lionel accessory

offerings have been so abundant that Lionelville itself may be more aptly renamed Lionel City!

Most desirable, of course, are the renowned Lionel operating accessories. As was the case with operating cars, Joshua Lionel Cowen's attention was continually drawn to development of a full line of accessories that would give the model railroad some purpose for being. Especially high on his list were accessories that would interact with the trains. It was fine to have a car that could unload something, but what about also creating an accessory that could reload that same car so the action could continue in a cycle, rather than end with a single activity?

First offered in 1946, the Triple Action Magnet Crane is the ideal interactive accessory. Operators can pick up, move, and deposit metal loads by remote control, and from any location around the layout.

Operating water towers supply "water" to thirsty Lionel steamers, and fuel station workers attend to the needs of diesels. Laborers shuttle loads of freight and baggage around the operating freight station. Coal ramps and loaders unload and load coal, and culvert loaders and unloaders do likewise with massive pipe sections. Magnetic cranes, under full control of young and young-at-heart Lionel engineers, retrieve metal scrap from the yard and then deposit the load in a waiting gondola. The rocking arms of oil derricks and pumping stations relentlessly extract "liquid gold" from beneath the earth, and the product itself can be seen bubbling through the pipes. Sawmills magically transform uncut logs into finished lumber, and Intermodal cranes lift trailers from waiting flatcars. There really is no end to the activity in and around Lionelville, and the work continues around the clock, thanks to the illumination provided by searchlight towers, street lamps, yard lights, and the great array of illuminated structures.

The rail line itself is alive with action and illumination. Crossing signals flash and crossing gates lower as a train approaches. Block signals, semaphores, signal bridges, and dwarf signals inform Lionel engineers of conditions along the route ahead. Control tower and switch tower operators scurry about to keep things running smoothly, and the ever-present Lionel Gateman, the single most enduring and

This Shell Oil Derrick is one of a number of operating oil derricks offered by Lionel over the years. An entire oil field could easily be constructed with the wide and colorful varieties that have been released.

If the accessory is located between two parallel tracks, operators can load and unload coal with the #97 Electric Coaling Station. The original #97 was introduced in 1938, and Lionel reissued this classic accessory in 2001.

The Lionel trackside accessory line includes these handsome, and functional, single- and double-track signal bridges.

endearing item in the Lionel operating accessory lineup, faithfully emerges from his shanty and swings his lantern as each train passes.

Even accessories only remotely related to the railroad itself are alive with lights and action. Rotary beacons warn low flying aircraft, including helicopters launching from the operating heliport, while revolving radar dishes track the movements of all aircraft, both friend and foe. Animated billboards provide Lionelville's motorists with alternating displays, and they can always stop by the operating newsstand to pick up a copy of their favorite newspaper or magazine. For entertainment, the citizens of Lionelville can visit the carnival, where the operating Ferris wheel and operating carousel will provide them with a fun-filled afternoon or evening. Or, they might elect to visit the operating aquarium, which is stocked with new finds from the ocean's depths by one of the many Lionel Aquarium Cars. Along the coast, a Lionel lighthouse continually warns passing ships of dangerous shoals in their approach to Lionelville's harbor.

And this is really just a small sampling of all of the operating and non-operating accessories available to Lionel railroaders. Of course, not all are available in the current

catalog—that would make for a very large catalog indeed! But even accessories made some years ago can still be found at train shows, auctions, and at dealers who stock previously issued items. For a more complete description of the entire line, consult a current Lionel catalog and the Lionel accessory books listed in both the Postwar and Modern Era References sections of Appendix A (see page 116).

The real world is full of the hustle and bustle of commerce, industry, and the everyday actions of the citizenry, so there's no reason that your modeled world shouldn't display this same level of activity. With Lionel accessories, adding life-like action to your layout is both easy and fun.

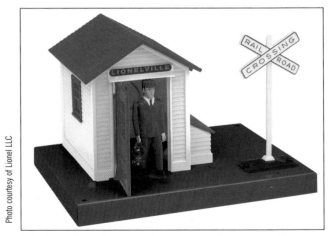

The longest-existing operating accessory in the Lionel lineup is the ever-vigilant Lionel Automatic Gateman. He's a big fellow who may intimidate the rest of Lionelville's citizenry by sheer size alone, but no Lionel layout is considered truly complete unless this dedicated and tireless worker is at his post.

Chapter 4

Getting started in Lionel railroading

Photo courtesy of Lionel LLC

The New Haven Command Control Set exemplifies one of the full-featured Lionel starter sets. This set is equipped with the Odyssey System and TrainMaster Command Control System, but it can also be operated with a conventional transformer.

Perhaps the most common form of introduction to Lionel railroading is with a Lionel starter set purchased during the holiday season for use around the Christmas tree—a tradition that has become closely linked to that event—or when a Lionel set is received as a gift on that or another occasion. If that's what sparked your interest in Lionel trains, you've joined countless thousands of others who, over many generations, have entered this fascinating hobby in a similar manner.

But regardless of whether you are still contemplating the purchase of your first set, have already done so, or have been given a Lionel set as a gift, this chapter provides a number of useful tips that will guide you in making the right selection and thoroughly enjoying your Lionel train set once you have it in hand.

• Selecting your first Lionel set

The first logical question you might ask yourself when considering the purchase of a first train set is: Why Lionel? If you have already read the first chapter of this book—Frequently Asked Questions—you'll recall that was the first question dealt with there. Still, it's worth reviewing the highlights here, and perhaps expanding on them a bit. Among the many good reasons for choosing Lionel are the following:

➤ History—Lionel trains have been around for more than a century. A study of the history of Lionel trains could easily be a hobby in itself, but what's important is that this

long tenure in electric toy train manufacturing has led to a product that is reliable, durable, and continually improved upon with the latest in technological advances.

➤ Size—Lionel O gauge trains are small enough to fit comfortably in the home without interfering with the normal living space, yet they are large enough to be easily seen, admired, handled, and enjoyed by young and old alike. They are nearly the perfect size for family model railroading activities.

➤ Durability—The fact that many Lionel trains manufactured nearly 100 years ago are still in fine running condition today attests to the lasting durability of the Lionel product line. No other electrical/mechanical toy can assert such a long and continuous history of product reliability.

➤ Ease of operation—Setting up and operating Lionel trains is both easy and fun. The distinctive Lionel three-rail track eliminates any fuss or bother over complex wiring arrangements, regardless of how you might wish to configure the trackwork on your layout.

➤ Quantity and variety—Because Lionel has been around for so many years, and in light of the fact that virtually all Lionel items produced since World War II are fully compatible with the Lionel trains being made today, you have a truly astounding assortment of items to choose from.

➤ Accessories—No other toy train maker has ever come close to matching Lionel in terms of the tremendous assortment of accessories offered over the years. These range from static items such as signs, billboards, and telephone poles to the vast array of Lionel operating cars, signals, and other accessories.

➤ Value—There is something for nearly every budget in the Lionel lineup. Best of all, your investment in the hobby can be gradually expanded in increments of just a few dollars or so, as your hobby budget permits.

➤ Collectibility—Lionel trains are prized and ever-popular collectibles. These great toys can be collected in any number of different ways, and for a variety of different reasons. As your involvement in the hobby grows, so, too, will your own collection, even if you don't consider yourself to be a collector.

➤ Educational value—Lionel trains offer an excellent entry into a hobby that can provide a rewarding educational experience for you and every member of your family. In the process of constructing a Lionel layout, you'll increase your understanding of railroad history and operations, carpentry, electricity, the art of creating scenery, and a variety of other facets that, taken together, constitute a very diverse and meaningful learning experience.

This is an impressive list of benefits, demonstrating that Lionel is, indeed, a great way to enter the model railroading hobby. After all, a good majority of today's hobbyists in all scales got their start with Lionel! In fact, many who moved on to other model railroading scales in their adult years have since returned to Lionel railroading for the simplicity, diversity, and just plain fun that it offers.

As noted earlier, if this is your first exposure to Lionel trains, the customary way to get started is with a Lionel starter set. The term "starter set" is generally applied to an assortment of components that include everything needed to assemble a basic train layout—normally in the shape of an oval—complete with a train and a power source. Typical starter sets usually include a locomotive, freight or passenger cars, enough track sections to form a complete oval, a transformer, a track Lockon with wires to connect the transformer to the track, and the owner's manual. Nevertheless, you should be aware that some Lionel sets include a locomotive and cars, but do not include the track or transformer. These are usually specialty sets with matched items for a particular railroad or a special type of train, and most of these sets are a bit more costly than a basic starter set. If you elect to buy one of these special sets, you'll need to purchase the track, transformer, connecting wires, and Lockon separately.

The logic for beginning with a starter set is rather straightforward. Starter sets are usually less expensive than individual components purchased separately, and they provide a good foundation for learning what Lionel trains are all about. New and different Lionel sets are offered every year, so it's a good idea to obtain a current Lionel catalog to see what's available. Your local Authorized Lionel Dealer has catalogs available, or you can order one directly from Lionel. While visiting a Lionel dealer in your area, you can also review the assortment of starter sets that he or she will have in stock, and ask a few questions to see if one of those sets might be right for you.

The purchase of your first train set is, of course, a personal decision based on your individual needs and interests. If you already have a favorite prototype railroad, the choice may be somewhat easier because you'll likely be attracted to a set with that railroad's paint scheme and markings, assuming one is available. If there isn't a complete set available in the roadname you prefer, you might explore the option of purchasing the components individually. Although this may cost a bit more, the result will be a "customized" set that appeals to your special interests, and one that can expand as your involvement in the hobby grows.

Another decision you will need to make relates to the specific type of train set you want. Would you prefer a passenger set or a freight set? Do you want the set to be headed by steam or diesel power? There are no right or wrong choices in this regard, since it truly is a matter of personal preferences. If you remember riding a real passenger train at some point in your lifetime, nostalgia might draw you to a diesel-powered passenger set. If you have always been fascinated by the brute power and flashing side rods of a steam locomotive, then that type of motive power, heading up a fast freight, might be your first choice. It's *your* railroad, so go for whatever appeals most to *you*!

• *Where to buy Lionel trains*

The best place to purchase your new Lionel train set is from a Lionel Authorized Dealer in your own hometown. Although alternative sources are available, your authorized dealer is there to assist you in selecting the right set and accessories, and he or she will be there when you need a few more sections of track, a new piece of rolling stock for your roster, some scenic materials, or when you just want to take a first-hand look at the latest releases from Lionel. Most important, your local dealer will be available to answer any questions you have about setting-up, operating, and maintaining your Lionel trains, and to assist with any repair issue that may arise later.

If you live in an area where there are no Lionel Authorized Dealers within a convenient distance of your home, you can also purchase your trains from authorized dealers who provide a mail order service for their customers. Many of these dealers advertise regularly in *O Gauge Railroading* and *Classic Toy Trains* magazines. You'll find that many major dealers also have Web site addresses on the Internet, where you can examine their in-stock list and even place orders.

Regardless of where you decide to buy your Lionel trains, it pays to shop around a bit before deciding on a purchase—especially a major purchase. Compare prices, and be sure to take into account any "value added" incentives associated with the source you are buying from. A local dealer, for example, may have the item you're looking for priced a bit higher than what is being asked by a mail order firm 800 miles away, but you'll know that you can count on the local dealer to be there for you when you have questions, or when your trains are in need of service. For your first train set purchase, it's best to stick with your local Lionel Authorized Dealer, if at all possible.

• Assembling a basic train set

Assembly of your Lionel starter set is covered in the owner's manual that is packaged with every set, but the steps presented here provide some additional tips that you may find helpful. Assuming that you have never before assembled an electric train set, and would like some specific guidance concerning the procedures to be followed, here are the basic steps:

1. *Unpack the set box, and examine all of the components, including the individual sections of track, to determine if any of the items have been damaged in shipping.*

2. *Locate the owner's manual, warranty card, and any other printed information that came with the set, and take the time to read these materials completely before you do anything else with your new train set.*

3. *If any pre-operation lubrication is specified in the owner's manual, attend to that before attempting to set-up and run the train. Always remember that too much lubrication is as bad as, or worse than, no lubrication at all. One drop of oil or lubricant in the proper location is usually all that's needed. Refer to Chapter 12 for more information regarding maintenance procedures.*

4. *Find a suitable location for the oval of track that came with your set. Assuming that you have not yet purchased any additional track sections, the oval of track that comes with an O27 set should fit in an area measuring about 6 feet long by about 3 feet wide. An O gauge set will require an area about 7 feet long by about 40 inches wide.*

Although your train set can be placed on the floor or carpet, at least temporarily, you'll be a whole lot better off if you use a platform of some type. In any case, avoid setting up your train on deep-pile or shag carpeting, since carpet fibers may find their way into the operating mechanisms, resulting in operational problems. If an on-the-floor layout is the only option available, consider purchasing a suitably sized section of inexpensive indoor/outdoor carpeting to protect your expensive home carpeting. Even better, use a sheet of 1/2-inch thick plywood for the on-floor foundation, even if you don't yet have a framework and legs for the platform. You could even equip the underside with felt protective pads, of the type sold at most home improvement stores,

and temporarily set the layout atop a dining room table or even on a large coffee table.

5. *Assemble the track, starting with the curved sections. A total of four curved sections are needed for each end of the oval. Because Lionel track sections are designed to fit together tightly, it's a good idea to wear a pair of heavy work gloves while fitting the sections together. The gloves will give you a bit more leverage and help provide a better grip. They will also prevent scraping your hands while you're working with the tight-fitting metal rails and ties.*

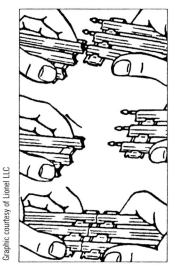

Graphic courtesy of Lionel LLC

If you find it difficult to insert all three track pins into their adjoining rails simultaneously, you can widen each hole by inserting a single track pin into each rail separately, thereby widening the hole a bit for an easier fit.

Grasping one section of track in each hand, align the track pins of one section with the rail openings in another section. It's easiest to do this if you align one outside pin on one section with its matching hole on the adjoining section, and then progressively align the center and remaining outside pin with their respective holes. When you are sure that all three pins have been properly mated with the corresponding holes on the adjacent section, join both sections together by wiggling them slightly while exerting sufficient force to push them together firmly, forcing the pins into the holes. If you find the track a bit too difficult to connect, you can "break in" a the new O27 track sections by first inserting, and then withdrawing, a single track pin into one rail at a time before attempting to join the entire track section. Make sure the sections are joined as tightly as possible, so there are no large gaps between the ends of the two sections.

After the two curved end sections of the oval have been formed, go ahead and join the straight sections together in a similar manner, creating two equal-length straight sections. Always remember that your trackwork must be symmetrical, meaning that whenever you add a straight section to one side of the oval, you must also add an equal-length track section to the opposite side. This applies to both a simple oval and to the more complex trackwork that you will have as your layout grows.

After the curved and straight sections of the oval have been constructed, go ahead and attach one curved end of the oval to each of the two assembled straight sections, again being careful to join the track tightly together. Then add the other curved end to complete the oval.

If your trackwork is being temporarily set up on the floor, it is recommended that you use Lionel Track Clips to keep the track sections tightly joined. Packages of these inexpensive clips can be obtained from any Lionel dealer (part #6-62901 for O27 gauge, and part #6-12743 for O gauge). You will need one clip for each track joint, and each package contains enough clips for a basic oval comprised of eight curved sections and eight straight sections. If you didn't purchase these clips when you bought your set, there's no need to worry about it at this time because it's not at all likely that the tight-fitting track sections will work their way loose in the course of a moderate number of train operations. However, if you plan to keep the trackwork on the floor for an extended period of time, be sure to pick up a package of these clips during your next visit to the hobby shop.

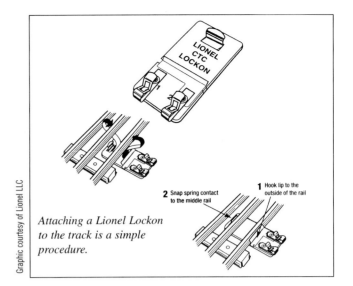

2 Snap spring contact to the middle rail   1 Hook lip to the outside of the rail

Attaching a Lionel Lockon to the track is a simple procedure.

O27 track clips, for use on temporary layouts.

O gauge track clips, for use on temporary layouts.

6. Determine where you want to locate your transformer, and attach the Lockon to a straight section of track in that general area. To attach the Lockon, slip the rigid hooked lip onto the bottom edge of one outside rail, and apply pressure to the spring contact clip from beneath the Lockon until that movable clip snaps securely onto the center rail.

7. Review the operating instructions for your transformer. Most older Lionel transformers are a self-contained unit, while many new models consist of two components: A power pack and a controller unit. The power pack on these new units is actually the transformer, and the controller is the console that holds the speed control throttle, whistle/horn button, and direction button.

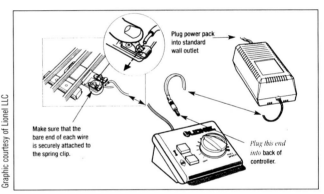

Plug power pack into standard wall outlet

Make sure that the bare end of each wire is securely attached to the spring clip.

Plug this end into back of controller.

Connecting you starter set transformer to the track is both quick and easy, as illustrated here.

Examine the transformer carefully to make sure that the case, control knobs, and any other visible components and wires (on newer models) are undamaged, and that the AC power cord is intact and not loose, cut, or damaged in any way.

If you are using an older Lionel transformer, locate the two posts that, per the instruction manual, are used to supply variable power to the track. Connect a length of wire from one post of the transformer to one of the clips on the Lockon. Connect a second length of wire from the other variable power post on the transformer to the second clip on the Lockon. Be sure that both ends of the wires are bare, and making good contact with the posts and Lockon clips. After all connections have been made, go ahead and plug the transformer into an AC outlet or terminal strip. After doing so, make sure that the throttle knob or handle on the transformer is set to the zero-voltage position.

HOW TO CONNECT TRANSFORMERS TO "O" AND "027" TRACK

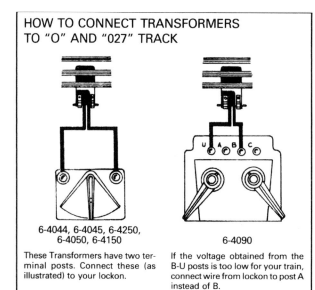

6-4044, 6-4045, 6-4250, 6-4050, 6-4150

These Transformers have two terminal posts. Connect these (as illustrated) to your lockon.

6-4090

If the voltage obtained from the B-U posts is too low for your train, connect wire from lockon to post A instead of B.

HOW TO CONNECT OLDER TRANSFORMERS TO TRACK – (Many older types still may be available in stores)

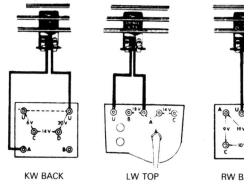

KW BACK
The two U posts in this transformer are connected internally so that either U post can be used for "ground."

LW TOP
The two A posts in this transformer are connected internally. Either one can be used for "ground."

RW BACK
If the voltage obtained from the B-U posts is too low for your train, connect wire from lockon to post A instead of B.

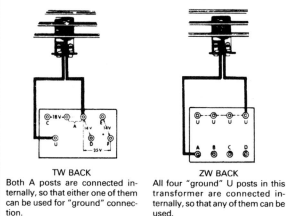

TW BACK
Both A posts are connected internally, so that either one of them can be used for "ground" connection.

ZW BACK
All four "ground" U posts in this transformer are connected internally, so that any of them can be used.

Graphic courtesy of Lionel LLC

Lionel has produced a variety of transformers over the years, and the connection points between track and transformer may vary a bit depending on the model. Depicted here are examples of track connections for a number of the most popular older transformers.

If you have the newer two-component transformer configuration, connect the controller wires to the two clips on the Lockon. Next, insert the small plug end of the power pack into the back of the controller, and plug the AC power cord into a standard household outlet. Make sure that the throttle knob or handle on the controller is set to zero-voltage position.

8. After reviewing and performing any pre-operation lubrication instructions noted in the operator's manual, place your locomotive on the track, making sure that all wheels are properly positioned on the running rails. Also check to make sure that the center-rail pickup rollers beneath the locomotive and on any operating cars move up and down freely, and that the rollers themselves spin freely when you flick them with your finger.

If your locomotive is equipped with a smoke unit, add the appropriate number of drops of Lionel Smoke Fluid through the top of the smokestack (the operator's manual will tell you how many drops to add). Be sure to keep the smoke unit supplied with fluid at all times when it is operating; otherwise it may run dry and risk damage to the internal heating coil that converts the fluid into a harmless smoke. Also, be careful to not overfill the smoke unit, because that will only diminish smoke output, and perhaps cause smoke fluid to overflow on both the inside and outside of the locomotive. Always wipe off any excess or spilled smoke fluid with a clean piece of cloth.

9. Now advance the throttle on the transformer slowly until the locomotive lights come on. Advance it a bit further to see if the locomotive begins to move. If it doesn't move after you have applied about 6-8 volts, depress the direction button on the transformer one time to cycle the locomotive's reversing unit to the next position (you can also do this by turning the throttle knob or handle to zero, and then turning it up again). The locomotive should start moving in one direction or the other—normally forward. All of today's Lionel locomotives are equipped with silent and efficient electronic reversing units that allow for three sequential operations: forward, followed by neutral, followed by reverse. The sequence repeats itself, with a neutral position between each forward and reverse, each time the direction button is depressed, or each time the throttle is returned to the zero position and then re-activated.

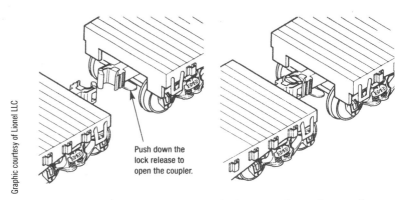

Push down the lock release to open the coupler.

Another way to couple cars is to place both cars on the track; open the coupler on at least one of the cars by pushing down on the locking lever that protrudes from the bottom side of the coupler; and then push the cars together until the couplers snap closed.

One way to couple or uncouple cars by hand is to lift the end of one car and slide the knuckle couplers together. After you have joined the cars, give a firm but gentle tug on the last car to assure that all couplers are securely closed. Check to see that all wheels are sitting properly on the rails before moving on to the next car.

10. *If the locomotive is operating properly, give it a bit of "running-in" time before adding any cars to the track. This will help to fully and evenly distribute the lubricants, and assure that all gear mechanisms or other moving parts are performing properly. Run the locomotive both forward and backward at various speeds (but not so fast that it will derail) for a total of ten to fifteen minutes in each direction.*

11. *After you are satisfied that the locomotive is operating properly, and have gained some feel for the various knobs and buttons on the transformer that control the locomotive's movement, speed, and features (such as bells, whistles, horns, and the like), it's time to add the* cars to your train. First, makes sure that the track power is turned off. Track power should always be off whenever you are adding something to, or removing something from, your track. As you add each car to the track, make sure that all wheels are properly seated on the running rails, and that the car is securely coupled to the locomotive or to the car in front of it. Also, give a gentle tug on the rear of the car to make sure it is firmly coupled to the car ahead of it.

Congratulations! You are now an official Lionel engineer, and well on your way to many years of fun and relaxation in this great hobby!

Chapter 5

The tried-and-true Lionel track system

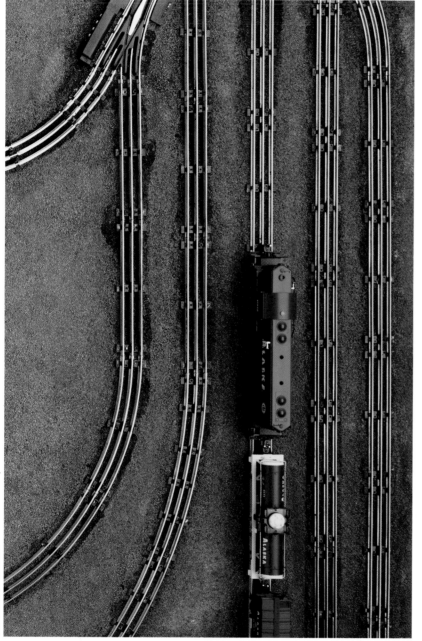

The Lionel tubular three-rail track system ranks among the most versatile in all of model railroading.

tions. It's important to keep in mind, though, that Lionel track has been available to hobbyists for far longer than any other system—since 1906, in fact—and these reliable track components have proven themselves over many years of use on countless thousands of three-rail layouts, ranging from around-the-Christmas-tree circles of track to large, permanent layouts that occupy an entire basement. Lionel track is rugged, affordable, easy to assemble, and designed to last a couple of lifetimes or more, so be sure to give it full consideration before you go out and spend more for other brands.

• O27 and O gauge three-rail track components

Lionel manufactures tubular track and switches (known as "turnouts" in most other scales) in two sizes: O gauge and O27 gauge. By "tubular" we mean that the track is made of rolled steel strips that, after being formed, are hollow in the middle. Tubular track also has a rounded railhead (the top portion of the rail), as opposed to the flatter "T" shape seen on some other model train track and prototype rails. A tubular-shaped railhead was selected by Lionel because it has been shown to minimize the wheel wear that may result when wheels roll over a flat, T-shaped surface. Each section of Lionel tubular track, regardless of whether it is O27 or O gauge, is made up of several common components.

The name of the game is, of course, model *railroading*! This implies that you have a "road" made of rails upon which to operate your Lionel trains.

If you shop around a bit, you'll find that there are a variety of three-rail O gauge track systems being offered today, each of which has its own advantages and limita-

First, there are the rails themselves. Each track section has three tubular metal rails—two outside running rails, and a centered power rail that is identical to the running rails except for how it is affixed to the supporting ties. The center rail is insulated from the metal track ties by a fiber insulating pad positioned between the bottom of the center rail and each tie to which the rail is attached. This insulating material assures that electric current provided to the center rail stays within that rail, and is not conducted through the ties to either of the outside running rails, which would result in a short circuit.

Each track section also has three metal ties—the rail supporting devices that keep the rails in proper alignment, and which electrically connect both outside rails in what is known as a "common" connection. With both O27 and O gauge track, ties are positioned at each end of the track section, with one tie located in the center of the section to maintain proper alignment there. The ties also feature pre-drilled holes, located between the power rails and the running rails, which permit the track section to be screwed securely to a firm platform.

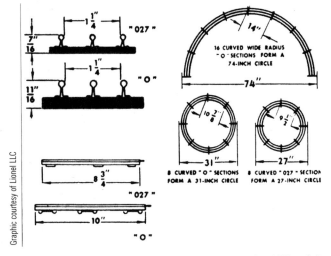

Graphic courtesy of Lionel LLC

A comparison of dimensions and measurements for O27 and O gauge track.

Finally, each section of track comes fitted with three metal track pins fitted in one end. These pins allow the section to be tightly joined to an adjacent section. The track pins are tight (or certainly should be), but they can be carefully pried loose with diagonal cutters or a pair of pliers to replace the metal pin with a fiber insulating pin, if necessary.

The "gauge" of both O27 and O gauge track is identical. Gauge is the measure of distance between the inside top edges of the two outside running rails, and this is an all-important measurement in the sense that gauge determines how well the wheels of your locomotives and rolling stock will actually roll along your trackwork. Because O and O27 track are both considered O gauge, this measurement is 1-1/4 inches for both types of track. That being the case, it is even possible to join a section of O27 track to an adjacent section of O gauge track, if the O27 track is shimmed-up to

meet the rail height of the O gauge track, and if the ends of the O27 rails are spread a bit to accommodate the slightly larger O gauge pins. You can also purchase from Lionel customer service in Michigan or your authorized Lionel Service Center, an adaptor pin, part number 610-2948-010.

With all of those commonalties, one might logically ask why there are two types of track in the first place, and perhaps more importantly, why one type might be chosen over the other. So, it's useful to explore the differences between O27 and O gauge track.

As noted earlier, there are some obvious physical characteristics that distinguish Lionel O from O27 gauge track, and this becomes readily apparent if you compare a section of each track type side-by-side. The O27 track has a lower rail profile, and the ties are also lower, more flat in appearance, and painted brown. The O27 track measures 7/16-inch in height, when measured from the bottom of the tie to the top of the rail. Actually, a good number of hobbyists prefer the lower and more realistic profile of O27 track, although many larger layouts are constructed with O gauge track due to the availability of wider-radius curved sections and a different configuration of the O gauge switches, which allows for the passage of longer locomotives and cars.

Lionel O gauge track has a higher rail profile, along with ties that are black in color, and wider and deeper than O27 ties. Lionel O gauge track measures 11/16-inch high when measured from the bottom of the tie to the top of the rail—a full quarter-inch higher than its O27 counterpart. The ties on Lionel O gauge track also have a distinctive upward-flared ridge along their side edges.

Photo courtesy of Lionel LLC

As can be clearly seen here, Lionel O gauge track (left) has a considerably higher profile than Lionel O27 track (right).

There are also some differences in length of a typical section of track. A straight section of O27 track measures 8-3/4 inches long, while a comparable straight section of O gauge track measures 10 inches in length.

The difference in curved sections becomes obvious if you compare a standard O27 curved section with a typical O gauge curved section. The O27 section provides a tighter curve radius, which forms a circle 27-inches in diameter. O27 track is also available in 42-inch and 54-inch diameter curved sections. The smallest O gauge curved section forms a circle 31-inches in diameter, with 42-inch, 54-inch, and 72-inch diameter curved sections also available. If space for your Lionel layout is at a premium, you will be able to pack more railroading action into a given area by using O27 instead of O gauge track, all other things being equal.

In other respects the two types of track are nearly identical. A key point to keep in mind is that *all* of the somewhat smaller-than-scale O27 locomotives and cars will operate properly on either O27 or O gauge track. However, some of the larger and longer O scale models do require O gauge track, with its wider curve radius and wider clearances on switches. In some cases, even the 31-inch diameter of O gauge track is not adequate for proper operation of very large or long locomotives and cars, and the hobbyist may need to resort to 54-inch or even 72-inch diameter curves, both of which are available in O gauge. Before you purchase a Lionel locomotive or rolling stock item, it's a good idea to check the catalog description or the box label to determine what size curves are needed for the item to perform properly.

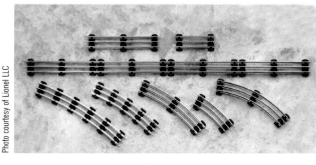

The O gauge assortment of straight and curve track sections.

Chances are that after you get your first Lionel set up and running for a while, even if it's just around the Christmas tree, you're apt to become anxious to expand that basic oval of track into something a bit more elaborate. At this point, you'll want to carefully consider whether O27 or O gauge track is best for you in terms of your long-term goals. If space is limited, and likely to remain so for some time, you may want to stay with O27 track components. That also holds true if you are especially fond of the smaller locomotives and rolling stock, and plan to continue with those types of items, or if you want to have more of your layout area available for scenery and operating accessories.

However, if you envision someday acquiring larger locomotives and operating very long freight or passenger cars, you may want to give serious thought to switching over to the O gauge track line before you invest in a lot of new O27 track, switches, crossovers, and the like. It's really just a matter of individual preferences and available space. There is no "right" or "wrong" choice, and there really is no "best" solution. Do what works well for you in your particular circumstances. For that matter, there's also nothing wrong with changing your mind later on.

Regardless of whether you elect to stay with O27 track, or decide to switch to O gauge components, you'll eventually want to acquire some additional track, along with one or more switches, and perhaps even a crossover. Before you do that, take some time to really think about what type of railroad you want and what type of track plan might best suit that concept and the available space. Read Chapter 7 (see page 59) to get a better idea of how to proceed, and study the various track plans presented in Chapter 8 (beginning on page 69) to see if any of them—even in a somewhat modified version—might suit your needs and interests. The track plans presented there are simply suggested arrangements, and all of them can be modified in a number of ways to better suit your own requirements. Also take time to read some of the many other books and magazines about the hobby. Almost all of them provide a variety of alternative track plans that you may want to consider—some simple, and some very complex. Use these as "food for thought" as you begin your own layout planning. You'll find a comprehensive list of reference materials in Appendix A (page 116).

When the time comes to purchase some additional track components, try to avoid being penny wise and pound foolish. Although it's easy enough to find old sections of Lionel track at flea markets, train shows, and the like, and often at very reasonable cost, you would be well advised to seriously consider investing in new track sections if you're building your first layout. Solid and reliable trackwork is absolutely critical to smooth, continuous, and trouble-free operations, and new track will meet all of the criteria. Often enough, any problems you're likely to encounter with old track and switches aren't related to rusty or dirty outside surfaces, which can usually be restored with some of the chemical cleaners designed for metals, along with a bit of elbow grease. Rather, the potential source of problems comes from damaged or missing rail insulator pads, or even from rust or corrosion inside the rails, in areas you can't easily see. Track pins in well-used track can also be a source of problems. Old pins should always be removed and replaced with new ones if you're determined to use older track. And, each insulating pad must be carefully examined, and replaced if necessary, to assure that no short circuits will occur.

Even with shiny, new, fresh-from-the-dealer track, you should take a few

Lionel Track Packs provide an easy and affordable way to expand your layout.

moments to inspect each section carefully to make sure everything is as it should be. First, check to see that all of the insulating pads beneath the center rail are in place and properly seated so no direct contact is made between the metal rail and the metal tie. Then, use your fingers to pull on and wiggle each of the track pins a bit to make sure that none of the pins are bent or loose. If they are bent, you may be able to straighten them with a pair of pliers. Or, you can use a cutting pliers to pry them loose from the rail and then replace them with new pins. Likewise, you can use a pair of pliers to tighten the pins firmly to the rail by squeezing in on the sides of the rail at the railhead and in the area just beneath the pin. Also check to see that the track sits level, and that it doesn't have a tendency to rock from side to side when sitting on a flat surface. It's possible that even some new track may have become slightly warped from rough handling at some point along the line. If you do all of these quick inspections while you're still at the dealer's store, you can easily point out the problem to the salesperson, and then substitute any problem piece for a good-to-go section.

When you begin to lay track on your new Lionel layout, it's also a very good idea to connect a transformer at an early stage, and use a locomotive to check things as you go along. Connect several sections of track, and then run the locomotive forward and backward over each new section. It's a whole lot easier to identify any track-related problems while you're still laying the track than it is to locate the problem area after all of the track is in place.

You'll note that Lionel straight track, in both O27 and O gauge, is also available in extra-long sections, as well as in half-sections. Since fewer rail joints tend to equate to fewer conductivity or tracking problems, it's advisable to use the extra-long straight sections in any area where you have at least four regular straight sections running end-to-end, in an uninterrupted manner. This will provide a nice, straight mainline, and you won't have to worry about loose pins or any other such problems along the length of that 35-inch (O27) or 40-inch (O gauge) straight-away.

Half sections can be used to extend the mainline or sidings just a bit, and they can also be used to provide slightly more gentle curves, if space permits. Just begin the curve with a normal curved section; then add a half-straight section between that section and the next curved section. Continue doing that around the full length of the curve, and the result will be a somewhat more sweeping curve. Again, keep in mind that this technique will involve more total space for the curve, so it may not be feasible in all situations.

It's also possible to cut a straight section of Lionel track to some other length, if the half-sections don't quite provide you what you want or need. All you need for cutting is (preferably) a table-mounted vise, a hacksaw, a small file, and a piece of old cloth or some other padding material to protect the rails from the jaws of the vise. If you don't have a vise available, you can also carefully cut the track right on the workbench, as long as you are able to hold it firmly in place (C-clamps and a scrap of wood may help in that regard). Saw into the rail only on the down stroke so you

don't risk lifting and damaging the rails. After you've completed your cut, use a file to clean off any burrs and to smooth the cut ends, and then insert the new track pins. If you place the track at the edge of the workbench so the cut and filed end of the track is flush with the edge of the bench, you can use a small hammer to gently tap the track pins into place in your newly cut rails.

Although straight sections can easily be cut to fit a specific requirement, it's not advisable to employ this technique with curved sections. For one thing, getting all three rails cut to precisely the proper angle is difficult at best, and cutting a curved section will also alter the rest of the curve.

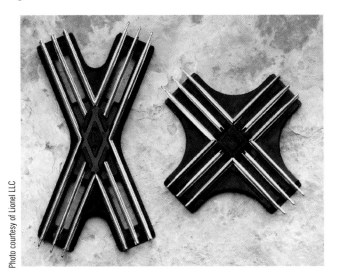

Lionel crossings are available in both the O27 and O gauge track assortment. The examples seen here are from the O gauge line, with a 45-degree crossing on the left, and a 90-degree crossing on the right.

One other category of basic track components warrants some mention: Crossings. Crossings are normally used to form "figure eight" layouts, in which a train completing a continuous circuit bisects the route it originally traveled, at the same level. In other words, it crosses over itself. You'll see some examples of a figure-eight arrangement in several of the track plans presented in Chapter 8. Lionel offers 45-degree and 90-degree crossings in both the O27 and O gauge lines. On a 90-degree crossing, the tracks intersecting at right angles to each other, while a 45-degree crossing allows for a more gradual approach and longer loops at both ends of the "8." A figure eight track plan, including the appropriate crossing, gives your train a somewhat longer and more varied route to follow, and is regarded by some as more interesting to view than a simple oval. With the three-rail system offered by Lionel, no special wiring is required if you decide that a figure-eight track configuration will work on your layout.

Since O27 track components are what most folks start out with, let's begin exploring the Lionel track assortment by reviewing all that's available in that line. If you've decided to use O gauge track components, that's fine, too, since all of the O gauge items are also listed in this chapter.

O27 Basic Track Components:

6-65038	Straight Track (8-3/4" long)	Standard straight section.
6-65019	1/2 Straight track (4-7/8" long)	Standard 1/2 straight section.
6-65024	Extra Long Straight Track Section (35 inches long)	Replaces four separate track sections.
6-665033	Curved Track (9-5/8 inches long)	8 sections form a 27-inch diameter circle.
6-65014	1/2 Curved Track (5-7/16 inches long)	
6-65049	O42 Wide-Radius Curved Track (10-7/8 inches long)	12 sections form a 42-inch diameter circle.
6-65113	O54 Wide-Radius Curved Track (10-3/8 inches long)	16 sections form a 54-inch diameter circle.
6-65020	90-degree Crossover (7-3/8 inches square)	Used to form a figure-eight layout.
6-65023	45-degree Crossover (10-1/4 inches square)	Used to form an elongated figure-eight layout.
6-65041	Fiber Insulating Pins	Used to replace steel pins in creating insulated sections.
6-65042	Steel Track Pins	Used to join track sections (3 per section needed).
6-62901	Ives O27 Track Clips	For securing track on temporary layouts.
6-62900	Lockon	Used to attach wires to track.
6-62905	Lockon with Wires	Includes Lockon and wires.
6-22966	O27 Add-On Track Pack	Includes one 90-degree crossover and four curved track sections for converting a starter set oval to a figure-eight layout.
6-22967	O27 Double-Loop Add-On Track Pack	Includes two curved sections, 10 straight sections, one left-hand manual switch, and one right-hand manual switch to expand starter set track into a double loop, an oval with two sidings, or a double oval.
6-22968	Double-Loop Compete Track Pack	Includes 10 curved sections, 18 straight sections, one left-hand manual switch, and one right-hand manual switch to create a complete double loop, an oval with two sidings, or a double oval without any additional track.

O GAUGE BASIC TRACK COMPONENTS:

6-65500	Straight Track Section (10 inches long)	Standard straight section.
6-65505	1/2 Straight Track Section (5-1/2 inches long)	Standard 1/2 straight section.
6-65523	Extra Long Straight Track Section (40 inches long)	Replaces four separate track sections.
6-65501	O31 Curved Track (10-5/8 inches long)	8 sections form a 31-inch diameter circle.
6-12925	O42 Curved Track (10-7/8 inches long)	12 sections form a 42-inch diameter circle.
6-65554	O54 Curved Track (10-3/8 inches long)	16 sections form a 54-inch diameter circle.
6-65572	O72 Curved Track (14 inches long)	16 sections form a 72-inch diameter circle.
6-65504	1/2 O31 Curved Track (6 inches long)	
6-65540	90-degree Crossover (8-5/16 inches square)	Used to form a figure-eight layout.
6-65545	45-degree Crossover (11-3/4 inches square)	Used to form an elongated figure-eight layout.
6-65551	Steel Track Pins	Used to join track sections (3 per section needed).
6-65543	Fiber Insulating Pins	Used to replace steel pins in creating insulated sections.
6-12743	O Gauge Track Clips	For securing track on temporary layouts.
6-22969	O Gauge Deluxe Complete Track Pack	Includes 20 curved sections, 22 straight sections, two 90-degree crossovers, and one 1/2-straight section to create a pretzel-twist layout with extended mainline run.

Note: Lockon and Lockon with Wires same as for O27

You'll notice that there are more varieties of curved sections available in O gauge than in O27. You'll also note that O27 gauge track sections are slightly shorter in length than their O gauge counterparts. Again, the important thing to keep in mind at this point is that an O gauge layout will require somewhat more space than an O27 layout, assuming that the same track plan is used for both. In most other respects, there isn't a whole lot of difference between the two track assortments, aside from the couple of additional "Track Pack" items that are available for O27 gauge.

• All about switches

Now let's take a look at the switches. Hobbyists in O gauge, and even real-life railroaders, have long called them "switches," but be aware that modelers in many other model railroading scales often refer to these devices as "turnouts" to keep from confusing them with electrical switches of the on/off variety. We'll use the "switch" terminology in this book, because that's what Lionel and most O gauge railroaders call them.

Lionel O27 manual switch (left) and remote control switch (right).

The purpose of a switch is to allow a train to safely move from one route to another, such as from one mainline to another, or to a siding branching off of the mainline. The main route through a switch is customarily referred to as the "through route," and the alternate route is known as the "diverging route." Most often, the straight section of track through a switch designates the through route—the path the train would follow if there were no switch present at that location. The curved portion of the switch normally forms the diverging route. If the diverging route curves off to the left as you view the switch from its leading end (the end with only one track), you have what is known as a "left hand switch." If the diverging route curves off to the right, it's a "right hand switch."

All switches—real and model—have some common parts. Arguably, the most important component of any switch is the device known as a "frog"—so called because it kind of resembles a flattened out critter of the same name. The frog is a critical component that helps to direct the wheel flanges on locomotives and cars into the pre-selected

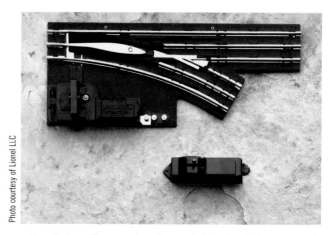

Lionel also offers a wide-radius switch in the O27 gauge track assortment. The curved portion of 42-inch radius switch is a matching fit for O42 curved sections.

routing. The other critical components in that regard are the "points" or "point rails," which are movable rails designed to actually form the path the wheels will follow. A switch stand or switch machine (which shows why the term "switch" is used), operated either manually or remotely, controls the movement and alignment of the points. Another important component of all switches—both those made by Lionel and the prototype variety—are guardrails, which help to keep wheel flanges properly aligned during a train's movement through the switch.

One special feature common to all Lionel switches in both O27 and O gauge, but not found on prototype switches, is the "non-derailing" feature. When you purchase a new O27 or O gauge Lionel switch, you'll notice that one running rail on both the through route and the diverging route is fitted with a fiber insulating pin in place of the usual steel track pin (if the pins are not already in place, the instruction sheet will show you where to place them). On a switch, these rails serve as non-derailing control rails. When a locomotive approaches an open switch from either the diverging or through route at the double-track end of the switch, its wheels bridge the control rail across to the other outside rail. This completes an electrical circuit to a coil inside the switch mechanism, which, in turn, causes the switch to be thrown to the correct position so the train can safely pass through. Obviously, if this did not happen, and if the switch was not properly aligned for the route the train was following, a derailment would occur at the switch. No insulated rails or pins are needed for a train approaching the switch from the leading or single-track end, of course, because a train approaching from that direction will just follow whatever route the switch was previously set for.

With Lionel O27 and O gauge remote control switches, the non-derailing feature can also be used to automatically direct a train through alternating track routes, thereby increasing its run without repeating a passage over the same section of track each time, and without operator intervention. This automatic track-routing feature does require the use of remote control switches, however, and it will not work with O27 manually controlled switches.

You can also use the power feature of Lionel remote control switches to activate certain lineside signals, such as block signals, dwarf signals, signal bridges, and semaphores. It's a simple process: Just connect the three wires from the accessory to the three posts on the switch machine. When the switch is thrown, the color of the signal's lamps will change, or the semaphore blade will change positions. This technique is especially useful in areas of a layout where the switch itself may be difficult to see from the operator's position.

Lionel O27 switches come in two types: Manually controlled and remote controlled. The manually operated O27 switches are the least expensive of all Lionel switches, and all it takes is a simple hand movement of a lever to throw the switch to the desired routing. No additional or special wiring is required, since there are no switch motors or mechanisms to drive. These switches perform well on a layout where they are easily accessible to the operator, but if you have a larger layout, or one that is located in an area where all parts of the layout cannot easily be reached—in the corner of a room, for example—you may want to consider using remote control switches so all of the action can be controlled right at your fingertips, on the control panel.

Lionel O27 switches do not have illuminated lamps on the switch machines or on the controllers. The O gauge line of switches do feature lighted indicators on both components. This may be a consideration if you plan to do a lot of operating in low room light, such as when you want to run your trains in a situation representing night operations.

Additional features of the physically larger O gauge switches include the ability to reposition the switch motor to the opposite side of the switch (useful in tight areas or where track runs close to the edge of the layout), and the ability to power the switch mechanism directly from a transformer, instead of relying on track power. All of the O27

and O gauge remote control switches made by Lionel normally operate with track power, which, of course, is variable depending on how fast you are running your trains. If the power received by the switch motor is too low, the points may not fully snap into place when you throw the switch. If you run a wire from the constant voltage plug on an O gauge switch directly to a constant voltage transformer post, there's no need to worry about this happening because a consistent amount of current will always be supplied to the switch motor.

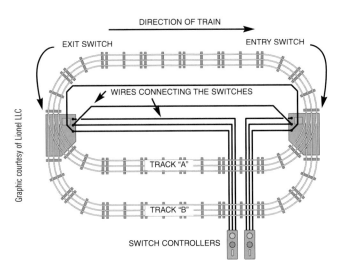

A pair of either O27 or O gauge switches can be wired for automatic control as shown here with O27 switches. A train operating on a track configuration similar to the one depicted will alternate routes automatically with each circuit of the layout.

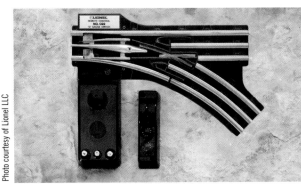

A Lionel O31 switch, in O gauge.

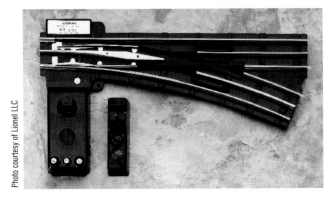

The O72 wide-radius switch.

A Lionel Block Signal can be wired directly to a switch so the lamps change from red to green when the switch is thrown. This works especially well in remote areas of the layout where the switch machine itself cannot be easily seen.

If cost is a major consideration, you may want to stick with O27 track and switches for your layout, especially if it is a relatively small one and you plan to operate similarly small locomotives and cars. For larger layouts, and in situations where you want or need the additional features and flexibility that remote control affords, give some consideration to remote control versions in either O27 or O gauge. And, if you intend to eventually operate large and long locomotives and car, and enjoy seeing lots of lights on and around your layout, the O gauge line of switches, including the wide-radius O72 switch, may be just the thing for you.

O27 Switches:

The straight sections and diverging route (curved) sections of standard Lionel switches are one-for-one drop-in replacements for similar lengths of O27 straight and curved sections, although the O42 switches replace 1-1/2 sections of these components.

6-65021	O27 Manual Switch (Left)	Hand-thrown switch (left diverging route).
6-65022	O27 Manual Switch (Right)	Hand-thrown switch (right diverging route).
6-65121	O27 Remote Switch (Left)	Remote-control switch (left diverging route).
6-65122	O27 Remote Switch (Right)	Remote-control switch (right diverging route).
6-65167	O42 Remote Switch (Left)	Wide-radius remote-control switch (left diverging route).
6-65168	O42 Remote Switch (Right)	Wide-radius remote-control switch (right diverging route).

O Gauge Switches:

Lionel O gauge switches are all designed for remote control operation, although they can also be thrown by hand by simply rotating the lamp housing. For added flexibility in layout design, the switch motor on O gauge switches can also be removed and relocated to the opposite side of the switch. Also, the switch may be powered directly from the transformer, if so desired, rather than by track power. This results in a more consistent and positive action when the switch motor is activated. The O gauge switches also come with a lighted switch lamp and lights on the controller. Like their O27 counterparts, Lionel O gauge switches are one-for-one drop-in replacements for a straight or curved section of regular O gauge track. The O72 switches require some additional track cutting and/or fitting for straight sections that they replace.

6-14062	O Gauge Remote Control Switch (Left)	Remote-control switch (left diverging route).
6-14063	O Gauge Remote Control Switch (Right)	Remote-control switch (right diverging route).
6-65165	O72 Remote Control Switch (Right)	Wide-radius remote-control switch (right diverging route).
6-65166	O72 Remote Control Switch (Left)	Wide-radius remote-control switch (right diverging route).

• Remote-control track sections

Remote control track sections in both O27 and O gauge allow you to uncouple cars at selected locations, and they are also often used to activate many Lionel operating cars, such as the milk car, cattle car, horse car, operating boxcar, automatic dumping coal and log cars, and a number of others.

Remote control sections in both gauges are one-for-one replacements for a straight section of track in their respective gauge. That being the case, you'll have little problem in adding a new remote control section to the layout as your layout expands, or changing the location of an existing remote control section as experience shows that an alternate location will work better.

In terms of its physical characteristics, the remote control section is essentially a straight section of track (8-3/4 inches long for O27 and 10-inches long for O gauge) fitted with a magnet on the center rail. A simple push-button controller, located on the layout's control panel or wherever the operator prefers, is wired to this magnet. When the button is depressed, the operating knuckle coupler of any Lionel freight or passenger car located directly over the magnet will be pulled open as the magnetic field exerts a downward force on a pin located on the bottom of the coupler. It is a simple and dependable way to perform coupling and uncoupling operations in a hands-off manner, although this operation can also be done manually if you so desire.

The primary use of the remote control section is, as noted, to uncouple cars, but these sections are also used to activate Lionel operating cars. So, if there's a particular spot on your layout where you would like to dump a load of coal or logs; have the dairy farmer deliver cans of fresh moo-juice; or provide the cattle and horses with an opportunity to stretch their legs a bit, you'll want to be sure to place a remote control section adjacent to each receiving bin, platform, or corral. It's a good idea to position these items at a spot on the layout where there will be at least one full regular straight section connected to each end of the remote control track section, if possible. You'll also want to consider where the remote control section will best serve the operation of your railroad before you place it on the layout. Ask

Photo courtesy of Lionel LLC

O gauge Remote Control Section, which is used to uncouple cars and activate operating cars.

yourself, "Where might I most often want, or need, to uncouple or activate cars?" and "What will I do with these cars after they are uncoupled?"

Be aware, too, that there are two types of remote control track sections available in the O27 line. The Remote Control Uncoupling Section is the type most often used, and it will allow you to uncouple cars and activate a good number of Lionel operating cars. However, some cars that are, or were, originally designed for use with the O gauge track system require a special five-rail track section, as seen on the O gauge Remote Control Track section. The bottom of these cars are equipped with special slide shoe contacts on the trucks which make contact with the two extra inner rails and provide power and control for their operation. The 6-12746 Remote Control Track, in O27, comes equipped with the five rails needed for those cars to operate on an O27 track system. If you plan to have lots of operating cars on your layout at some point in the future, you'll want to take a look at placing at least a couple of these special sections somewhere along the mainline.

O27 UNCOUPLING AND REMOTE CONTROL TRACK SECTIONS:

6-65149	Remote Uncoupling Section (8-3/4 inches long)	Used to uncouple cars and activate operating cars.
6-12746	Remote Control Track (8-3/4 inches long)	Allows O gauge operating cars to be activated on O27 layouts.

O GAUGE REMOTE UNCOUPLING TRACK SECTIONS:

6-65530	Remote Control Track (10" long)	Used to uncouple cars and to activate operating cars by remote control.

• Lionel insulated track sections

Insulated track sections are special sections that can be used to activate certain accessories such as trackside signals, crossing gates, and a whole lot more. They provide a reliable means for springing these accessories into action. Also, many Lionel trackside accessories come packed with a pressure plate activator called a 153C contactor. It is placed under a section of track and is activated by the weight of the passing train.

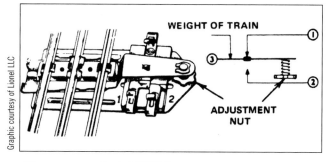

The pressure-activated 153C Contactor.

With a normal three-rail track section, a locomotive obtains its power from the center rail and both outer rails of Lionel track. If one of the outer rails is somehow "insulated" from the other outer rail, and is also insulated from each adjoining track section by replacing the steel track pin with a fiber pin at each end, any locomotives operating over that section of track will still run fine, because current still has a return path through the second outside rail. However, the insulated rail itself will be "dead" until the wheels of a locomotive or cars pass over it, thereby allowing current to flow from the non-insulated rail, through the wheels and axles, to the insulated rail.

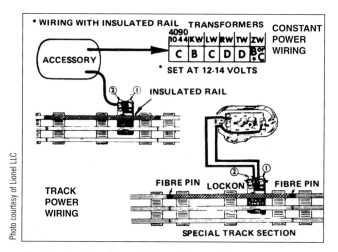

Insulated rail sections eliminate the need for pressure-activated contactors to control operating accessories. This is a real advantage on permanent layouts, where track is normally fastened down and/or ballasted. You can make an insulated section yourself, as seen here and described in the text, or you can purchase ready-made Lionel Insulated Track Sections.

If an accessory—a block signal, semaphore, crossing gate, or highway flashing signal, for example—is connected to the insulated rail, either by means of a Lockon or by soldering a wire to that rail, the accessory will only receive current, and thus be activated, when a train is passing over the insulated rail. In effect, the locomotive or car wheels act like a switch, supplying current to the insulated rail and briefly powering whatever is connected to that rail. After the train has passed, the accessory activation will cease. It's simple and it works very well!

Lionel offers ready-made insulated straight track sections in both O27 and O gauge. Again, these are one-for-one replacements for an ordinary section of straight track in each respective gauge, so installation, even on an existing layout, is a simple task.

You can, if you so desire, also make your own insulated track sections. Since Lionel only offers full straight sections of insulated track, you can even make your own insulated track sections out of half-straight, extra-long straight, or any of the various curved sections of track. You can also do this with sections you cut to some special length. Here's how to make an insulated section of track:

1. Remove one of the two outside rails from a section of track, either a straight or a curved section. Use a small, flat-blade screwdriver to gently pry up the metal tabs that hold the rail to the ties. Pry up the tabs on both sides of all three ties sufficiently to remove the rail. Then use a needle nose pliers to open the tabs a bit more, so they are pointing straight up.

2. Cut three small sections of an insulating material (about 1/2-inch square should do) to create insulators like those that are on the center rail. You could use insulators saved from a discarded track section for this, or you can make your own out of thin cardboard, such as that used on matchbook covers or the type used to retain the shape of a new shirt, or you could even use a bit of heavy electrical tape.

3. Place the insulators between each of the tabs, and then reinsert the rail, making sure that the rail does not contact the ties or the tabs at any point. Then use a large screwdriver blade to bend the tabs back down into position so they grip the rail and insulators securely.

4. Fit fiber insulating pins into each end of your new insulated rail, and you're ready to go!

Insulated track sections are great for activating accessories intended to do something, or to change in some manner, when a train passes a specific area. These special sections readily demonstrate why the three-rail track system has endured over so many years!

O27 INSULATED TRACK:

6-12841	Insulated Track (8-3/4" long)	Used to activate operating accessories. Drop-in replacement for one standard straight track section.

O GAUGE INSULATED TRACK:

6-12840	Insulated Track (10" long)	Used to activate operating accessories. Drop-in replacement for one standard straight track section.

• *Track tips:*

Here are three tips that will help to assure that your track is trouble-free before you install it, and that it will remain that way after it's in place on your layout:

1. Worth repeating: Always inspect each section of track—whether new or old—before you place it on the layout. This one tip alone will save you a whole lot of time and effort in trying to track down (pun intended) a loose track pin, or a misplaced or damaged piece of insulating material.

2. The Lionel Lockon is used to connect power and accessories to the track. The two clips on the Lockon are numbered "1" and "2." Keep in mind that the "1" clip connects to the center rail, and the number "2" clip connects to one or the other of the outside rails. When connecting a transformer to the track with a Lockon, the variable voltage post should be connected to the "1" clip, and the ground (U) wire should be connected to the "2" post. If you are attaching a Lockon to an insulated rail section—to activate an accessory, for example—you will not use the "1" clip. Attach the wire from the accessory to the "2" clip only.

3. If you decide to make your own insulated track sections you can check your work with a 14 to 18 volt lamp to assure that there are no short circuits. Begin by attaching a Lockon to the center rail and the outside rail that is not insulated. Connect clip "1" of the Lockon to any of the "hot" posts on your transformer and connect clip "2" of the Lockon to the ground or common post of your transformer. Now take your test lamp (even a street lamp from your layout will do) and touch one of its wire leads to Lockon clip "1" and the other lead to clip "2." Now slowly raise the transformer voltage until the lamp lights fairly brightly and leave the transformer set at that point. Take your lamp again and touch one of its wire leads to the center rail of the track section and the other lead to the insulated rail. If the lamp lights the rail is <u>not</u> properly insulated. If the lamp does <u>not</u> light then the insulated section is properly insulated and ready for use.

Chapter 6

Powering your Lionel trains

Photo courtesy of Lionel LLC

The renowned Lionel ZW transformer has long reigned as the "king" of O gauge power sources.

You certainly don't have to be an electrical engineer to qualify as a railroad engineer with Lionel electric trains, but some understanding of the basic principles and terminology that apply to electrically-powered model trains and accessories will help you understand how things work, and it will help you identify and remedy problems that you might encounter from time to time.

• *The basics of toy train electricity*

One of the easiest ways to explain how electricity works is to fall back on the old "water pipe" analogy that is often used in high school physics classes. If you were paying attention during that particular session at your school, you will recall that the flow of electricity through a circuit is often likened to water being forced through a pipe by a water pump. If you substitute a wire for the pipe, and substitute an electrical generating source for the water pump, this closely approximates what, in the world of electricity, is the fundamental nature of controlled electrical current. All that's really needed are some common electrical terms to describe what happens:

Voltage can be likened to the water pressure—the force that is trying to push water through the pipe, such as when there is a pump on the line, or when you turn on the faucet supplying a garden hose. Volts are a measure of electrical pressure. The voltage available at the output posts of a model train transformer is known as "stepped down" voltage, because it has been reduced from about 110-115 volts to about 8 to 18 volts, which is normally what is required to drive most toy electric train motors. Voltage can also be "stepped up," but that application is not used in operating Lionel trains.

Current, or *amperage* (abbreviated as amps) can be likened to the actual quantity or amount of water flowing through a pipe at a given water pressure. Amps measure and describe the volume of current passing through an electrical circuit.

Resistance is a function of the pipe's actual length and diameter, two factors that restrict the passage of water through the pipe. A given water pressure can only force a finite amount of water through a pipe of a given diameter and length. Similarly, as electricity flows through a wire, the diameter or thickness of that wire, as well as its length, also imparts resistance. All things being equal, there is less resistance in heavier wire of a given length than in a lighter wire of the same length.

In order to increase the water flow (amperage), you must either raise the water pressure (voltage), or increase the pipe's diameter (lower the resistance), or perhaps do both of these things.

These three fundamentals—voltage, amperage, and resistance—are related through what is known as Ohm's Law ($E=IR$), where E=voltage, I=amperage, and R=resistance. Basically, what this says is that the pressure (voltage) required to force a given amount of current (amperage) through a conductor (wire) is equal to the amperage times the resistance. Knowing any two of the factors in this simple equation also allows you to calculate the third. For example: $I=E/R$ and $R=E/I$.

Wattage is a measure of the total power available, and is equal to voltage times amperage ($W=EI$). Again, simple algebra allows you to calculate any one of the values if the other two are known: Hence, $I=W/E$ and $E=W/I$. To put this in a model railroading perspective, assume that your train is operating at 12 volts and is drawing 1/2 amp of power (both values can actually be measured with a voltmeter and ammeter). The total wattage being used is 6, which is obtained by multiplying 12 times 1/2 (12v x .5a). This measure is also often referred to as "Volt Amps (VA)" for rather obvious reasons. As with ordinary light bulbs, which you purchase based on their rating in watts, the total power available from an electric train transformer is also a function

of the watts available at the output side. Generally, the higher the wattage rating, the more power will be available for operating trains and accessories.

The important thing to remember is that all four of these quantities—voltage, amperage, resistance, and wattage—are interrelated, and they cannot be separated. Together, they define the power potential of a given electrical circuit.

These values can easily be measured in your home, and on your model railroad. To measure voltage, for example, you'll need a voltmeter. Touch the voltmeter's two probes to both terminal posts on your transformer, or touch one probe to the center rail and the other to the outside rail of the track.

To measure current (amps), you must use an ammeter. To connect the ammeter, you first must remove one of the two wires leading from the transformer to the track, and place the meter's leads in that wire's place. Then, with one probe touching the terminal post on your transformer, and the other touching the track rail that was connected to that post by the removed wire, take your current reading.

To determine wattage, you don't need any measuring device; simply multiply volts times amps, and the resulting product is watts, or "Volt Amps," which is the same thing.

These definitions and principles are applicable to all forms of electricity. It's important to recognize that there really is only one type of electricity, but it behaves in different ways depending on how it is generated. So, by "forms," we mean the manner in which electricity can be made to act as it travels through a circuit after having been generated.

Direct Current (DC) is one of two forms of electricity, and DC involves a continuous flow of current in one direction from the positive (+) terminal of a generating source—a battery, for example—back to the source through a negative (-) terminal. Direct Current is used by most two-rail model railroading scales, and is the form of electricity produced by all types of batteries.

Alternating Current (AC)—the form of electricity that powers nearly all Lionel trains—is so named because current flowing through the circuit actually changes direction, or alternates, at a very high rate. The rate of reversal is known as the "frequency," and it is measured in a unit called "Hertz" (Hz), which designates cycles per second. A cycle is actually two reversals—positive to negative, then back again. The frequency for power distribution in the United States is standardized at 60 Hz, so the current reversal actually happens 120 times per second.

Alternating current can also be changed to Direct Current by means of a "rectifier." Conversely, DC current can be changed to AC current by means of a "converter," so there are indeed ways to reconfigure the form of electricity depending on its intended use.

Alternating current enjoys some advantage over DC when it comes to maintaining pressure over a long-distance transmission of electricity, such as from state-to-state by the electric utilities. Direct current has the edge in supplying clean, filtered power for circuit boards and computer chips. However, since AC can be rather easily converted to DC, and since the converse is also true, there really are no major advantages or limitations associated with either type of electric current in model railroad applications.

One additional point about electricity, be it AC or DC: Electricity must flow in a complete circuit, and whatever device it is intended to operate must be part of that circuit. If the current finds some way to bypass the device it is supposed to operate, regardless of whether that object is a light bulb, an electric train locomotive motor, or some other device, a "short circuit" will result. If left unattended, the short circuit can permanently damage the power source, which is why most such sources—Lionel transformers, for example—are equipped with automatic circuit breakers. These breakers are designed to activate well in advance of any real harm being done to the source.

• Locomotive motors

Over the years, the type of motor most commonly installed in Lionel locomotives has been what is known as an "open frame" motor—most of which are also "universal" motors, meaning that they are capable of running on either AC or DC current. Be aware, however, that some open frame motors are designed for DC-only operation, while others may be AC-only. Also keep in mind that some Lionel locomotives are equipped with a single motor, while others have two motors, both of which are electrically linked to perform as a single unit. Dual-motor units are usually placed in the larger diesels and articulated steam locomotives. The most recent version of the open-frame motor used in Lionel locomotives is the well known Pullmor motor, which has long been regarded as a rugged, dependable, and easy to maintain workhorse.

Basically, an open-frame motor like the Pullmor consists of a large, fixed field electromagnet (also known simply as "field"), one end of which is the north pole and the other the south pole. Keep in mind that all magnets, big and small, work in the same way: Opposite poles attract, and like poles repel. The moving part of the motor is called the "armature," and it is permanently positioned so that it will freely turn inside the two fixed poles of the field. The armature itself consists of three, five, seven, or more small electromagnets (magnets activated by electric current). When the motor is running, these small electromagnets constantly change their polarity by means of a "commutator," which is a plate-like device attached to one end of the armature. Electricity is fed into one side of the commutator by means of a carbon brush. It then runs through the windings of the armature and out the other side of the commutator through another brush. This causes each of the coils on the armature to spin rapidly, also causing each, in turn, to first become a south pole, then a north pole, and then a neutral pole. Here's how it works:

When electricity is initially supplied to the motor, the pole of the armature nearest the north pole of the field is a south pole, and it is pulled toward the field's north pole in a revolving motion (unlike poles attract). Once it reaches the point where the pull of the north pole is strongest, the commutator changes the polarity of the armature pole and that pole then becomes a north pole. Since like poles repel each other, the armature pole is repelled by the north pole of the field and it is subsequently attracted even further around toward the field's south pole. In the meantime, the next pole of the armature has become a south pole, and it is attracted to the north pole of the field. As the poles in turn continue to attract and repel each other, the armature turns. All of this frantic activity occurs very rapidly, and the armature turns continuously and smoothly, thereby making the motor run.

Open-frame motors are relatively simple and very durable devices. They have certainly passed the test of time, because open-frame motors installed in Lionel locomotives built a century ago still perform flawlessly today.

In recent years, increasing numbers of Lionel locomotives are being powered by sturdy, reliable, and virtually maintenance-free DC can motors, which are so-named because they are a sealed unit, basically resembling a metal can in shape, except for a drive shaft that protrudes from one end. The can motor operates on DC only, with the traditional AC track power being rectified to DC within the locomotive itself so it can be used by the motor. DC can motors have the advantage of being very quiet, cool running, and able to provide a very smooth transition in speeds, particularly if they are also equipped with a momentum flywheel to absorb and minimize the effects of any abrupt speed changes. Another distinct advantage of a can-type motor is their relatively low cost. Since there are no user serviceable parts to fuss with, these motors are simply removed and replaced when something goes wrong.

The latest Lionel innovation in locomotive power control is the Odyssey System. The Odyssey system is not really a motor, per se, since it combines high performance DC can motors with sophisticated electronic circuitry to provide a number of new features, including the ability to maintain an operator-selected speed setting regardless of whether the locomotive is moving up or down grades, negotiating tight turns, or passing through switches and crossings. The Odyssey System also interacts with the locomotive's sound system, if the locomotive is so equipped, so motor sounds and smoke output increase or decrease in sequence with the workload demanded of the motor, and regardless of whether or not the locomotive's speed has actually changed. The Odyssey System represents state-of-the-art technology that marks the next level in realistic operator control over every locomotive function.

The type of motor (or motor system) used in a Lionel locomotive you intend to purchase can be determined from the catalog description. All are designed to operate reliably with any Lionel AC transformer, so you can be assured of full compatibility across the range of offerings.

• Lionel transformers—past and present

Of course, the true heart of any O gauge model railroad is the transformer that provides the current needed to operate locomotive motors and accessories. Over the years, Lionel has produced a wide variety of transformers, ranging from the small units packaged with most starter sets to the robust and renowned ZW, with enough output power to operate several trains and a good number of lighted or operating accessories.

Lionel 40-watt power supply is the basic transformer that comes in many starter sets.

In terms of how it functions, a transformer is not a terribly complex device. Essentially, what it does is "transform" ordinary—and extremely dangerous—110-115 volt Alternating Current (AC), of the type delivered to your household outlets, into the safe, low (about 6-22 volt) range of AC voltages used to operate toy trains. Most three-rail O gauge trains manufactured today are designed to operate with the low range AC current provided by a transformer, but you should also know that in the world of two-rail model railroading, and even in the case of a very few three-rail train sets (none of which are currently offered by Lionel), a device called a DC "power pack" is used to power and control the trains. A DC power pack looks very much like a transformer, and it functions in the same way. The only significant difference between a transformer and a power pack is that a power pack takes high-voltage Alternating Current (AC) on the input side, and converts it to low-voltage Direct Current (DC) at the output posts that supply power to the track. A transformer simply converts high-voltage AC at the input side to low-voltage AC at the output terminals.

The thing to keep in mind at this point is that all Lionel transformers produced today transform high-voltage AC into low-voltage AC. At certain points in its long history, Lionel did provide DC power packs to power DC-type motors in some locomotive models, but this is no longer the case. If you purchase or are given an older Lionel train set, it's a good idea to check the package label or operator's manual to see if it was intended for DC-only operation. If the packaging or manual isn't available, check with your local Lionel dealer, or consult one of the references listed in Appendix A (page 116) before attempting to operate the train on your AC-powered layout. Applying the wrong type of power to a locomotive may damage or even ruin the motor.

Being inquisitive by nature, many of us are tempted to take things apart to see "what makes it tick." Avoid this temptation with any transformer or power pack! Unless you

are a trained electrician, what you find inside could shock—or even kill—you. **NEVER** attempt to open a toy train transformer to "see how it works!" They're difficult to open in any case, because most transformers and power packs are intentionally manufactured as sealed units, which require special tools to open. If you're truly curious about what goes on inside these magical black boxes as they convert high-voltage current to low voltage, here's a brief description of what occurs:

Basically, there are two separate coils of enamel-coated wire inside the transformer. These wire coils are wound around a common core made of soft iron, but they are situated in such a way that neither coil comes into direct contact with the other. One of these coils in made of fine wire that is wound around the core many hundreds of times to produce what is known as the "primary" or "high-voltage" coil. The other coil, which forms the "secondary" or "low-voltage" coil, is comprised of a heavier gauge wire that is wrapped around the core about 1/5 to 1/10 the total number of turns as the primary coil.

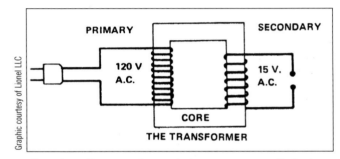

Two wire coils wrapped around a common core are the basic components of a reduction transformer of the type that power Lionel Trains.

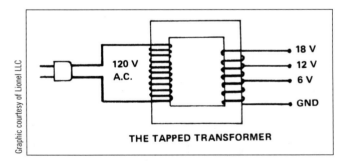

On the fixed-voltage outputs of a transformer, the specific voltages are obtained by "tapping" the secondary coil at select locations along the coil.

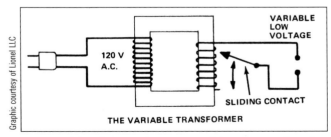

In a variable-voltage configuration, a sliding contact along the secondary coil permits a full range of output voltages to be used.

The two ends of the primary coil wire are connected to the AC line cord, which, in turn, plugs into an ordinary household outlet. When electricity passes through the primary coil, a magnetic field is generated, and this, in turn, results in a low voltage current flow within the secondary coil.

The secondary (low-voltage) output coil is what supplies current to your trains and accessories. This coil can be "tapped" into at one or more points along the coil turns to provide fixed voltage of a predetermined amount to, for example, light and/or operate accessories. However, if one end of the secondary coil wire leads to a common post on the transformer housing, and the other end is instead connected to a sliding contact or a "rheostat" that adjusts the amount of resistance in the circuit, varying levels of current can be obtained from the secondary coil. The amount of current being delivered can be controlled by the operator, by using a knob or lever outside the transformer case. This feature provides the variable voltage, from 0 to as much as 24 volts, that is used to power your locomotive's motor, causing it to move in a steadily increasing range of speeds up to its maximum limit, and back down again.

For safety, every Lionel transformer is also equipped with an automatic circuit breaker that will trip before the current demands become too great for the transformer to safely handle, such as when a short circuit occurs. If you overload the capacity of your transformer by trying to run too many trains or accessories at the same time, the internal circuit breaker will trip almost instantly, shutting everything off. The same thing will happen if a metal object or a train derailment causes the center rail of your track to come into contact with one of the outer rails. The circuit breaker will automatically reset itself, but *only* after the cause of the short circuit or overload has been removed or corrected.

All Lionel transformers also carry an Underwriter's Laboratory (UL) approval rating, further assuring you that, when properly handled and used as intended, these devices meet high standards of consumer safety. The phrase "when properly handled and used as intended" encompasses the following safety tips, which apply to all Lionel transformers:

➤ Always read, carefully and completely, all of the instructions that came with your transformer *before* putting it to use.

➤ Transformers are not intended for use by children under eight years of age.

➤ Inspect the exposed parts of your transformer, and particularly the line cord, on a regular basis. If a problem is detected, return the transformer to an authorized Lionel Service Center.

➤ Lionel transformers are designed for indoor use *only*. Do not use your transformer outdoors, or in any area where it may be exposed to moisture.

➤ NEVER use the transformer for other than its intended purpose, which is to operate Lionel locomotives with AC or universal motors.

➤ Lionel transformers are designed to operate on 110-120 volt, 60 Hz AC power only.

➤ NEVER attempt to disassemble any Lionel transformer.

➤ Do not leave your layout unattended with the transformer power on.

➤ If the circuit breaker trips, first turn the speed control lever or dial to the "off" position. Then correct the problem, and allow the circuit breaker to reset itself before again advancing the throttle. Failure to turn the speed control off may result in the locomotive surging forward when the circuit breaker resets.

➤ Turn off and unplug the transformer when it is not in use.

• *Connecting the transformer*

A transformer by itself, even with the AC cord plugged into a wall outlet, is not of much use to anyone. Something needs to be connected to the output posts for the available power to do any real work.

The most basic of Lionel transformers have only two posts or terminals, which are used for linking the transformer to the track. A wire from one of these terminals connects to the center rail of the track by means of wire and a Lockon (the #1 clip on the Lockon connects to the center rail). The second terminal is similarly connected to the other clip on that same Lockon (the #2 clip connects to either outside rail). Snap the Lockon onto the track; connect the two wires from the transformer posts to the Lockon; plug the AC line of the transformer into an ordinary household outlet; and you're ready to run your train. That's really all there is to it!

The 80 watt/5 amp Lionel Transformer is included in many of the higher-end Lionel sets.

A few small, lighted accessories can still be used with even the smallest transformers, consistent with the power requirements of the train itself. These accessories would need to rely on track power, however, and the reliability of their operation (including the brightness of their lights) will vary depending on how much voltage is being applied to the track at a given point in time. As your inventory of operating or lighted accessories expands, you will want to purchase a second, larger transformer to handle the power requirements of the trains. Then, your smaller transformer can be used exclusively as an accessory power source. The current supplied to accessories can then be regulated, so you can, for example, reduce bulb brightness, which will help to prolong the life of the lamps. You can also adjust the pace of action of many operating accessories in a similar manner.

The larger and more powerful transformers—those intended to operate more than one train, or those which also provide separate fixed voltage posts for powering a number of accessories—are equipped with several connecting posts or terminals on the outside of the transformer case. Each of these posts is normally labeled with a letter. On most (but not all) Lionel transformers, the "U" post on the transformer is connected to the #2 clip on a Lockon. Some Lionel transformers may have more than one "U" post, but since all are connected internally, any one of them can be used. The other posts, which are labeled "A" through "D" depending on the type of transformer you have, provide variable or fixed voltages (or both) in different ranges, again depending on the transformer model. These posts are connected to the Lockon's #1 clip. The operator's manual that comes with each transformer clearly explains the proper wiring and operation of that particular model.

Your Lionel transformer requires no operator maintenance of any kind, other than a periodic inspection of the power cord for safety purposes, as noted above. If you find any damage to the cord or the transformer housing, do not continue to use the transformer. Instead, immediately return it to an authorized Lionel Service Center for repair. Also, be sure to disconnect your transformer from the AC outlet when you are not running your trains, since none of the current line of Lionel transformers are equipped with an integral on/off switch. Plugging your transformer into a surge-protected power strip with a built-in on/off switch is a good way to gain an extra measure of protection, because you can easily flick the switch off when you have completed your operating session.

• Power distribution through auxiliary "feeders"

As your layout expands, you may find that trains tend to slow down along certain portions of the track—especially in those areas furthest away from the primary track power connection. This may be the result of voltage loss caused by the more extensive loop of track, along with some power loss that normally occurs where individual track sections are joined together. You can solve this problem by providing additional "feeders" to distribute transformer power more

evenly over a larger layout. Essentially, this involves nothing more than installing additional Lockons every 6-15 track sections, and running a wire from the #1 clip of the first Lockon to the #1 clip of the second (or subsequent) Lockon, and then running another wire to similarly connect both #2 clips on these Lockons. Be sure that all the #1 clips on all of the Lockons are connected to each other, and that the #2 clips are also connected only to other #2 clips—otherwise a short circuit will result.

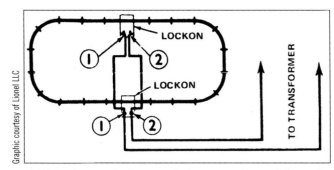

Additional power feeders attached to remote areas of the track, especially on larger layouts, will help to assure an even distribution of track power over the entire layout.

If you prefer, you can eliminate a "spaghetti bowl" wiring effect under your layout by installing a ground loop of wire in an oval shape underneath the layout. Use a continuous length of 18 gauge or 14 gauge wire (the lower the number, the thicker the wire) to form a large oval that approximates the shape of the track on the top side of the layout, then join and solder the wire ends together so it forms a continuous loop. This, in essence, will provide two paths for the current to return to the transformer. You can enhance the circuit even more on a large layout by soldering additional wires, spaced several feet apart, crosswise between the two sides of the oval, thereby forming a sort of "grid." For each transformer that you use on the layout, run 14 gauge wire from one common post on each transformer to the nearest and/or most convenient point on the wire oval you created, and solder the connecting point. The "electric highway" you have created will save you a whole lot of wire, and will reduce overall costs and effort in wiring a larger layout.

• Increasing your layout's power potential

At some point, as your involvement in the hobby grows and as you acquire more locomotives, cars, and accessories, you'll likely find that your original transformer no longer meets the power requirements of your ever-expanding layout. What should you do then?

Well, one viable alternative might be to purchase a more powerful transformer, such as the renowned Lionel ZW, which will handle up to four trains independently (or two trains and a good number of accessories). This doesn't mean that you can no longer make use of your original, small transformer. As noted above, it could be used to power accessories on the layout, such as streetlights or floodlight towers. It might also be used to power a separate loop of track that is independent of others on the layout. Or, perhaps it could power a point-to-point trolley line running through the town on your layout. If the track is fitted with a bumper at each end of the line, your Lionel self-reversing trolley can continually shuttle back and forth without any special operator attention.

Another less costly alternative is to use two or more smaller transformers together so they can power a layout that has been electrically divided into separate "blocks," wherein one transformer powers and controls train movement in a certain block, and the other powers and controls an adjacent block. Two Lionel 80 watt/5 amp Transformer/Controller units would be ideal for this application on small and medium-size layouts. However, the use of two or more transformers together requires physically connecting the transformers in parallel, and assuring that both transformers are synchronized, or "phased." Phasing assures that the Alternating Current, which, as noted previously, continually changes direction at 60 Hz per second, does this in a way so the directions of movement are the same (phased) at the secondary coils and output posts for both transformers. It is absolutely critical that two or more transformers intended to be used together on the same circuit be properly phased. If they aren't, you will experience a short circuit whenever a locomotive moves from the insulated block controlled by one transformer to the insulated block controlled by the other.

You won't have to worry about phasing newer Lionel transformers, because all of them are equipped with polarized AC plugs (one prong is wider than the other) so the transformer is automatically phased when it is used with a similarly equipped second transformer. However, if you are using one or more older Lionel transformers, with prongs on the AC cord that are the same width, you will definitely want to make sure they are properly phased. Here's the simple procedure for phasing two or more older transformers:

1. Connect a wire between the "U" posts on both transformers.

2. Set the throttle control on both transformers to full power.

3. Plug both transformers into a wall outlet or, preferably, an outlet strip.

4. Using an 18 volt lamp touch one lead to the "A" post of one transformer and the other lead to the "A" post of the second transformer. If the lamp does not light or burns very dimly the transformers are in phase and no further action is required. If the lamp burns brightly, the transformers are out of phase. This can be corrected by simply reversing the wall plug on only one of the transformers. Repeat the lamp test to confirm that both transformers are now in phase.

5. With a small dab of paint or nail polish, or a piece of colored tape, mark the wall plugs of both transformers to indicate the proper configuration. If you have to unplug the transformers, the color code will indicate the proper orientation for the next time they are plugged in. That's one reason why the use of a multi-outlet terminal strip is highly recommended. You can leave the transformers plugged in, and then use the on/off switch on the terminal strip to turn off the power to both transformers. Or, you can simply unplug the terminal strip from the wall outlet if there is no on/off switch.

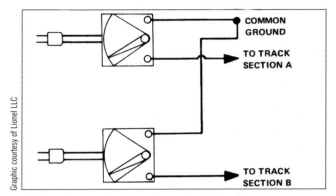

Wiring diagram for connecting and phasing of two or more transformers. Be sure the transformers are phased in accordance with the procedure described in the text.

If two transformers are being used to control trains operating on two electrically independent loops of track—a separate trolley line that does not connect to the main line at any point, for example—it stands to reason that the transformers do not need to be phased, because there will be no point where the wheels of a locomotive will cross over, or bridge, one electrical circuit or block while moving to the other.

However, it these same two transformers are going to power two trains operating along the same mainline, or will be used to power sidings, a yard area, or additional loops that *are* physically connected to the first mainline at any point, the transformers *must* be in phase so they can independently control trains within their own assigned "blocks."

• Basic block wiring and control

"Blocks" are electrically isolated sections of track that enable you to run two or more trains on the same physically connected track network while still maintaining independent control of each train by means of a separate power source, or with a transformer capable of multi-train operation. Blocks are particularly useful for separating a yard area from the mainline, for example, or for isolating individual tracks within that yard. A switcher can be put to work performing various movements in the yard, while another train continues to operate along the connected mainline. Or, block control can be used to allow parallel and physically connected double mainlines to operate two trains independently, each under separate control. And, they can even enable you to operate two or more trains along the same track network, assuming the blocks themselves are long enough to accommodate such movements.

Keep in mind that an insulated *block* differs from the insulated *track section* that was described in Chapter 5. In making the insulated track section, an outside rail was converted into an insulated rail that could be used to activate accessories. With an insulated block, the power or control rail—the center rail of the track—becomes the insulated rail. It's generally a good idea to decide where you want and need insulated blocks in the layout planning phase, before you proceed with construction and permanently install the track, because this will save you from going back and re-doing your work later on.

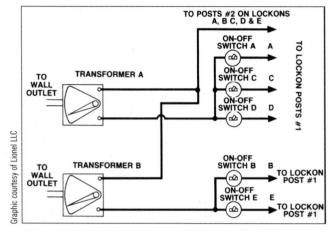

Diagram for wiring blocks controlled by multiple transformers.

Creating an insulated block is very easy. You simply replace the center rail steel track pin with a fiber pin at the point where you want the block to begin, and you do the same thing a number of sections further along where you want the block to end.

If you did nothing else at this point, a train will run normally until it hits that first fiber-pin-equipped section of track. At that point, the train will simply stop, and remain stopped, because it is no longer drawing current from the center rail in the about-to-be-entered block. So, something must be done to supply power to that "dead" block so the train can at least continue on its way.

If you are using only one transformer with single train capability to power your layout, you'll need to provide some means for turning each block off and on when you want a train to continue on an uninterrupted journey, or when you want to supply power to an insulated siding to allow a train to enter, park on, or exit the siding. A simple on/off toggle or sliding switch, located at your control panel and wired so one side connects to the power output post on the transformer, and the other side leads to the #1 clip on a Lockon installed within the block, will do the trick. When the switch is turned to the "on" position, power reaches the track. When it's turned "off," the power is cut.

If you are using two transformers, or a single transformer with multiple train controls, in your block control scheme, you can employ DPDT center-off toggle switches (double-pole, double-throw switches with a center-off position) to provide power to the track from one or the other of the transformers, or from neither of them if the toggle is set to the center-off position. These types of toggle switches are available at most electronics stores. This arrangement gives you the option of using one transformer or the other to operate the entire layout (assuming each has the output power to do so), or you can mix-and-match, using one transformer to control select blocks, and the other to control certain other blocks. Keep in mind that these blocks can be segments of the mainline loop; an independent second loop; passing sidings; an entire yard area or select tracks within a yard; and stub-end sidings. With this arrangement, you'll be able to control exactly where either of your two independently controlled trains go, or don't go.

A point to keep in mind: If you have a block system controlled by two transformers, and are running a single locomotive from a block controlled by one of those transformers into a block controlled by the other, the speed control levers on both transformers will need to be set at the same level in order for the locomotive to properly bridge the insulated gap between the blocks.

THE NEW TECHNOLOGY: TRAINMASTER COMMAND CONTROL

TrainMaster Command Control (TMCC), from Lionel, has revolutionized toy train operation and control, allowing the operator to control trains, switches, and a variety of accessories from any location around the layout, all by means of a convenient hand-held, wireless controller that is about the size of a TV remote control unit.

If all of the locomotives you operate are TMCC equipped, you won't even need insulated blocks for controlling trains on your layout.

To take full advantage of the capabilities of the TMCC system, you'll need at least one TMCC-equipped locomotive on your roster. These locomotives, designated in the catalogs and in advertisements as "Command ready" or "TMCC equipped," are packed with special features that allow for full and independent operator control over a variety of features, including smoke, horn or whistle, lights, a range of locomotive and crew sound effects, operating couplers, and more.

Photo courtesy of Lionel LLC

With Lionel TrainMaster Command Control (TMCC) total control of your trains is as close as your fingertips, regardless of where in the room you happen to be.

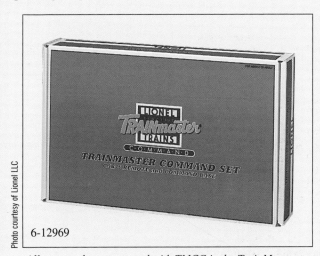

Photo courtesy of Lionel LLC

6-12969

All you need to get started with TMCC is the TrainMaster Command Set. Included in the set are the TrainMaster Cab-1, which allows for total walk-around control of your trains and accessories, and the TrainMaster Command Base, which receives signals from the Cab-1 and communicates with Command Controlled items on your layout.

Photo courtesy of Lionel LLC

6-12868

TMCC Cab-1 Remote.

TMCC affords total walk-around freedom and control of all aspects of your layout, including individual control of multiple locomotives operating on the same track. In fact, there's such a high level of total control with TMCC that you'll almost never have to stay at or near your transformer and control panel once you have TMCC installed.

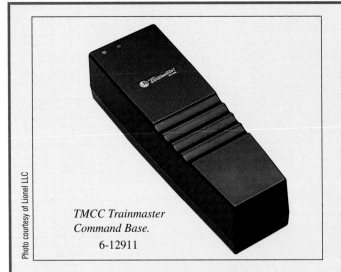

TMCC Trainmaster
Command Base.
6-12911

Getting started with TMCC is quite simple. If you have one of the outside rails of your track wired to your transformer as a common ground, and are feeding power to the center rail (the configuration for normal transformer operation), all you'll need is a Lionel Command Base and Cab-1 package, along with the transformer you are already using, as long as it can deliver 12 to 18 volts to your track. Your layout, regardless of size, requires only *one* Command Base to control the entire layout, so this is a one-time purchase. You could also use TMCC's PowerHouse power supply instead of a transformer to provide power to the track, but for getting started with TMCC we'll assume that you already have a conventional transformer, and prefer to use that to provide track power. Here's how to set everything up (see Figure 1):

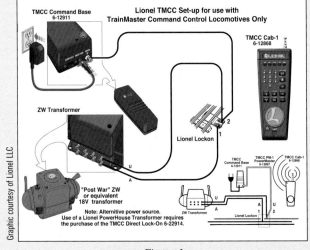

Figure 1

1. *Connect a wire from the Command Base terminal to your outside (common) rail—that's the #2 clip on the Lockon that you're currently using to connect your transformer to the track, or the #2 clip on a Lockon that you install elsewhere on the layout (the #1 clip in that second instance would have no wire leading to it). As an alternative, you can also connect the*

Command Base to the "U" (common) post on your transformer.

2. *The Command Base comes with a wall pack power supply. Plug the wall pack into a wall outlet, and plug the round Command Base power connector into the Base power jack located next to the "U" terminal post at the front of the Base unit.*

3. *Install 4 fresh AA batteries in the Cab 1 controller, and place a TMCC-equipped locomotive on the track.*

4. *Now set the power on your transformer to about 14 volts, and leave it set at that position. The operator's manual that comes with TMCC may specify setting the speed control to 18 volts, but operators have found that 14 volts works fine in most applications, and the lower voltage helps to extend bulb life in locomotives, lighted cars, and other track-powered devices such as switches.*

5. *Press the "ENG" button on the Cab-1; followed by the "1" button; then the "Boost" button. Your TMCC-equipped locomotive should now start up. Use the large red dial to control the locomotive's speed. Other buttons on the Cab-1 allow you to activate the whistle or horn, bell, lights, brakes, couplers, and any other features that the locomotive may have. That's really all there is to it!*

6-22914

The Lionel TMCC Direct Lockon is disguised as a trackside electrical utility shed, and is used to connect a PowerHouse Transformer to the track. It eliminates the need for a PowerMaster if you use only TMCC equipped locomotives, and provides over-current protection with automatic reset.

You can also run conventional, non-TMCC equipped locomotives with your TMCC system's Cab-1, with the addition of a PM-1 PowerMaster distribution system. Here's how that configuration works (see Figure 2):

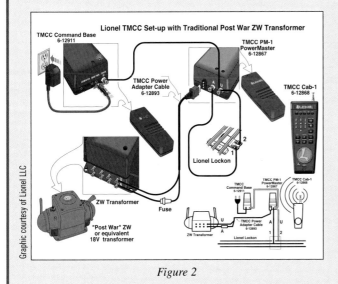

Figure 2

1. The PowerMaster distribution center connects to your conventional transformer by means of a special Adapter Cable that has a plug at one end and two wires at the other end. The plug end goes into the back of the PowerMaster, and the two wires connect to the same terminals on the transformer that normally would be connected directly to the track. The Adapter Cable is not needed if you're using a TMCC PH-1 PowerHouse Transformer as part of your system.

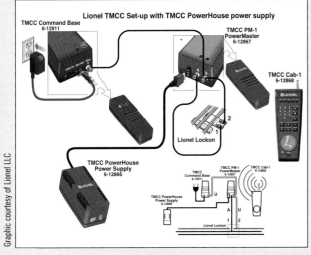

Figure 3

2. (See Figure 3.) The Mode Switch on the PowerMaster should be set to the "Conventional" position. On the back of the PowerMaster are two binding posts, labeled "U" and "A". Connect a wire from the "A"

post to the #1 clip (the one that powers the center rail) on a Lockon that is attached to the track. Connect the "U" post to the #2 clip on the Lockon. If you have more than one track or insulated block, and if each of these tracks or blocks is electrically independent of any others, use a separate PowerMaster for each track or block (up to a total of nine separate tracks and/or blocks).

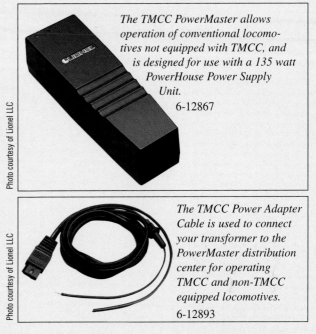

The TMCC PowerMaster allows operation of conventional locomotives not equipped with TMCC, and is designed for use with a 135 watt PowerHouse Power Supply Unit.
6-12867

The TMCC Power Adapter Cable is used to connect your transformer to the PowerMaster distribution center for operating TMCC and non-TMCC equipped locomotives.
6-12893

3. The Cab-1, in this configuration, will communicate your instructions to the PowerMaster, which will then control track power and, ultimately, the locomotive. To activate the track, press the "TR" button on the Cab-1, and then press the number "1" on the keypad. This sets that track's identification to Track 1. You can address other independent blocks or tracks in this same way, from "1" through "9".

4. Use the red throttle dial or the "Boost" button to initially power-up the locomotive. Then rotate the throttle to start the locomotive moving in the forward direction.

5. When the locomotive is running, you can use the "DIR" button to change direction. Pressing "DIR" one time will stop the locomotive, and pressing it again will reset the locomotive so it will move in the opposite direction. Turn the red throttle dial, and the locomotive will begin moving. You can use the "BRAKE" button to slow the locomotive, or turn back the throttle to stop it completely.

6. If your locomotive has horn (or whistle) and bell features, the buttons designated for those functions on the Cab-1 will activate these features—one push of

the bell button will turn the bell on, and another push will turn it off. Pushing the horn/whistle will activate the horn/whistle as long as the button is held down.

7. *If the TMCC PM-1 PowerMaster is added to your layout along with the TMCC Command Base, you will have CAB-1 wireless control of all your Command and conventional locomotives.*

There are numerous other features and functions that can also be controlled by TrainMaster Command Control and the Cab-1. If the locomotive you're operating is equipped with Lionel RailSounds (which will operate just fine without TMCC), you'll find that TMCC expands the variety of sounds available. TMCC also allows you to operate two or more locomotives on the same track, without requiring any complex blocks or additional wiring, and you can even couple two or more locomotives into a "lashup" to operate as a single unit.

It's also possible to operate two or more TMCC-equipped locomotives simultaneously with your Cab-1 by programming each locomotive with its own identification number so it will receive and execute commands addressed only to it—many hobbyists use the last two numbers of the locomotive's road number (located under the cab windows) to make it easy to remember the unit's TMCC address. All TMCC locomotives are programmed at the factory with an address of "1", so it is necessary to follow this "addressing" procedure, as described in the operator's manual, to give each locomotive a distinctive identity.

TMCC can also control switches, activate accessories, and turn sidings on and off by means of a TMCC SC-2 Switch Controller, available separately. The SC-2 can handle up to six switches and up to twelve accessories, all controlled remotely through your Cab-1 controller.

TrainMaster Command Control has brought new levels of operating excitement to Lionel railroading, and it's a system you'll certainly want to consider adding to your layout. A number of other manufacturers have also jumped aboard the TMCC express, and they are offering command-equipped locomotives that will perform all of the various functions without further modification. For that matter, a good many older Lionel locomotives can also be retrofitted with TMCC, so the possibilities for increased railroading fun are expanded even further.

Lionel Trainmaster Command Control with Traditional (Non Command) Setup

For those who wish to continue to operate their railroad empire with conventional non-command locomotives only, Lionel Trainmaster components can give you the ability to run your trains by remote control. With the Cab-1 Remote Control and PM-1 Powermaster combination, along with your existing or new transformer, you too can enjoy wireless walk-around control of your trains.

For the simple easy to follow wiring to enhance your layout, see Figure #4:

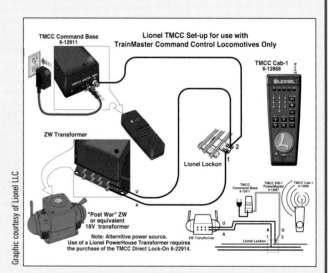

Figure 4

Chapter 7

Planning a Lionel layout

Although Bill Heron's spectacular Alamoosook Junction certainly represents a decidedly more ambitious project than the first-time layout builder is likely to tackle, it does provide an outstanding example of what can ultimately be accomplished in the hobby with careful planning and preparation. Bill's beautifully detailed O gauge pike was constructed by custom layout builder Clarke Dunham in his workshop, and then shipped to Bill's home in sections. Note how the displays and other furnishings in the train room nicely complement the layout. A closer view of the imposing trestle can be seen in Chapter 11.

Spending time to plan your Lionel layout—regardless of whether it's your first one or your tenth—is definitely time well spent. The planning phase is where you will decide where you're going to put your layout; what size it will be; what you want your railroad to be; and how it will be designed to operate. This is also a time when thought can be given to scenery and accessories, and to imagine how you can freely express your ingenuity and creativity without making a big dent in your hobby budget. Once this phase is complete, you'll have a better understanding of where you are going, how to get there, and what tools and supplies will be needed to reach your goals. You'll also have a much better idea of how to proceed with actual layout construction, because, like an architect planning a new home, the advance work you do will serve as your blueprint.

There is one planning pitfall to be aware of: Some folks tend to become so involved with planning that they never

really get around to starting construction of their layout. That's something this chapter is designed to help you avoid, because the true enjoyment of Lionel railroading comes from actually running the trains and expressing your individuality and creativity through the surroundings you create for them.

By the same token, other hobbyists go to the opposite extreme: They don't do any real planning! They simply find a place to put the layout; build a platform of some type to hold it; and then start putting down track in a random manner to see if they can come up with a satisfactory arrangement that fits the available space. While there's really nothing terribly wrong with this approach, it will save you time, money, and possible frustration if you'll just spend a modest amount of time looking before you leap. Do spend some time planning; just don't over-plan to the point where you become what is known as an "armchair model railroader."

• *The Golden Rule of model railroad planning*

Let's start the planning process with what might best be called the Golden Rule of Model Railroad Planning: *Start small, keep it simple, and plan for expansion.* This "rule" is applicable to model railroading in any scale, and it is particularly relevant if you are new to the hobby. Since there are three parts to the "rule," it's useful to explore each component in turn.

Start small. . .

Starting small truly is sound advice. Many newcomers to model railroading seem to feel that enjoyment of the hobby somehow relates to the amount of space available for an extensive network of track on a platform that fills an entire basement, garage, or attic. Nothing could be further from the truth!

When it comes to model train layouts, bigger is not necessarily better, or even more rewarding. Bigger *is* more labor intensive and time consuming, and bigger *is* often far more expensive. But that's about it! Even the largest model railroad enjoys no particular advantage over its smaller cousins in regard to its potential for creative expression and personal satisfaction. The danger in starting out with ideas and plans that are overly complex and ambitious is that building your railroad may become more of a compulsion than a hobby, and you are apt to become frustrated and discouraged far short of reaching your lofty goal.

There are a number of advantages to "starting small," including:

➤ Smaller model railroads are easier to maintain.

➤ Planning, designing, and building a small layout provides good hands-on exposure to the tools and techniques that might be used for a larger layout later on.

➤ Building a layout in small and manageable phases helps to focus attention on actually completing and detailing an individual segment or scene before moving on to the next.

➤ Even the smallest layout is never really complete when you consider the myriad of small details that can be added over time. As a result, you'll almost never run out of new and imaginative things to do.

➤ Hobbyists with limited space can enjoy the benefits of "building small" at home, and then join with local groups for expanded "big time" model railroading on more extensive club layouts, or on layouts made up of transportable modules.

➤ "Small" also implies accessible. There's little point in constructing a layout if you can't conveniently get to

every part of it when maintenance is needed, or when you want to add more scenic details. Operators of very large pikes also quickly discover that the worst derailments or electrical problems almost always seem to occur in the most inaccessible areas.

Keep it simple. . .

A common problem with many model railroads is that there is often too much railroad and not enough environment for the railroad to operate in. In other words, there's a tendency on the part of some hobbyists to cram as much track as possible into a given amount of space. Resist that temptation! Aside from yard areas, you'll notice that real railroads generally get by with the minimum amount of trackwork needed to transport people or freight from point "A" to point "B." You should strive to do the same with your model railroad.

On a small layout, for example, a single mainline, with perhaps a passing siding to accommodate a second train, and a couple of spur sidings to serve trackside industries, is quite enough to provide a whole lot of operating potential. Rather than fill the remaining space with more track, plan to make good use of that area by adding accessories, scenery, and other details that will support and reinforce the theme you have chosen for the railroad (theme development is discussed later in this chapter). The knowledge and experience gained from constructing, wiring, detailing, and operating a simple layout will serve well in any future expansion efforts, which takes us to the final part of our Golden Rule:

Plan for expansion. . .

That smaller layout you start with can almost always be expanded later by adding new sections to one end or the other—especially if you gave some realistic thought to future expansion in your initial planning phase. For example, a 4 feet by 8 feet layout can easily be expanded by adding another 4 feet by 8 feet platform to one end of the layout. The extended layout could also be configured in an "L" shape, to fit the corner area of a room. There's also nothing to prevent you from expanding it to some greater or lesser length, or giving it some other configuration altogether, depending on the space available.

By "plan for expansion," we don't necessarily mean that the entire layout of your dreams has to be designed and committed to paper at this time. Until you've become accustomed to working with Lionel trains, there's no need to go to that extreme. Rather, what we mean is that, in the early planning stages, you should give at least some consideration to how the layout might grow in the future. If you eventually want to extend the mainline, for instance, where would you connect into the existing mainline, and how might you accomplish that with a minimum of disruption to the existing phase? Would a switch installed in place of the first curved sections (both sides) at one end of the oval do it for you? If so, would you also want to consider extending the length of the inner mainline? During the layout design stage, these are considerations you'll want to keep in mind. Planning for expansion early-on just makes it all that much easier to accomplish when the time comes, and it gives you something new to look forward to.

• *Selecting a location for your layout*

With the "Golden Rule of Model Railroad Planning" now firmly in mind, it's time to begin thinking about where you're going to put your layout. You may have already chosen a location, of course, and there may be no other options are available. If so, that's perfectly fine, and you'll work with whatever space is available.

On the other hand, you may be one of those budding Lionel enthusiasts who feels that you simply don't have *any* space available for a layout. That's probably the most common concern expressed by individuals who would really like to operate their Lionel trains beyond the holiday season, but who have never attempted to do so because of concerns about space. The truth is, there very likely *is* some space for a Lionel layout in your home—you simply haven't yet discovered where it is and how to make the best use of it. So let's attend to that dilemma.

Those fortunate enough to have a fully finished basement beneath their home are blessed with an obvious, and often readily available, space for a model railroad. If the climate in the basement can be controlled, and the humidity level maintained at about 60 per cent or so (a portable dehumidifier will take care of that), this location provides an ideal environment for just about any model railroad. Best of all, most basements have ample open and unused space that could potentially house a good-size layout.

Unfortunately, homes in many parts of the country don't have basements. Here the challenge becomes a bit greater because the layout may need to compete with, or share, living area that is already dedicated to some other purpose. Still, all is not lost! Often enough, a bit of reconfiguring of the existing space will provide ample area for a

small or even a modest-size layout. Relocating a single piece of furniture may be all that's necessary to provide space for a first layout, and the layout itself will be a novel and attractive addition to an otherwise ordinary room.

The use of a portion of a family room or recreation room should certainly not be overlooked. These areas are often the focus of a family's leisure activities, and thus are ideal for a hobby pursuit, especially since other family members may ultimately be enticed to pitch in and help with construction and operation.

A spare bedroom also provides an excellent location for a Lionel layout. While it's often not possible for a growing family to devote a full room to hobby activities, "empty nesters," whose children are off on their own, may certainly put this area to good use—assuming, of course, that one's spouse agrees to such an arrangement!

There may even be space available in an attic or garage, if the climate and humidity in those locations can be controlled in a manner similar to what would be done in a basement. Some hobbyists with a garage have been known to employ a hoist arrangement to raise the layout to near-ceiling level when its not in use, thereby accommodating both the car and the train layout in the same space.

The point is: A bit of active exploration of the area inside your home, townhouse, or apartment, coupled with a bit of imagination, will almost certainly lead to some suitable space for your Lionel railroad. It may not be the grand rail empire that you ultimately hope to have, but there's nothing wrong with starting out in a far more modest way, and taking full advantage of the learning experience that comes with constructing and detailing a small layout. Indeed, that's the recommended way of doing things!

To this point, we've been discussing a Lionel layout in terms of the type most customarily seen: A sheet or multiple sheets of 4 feet by 8 feet plywood attached to some sort of supporting framework. But now let's try to think "out of the box"—to borrow a phrase often heard in the business community—and explore some alternatives to that conventional form of layout.

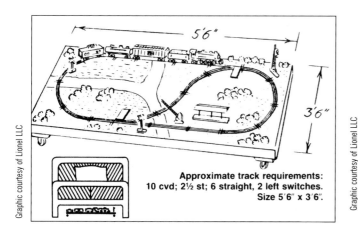

Graphic courtesy of Lionel LLC

Approximate track requirements: 10 cvd; 2½ st; 6 straight, 2 left switches. Size 5′6″ x 3′6″.

This compact Lionel layout is designed to be stored under a bed when not in use. Of course, taller accessories would need to be temporarily removed.

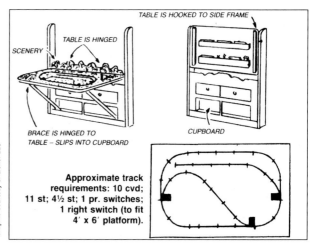

Graphic courtesy of Lionel LLC

Approximate track requirements: 10 cvd; 11 st; 4½ st; 1 pr. switches; 1 right switch (to fit 4′ x 6′ platform).

Another means of storing a Lionel layout—ideal for an apartment dweller. This hinged layout could become an attractive piece of furniture, with trains and accessory items stored in drawers beneath the layout cabinet.

If you have a long, open wall space available in some room of your home, you may consider mounting a narrow layout along most of the length of that wall, installing wider segments at each end to allow for the turnarounds. A "dog-bone" type of layout (described in more detail below) might work well in such a situation. Bookcases or shelves could be placed under the layout along its length, so that space would still be functional for other purposes, including the display of a collection of trains and accessories.

There are almost as many different kinds of layouts as there are locomotives. Here are five interesting types, each designed to meet specific needs.

Graphic courtesy of Lionel LLC

Alternative locations and configurations for Lionel layouts.

Similarly, you might consider installing an around-the-room shelf-type layout, mounted high enough on the walls to clear the tops of doorframes and windows, but still low enough so the trains and accessories can be seen and enjoyed as they run their extensive mainline. No return loops would be required for this arrangement because the mainline would completely encircle the room without interfering with other activities that take place there. The shelf could be wider along one or more lengths, again with tall bookcases or something else underneath, so you could still install a passing siding, spur sidings, and various accessories. Corner areas, which would need to be wider to accommodate the curved sections, might also be used for scenery and accessories. How about having each of the four corners devoted to a different season of the year, for example?

For that matter, you might consider a permanent but portable layout for your Lionel trains. The layout could be constructed on a lightweight base made of 1/4-inch plywood topped with a 2-inch-thick sheet of extruded Styrofoam, for example. The platform could be supported on folding, removable, or caster-equipped legs. Such a layout could easily be stored under a bed or in a closet or utility room, assuming that the trains and accessories can be removed for storage or display elsewhere.

In short, there's just about always some space available in your home for a Lionel layout if you'll just spend some time exploring the options. So put aside that "no space available" excuse, and let's move on with some planning and design considerations!

• *A theme for your railroad*

The next step in layout planning involves creating a theme for your railroad. A theme will tie everything together; give the railroad a logical reason for being; and, over the long term, even save you money. In a hobby where there is so much available in the way of locomotives, rolling stock, and accessories, a theme helps to keep your hobby budget under control by focusing attention on items that will logically support the theme.

Of course, a theme is by no means absolutely essential to creating and constructing a model railroad, but having a theme in mind, and striving to execute it faithfully, does make a difference. If you've ever had occasion to visit a number of model railroads, regardless of scale, you may have noticed that certain layouts tend to leave a marked impression on your mind, while others are rather quickly forgotten. Most times, the memorable ones are those that were unified in such a way that the trains and their surroundings looked like they belonged together. That is the hallmark of a properly executed theme layout!

The theme you select for your Lionel layout could be related to just about anything. Perhaps you are drawn to a favorite prototype railroad from your childhood, or one that you see operating in your hometown today. Or, maybe there's a particular type of railroading activity that appeals to you, such as passenger or commuter service, a logging railroad, a rail line that serves some specific type of industry, switching cars in a rail yard, or even a military railroad. For that matter, the theme might be something entirely fanciful, and not based on any real-life prototype. The list of possibilities is practically limitless!

To further enhance your theme, you may want to select a particular era from a prototype railroad's history, and perhaps focus on a specific geographic location along the railroad's route. Published historical references relating to the railroad will provide some good ideas. You may even want to consider joining that railroad's historical society to learn more about the line and its operations. Published photographs of the railroad in its real-life environment will even help you identify the proper accessories, structures, and trackside items to use.

If you don't already have a theme in mind, and aren't quite sure where to begin developing one, a good place to start is by first focusing on a general era in prototype railroad history that most appeals to you. If early steam locomotives have always drawn your interest, a theme related to the latter half of the nineteenth century, when the nation was still expanding westward, might be the way to go. If you're awestruck by more massive locomotives, a theme relating to the years prior to the start of World War II, when giant steam and electric-outline locomotives ruled the nation's

Photo courtesy of Peter Vollmer

Peter Vollmer changes the theme of his railroad, on occasion, by changing the prototype being operated at a given time. The scene here, for example is typical of the New York Central, with a Lionel Lines steamer thrown in for good measure, in the late 1940s and early 1950s.

Photo courtesy of Peter Vollmer

In this second view of Peter Vollmer's layout, the prototype being modeled is the colorful Santa Fe, again in the late 1940s or early 1950s. Lionel operators with more locomotives and rolling stock than they can possibly run at one time often alternate between several roadnames or eras as a way of changing the theme and adding some new variety.

rails, may form the basis for your model railroad. A theme set in the middle years of the twentieth century, when both steam and diesel locomotives were in common use, might be just the ticket for the hobbyist who would like to operate examples of each type of motive power. And, if large, contemporary diesel power is what you prefer, any period from the 1960s through the present will be appropriate as a starting point for your theme.

After you've narrowed your focus to a general era in railroading history, and have some idea of the type of motive power and rolling stock appropriate to that era, the next logical step might be to choose a geographic setting for your railroad. In part, this might be dictated by the real-life railroad you have chosen to model. For example, if the Santa Fe or the Union Pacific is your railroad of choice, perhaps western topography would be best. On the other hand, someone modeling the Pennsylvania Railroad or the Baltimore & Ohio would do well to consider an Eastern setting.

Beyond geographic location, you might even wish to model a particular season on the year. Fall is always popular because of the splash of vibrant colors evident in those months, but the other seasons also have their own advantages. Modeling winter scenery can be a real challenge, but the stark contrast between a "snow-covered" winter landscape and the colorful locomotives and rolling stock is perfect for really showing off the trains. Besides, challenges are part of what makes model railroading so creative, diverse, and so much fun!

The sky is the limit as far as theme selection with Lionel trains is concerned, simply because more than 100 years of production has resulted in a great diversity of products, some of which will almost certainly conform to virtually any interest.

Keep in mind that a theme may also help determine the physical dimensions of your layout. If you want to model a small logging line, or perhaps an industrial or yard operation, you can generally get by with smaller locomotives and cars, which can operate reliably on tight curves. If running large, articulated steamers or contemporary diesels is what you prefer, you'll need to plan your railroad with the broadest curves possible so these locomotives and their similarly large and long cars can negotiate the turns with relative ease.

Keep in mind that in both concept and execution, your railroad can really be *anything* you want it to be. You may decide to construct a railroad based solely on your imagination and individual creativity, with its own fanciful name, reason for being, geographic location, custom-designed paint scheme, and customized lettering and logos. There's absolutely nothing wrong with that approach. Some model railroaders even enjoy concocting detailed historical accounts of the fictitious railroad's founding and history, to the point of developing creative and fanciful stories about the daily activities of "folks" who work on the railroad or who live and labor along the line. Don't be bound by convention or what others advise you to do. Approach theme development, and every other aspect of building a rail empire, in whatever way *you* prefer!

One portion of the large Lionel layout built by Jeff James is completed as a winter scene. The other side is done as a summer scene. The upper level trestles, along with a town in the center of the layout, act as visual barriers so neither of the disparate seasonal scenes conflicts with the other. Seasons of the year are among the many themes that can be employed to unify a model railroad, and give it a distinctive personality and purpose.

• *Types of track plans*

Virtually all model railroad track plans, regardless of scale, fall into one of four basic categories, or some combination of the four. Despite the complexity of the trackwork on a completed layout, the overall scheme will incorporate one or more of these basic plans, which include the closed loop, the dogbone, the figure eight, and the point-to-point.

Closed loop:

The closed loop is perhaps the most common of track plans for model railroads. The track sections that come packaged with your starter set already form a closed loop—an oval—that affords continuous running of the train in what amounts to an around-the-Christmas-tree manner. You can subsequently add straight and curved sections to expand this circle or oval into a wide variety of sizes and distorted shapes, but it will still be a closed loop.

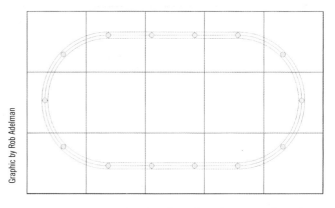

The majority of model railroads are based on an oval track configuration.

The closed loop track plan is generally preferred by hobbyists who enjoy just sitting back and watching their trains perform without any significant human intervention, aside from whatever is required to move a train onto or out of a siding, or to operate a particular car or accessory.

The only real disadvantage to the closed loop type of plan is that watching a train endlessly chase itself can become a bit boring, particularly if the layout is a small one with a relatively small oval of track. That's where the addition of operating accessories and various scenic elements comes into play. These features help break-up the repetitiveness of the action, and also make the layout appear larger than it actually is. It's also worth keeping in mind that a closed loop is not the way the real railroads actually operate, since none of them run in even very large circles, covering a good number of states or regions. Nevertheless, the closed loop is something of a standard in model railroading.

Dogbone:

The closed loop track plan described above may, of course, be configured into the shape of a dogbone—two long parallel straight sections connecting curved "bulges" at both ends—as was alluded to in the shelf type of layout mentioned earlier in this chapter. But such an arrangement would still really be a closed loop.

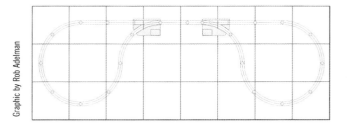

The true dogbone track plan involves reversing loops at each end.

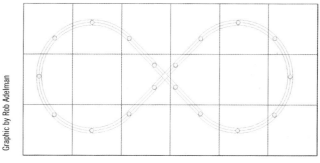

Figure eight track plans incorporate a 45-degree or 90-degree crossing.

A true dogbone track plan consists of a single length of straight track (or an extended mainline section comprised of both straight and curved sections), that is connected to what are known as *reversing loops* at each end. This track configuration is also known as a loop-to-loop type of plan. The reversing loop that forms each teardrop-shaped end of a dogbone does just what its name implies: It causes the train to traverse that loop and then head back, now moving in the opposite direction along the same straight route that it had previously traveled. At the opposite end, the turnaround activity repeats itself by means of yet another reversing loop.

In two-rail model railroading the principal disadvantage of the dogbone track plan is the complex wiring required to allow track to curve back into a single mainline at the end of each loop. What happens is that each reversing loop creates a dead short at the switch where it diverges from, and subsequently reconnects with, the straight section or mainline. This occurs because the polarity of the DC power used for two-rail moves in only one direction, and a reverse loop results in the current flowing in one direction colliding with the current flowing in the opposite direction. To see how this happens, draw a simple sketch of a two-rail reversing loop, and label one rail (+) and the other rail (-). Wherever a (+) meets a (-), you will have a problem!

With Lionel three-rail track, the center rail is always the power rail, so no matter what track arrangement you create, and regardless of its complexity, you'll never have power routing problems. The non-derailing feature of Lionel switches also will keep the points on your reverse loops properly oriented for continuous running, unless you want to change things to a different route. For these reasons, the dogbone track plan is a very viable option that you may want to consider, particularly if the space you have available calls for a long and narrow rail line.

Figure Eight:

In it's simplest form, a figure eight track plan requires the use of a special section of track, known as a 90-degree crossing, to allow a single mainline track to cross through itself at the same level, thereby creating a route that resembles the number "8". If space permits, a less severe 45-degree crossing (available in both O27 and O gauge) can be used to extend the length of the closed loops at the top and bottom of the "8". As with the reversing loop, the Lionel three-rail track system allows you to install a figure eight on your layout without the need for any additional wiring or special controls.

An over-and-under figure eight track plan can also be created without the use of a crossing, if the plan is intentionally designed so that the track passes *over* instead of through itself. To accomplish this, a significant number of track sections need to be gradually and progressively elevated until there is sufficient clearance at the point where the tracks cross to allow for unobstructed passage, under this crossing point, of your tallest locomotives or cars. Of course, the same consideration must be given to the downgrade portion after the train has reached the crossover point. The upgrade and downgrade portions of such a configuration require carefully planned and properly executed gradual grades—something the real railroads prefer to avoid, wherever possible. If you decide that this type of plan is what you want, you'll need to allow for ample space to construct the upgrade and downgrade segments—the goal being to keep the upgrade and downgrade portions as gentle and gradual as possible. Lionel offers a graduated trestle set that can be used to form a figure-eight arrangement, but the ideal way to achieve this effect is to construct a supporting platform to provide for much longer and more gentle changes in elevation. Another way to achieve gradual grades in a somewhat restricted space is to lower the elevation of the lower line as you increase the elevation of the upper line, although this is difficult to do if the lower line is permanently mounted on a flat platform, such as a sheet of plywood.

The conventional figure-eight track plan—the type that incorporates a crossing—offers the continuous running advantage of a closed loop plan without quite the level of boredom that results from watching a train chase itself around a circle or oval.

Point-to-point:

If true-to-prototype operations are what you want to duplicate on your Lionel layout, or if a long but very narrow space is all that you have available, then a point-to-point track plan is certainly worthy of consideration. After all, the prototype railroads almost invariably operate with point-to-point routing.

As the name implies, a point-to-point railroad consists of little more than a line, be it straight or full of twists and turns, drawn between two points. A train starts at point "A", or somewhere in between, and ends up at point "B", or at some intermediate destination. There may be passing sidings along the main route to allow a train heading in one direction to bypass a train heading in the opposite direction, and there may be numerous sidings, spurs, yards, or even interchanges with other railroads along the way, but the basic goal is to deliver loads in the most direct manner possible from point of origin to final destination.

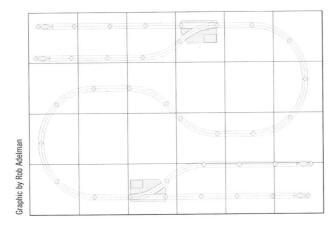

Nearly all prototype railroads operate as a point-to-point.

Graphic by Rob Adelman

An inherent problem with the point-to-point scheme, at least as far as model railroad operations are concerned, is the inability to conduct continuous running. Operators of a point-to-point rail line can't just sit back and watch the trains run around and around. They must be in control of their trains at all times, particularly when the train approaches one end of the line or the other. The railroad must also be equipped with some means of actually turning the locomotives at the end of the line, unless the operator is content with having trains operate in what is known as a push-pull fashion, where locomotives or locomotive control units are at each end of the train.

In the days when steam power ruled, a turntable at each terminus, and even at service points in between, was used to turn locomotives so they would be oriented in the proper direction. Diesel locomotives were also turned in this way. An alternative to the turntable, in areas where sufficient real estate was available, was a long Y-shaped network of track and switches called a "wye" that could be used to turn either a locomotive or an entire train. A train heading up the stem portion of the wye would move into one or the other of the branches. When it neared the end of the long branch line, it would reverse direction; a switch would be thrown; and the train would then back through a "saddle" route that connected the two branches. After it had moved fully into the opposite branch, and had cleared the opposite switch on the saddle, that switch would then be thrown and the train would

head back onto the stem en route to the main line.

In model railroading, either the turntable or the wye, or perhaps a combination of the two, offers a lot of fun and challenges for those who truly want to operate trains in a realistic manner. However, a good many model railroaders still prefer the comfort and ease of watching their trains operate in a continuous and uninterrupted fashion, and both the turntable and the wye do require operator attention when the train reaches the end of the line.

Keep in mind that all of the basic track configurations outlined here are just that: Basic! They can be combined and embellished in any number of ways to increase operational capabilities and to enhance your layout. You might, for example feature a closed loop configuration for your main line, but supplement it with a point-to-point trolley line elsewhere on your layout—especially since Lionel trolleys are equipped with bumper-activated reverse mechanisms that allow them to alternate between one end of the track and the other without operator intervention. And, of course, all of these basic track plans can easily be made more complex and interesting by adding switches almost anywhere along the line for passing sidings and spurs.

• *Layout design tips and techniques*

With some idea of the basic types of track configurations in mind, it's time to put this information to use in creating a track plan for your Lionel layout. You have already determined where you will locate the layout, and have a pretty good idea of what its overall dimensions will need to be, so now we'll devote attention to developing a track plan that will work in that predetermined space.

A well-thought-out track plan will permit you, in advance of actual construction, to determine how to make the best use of your available space, and it will allow you to explore various operational considerations that may be most important to you. Perhaps most importantly, it will help you to determine just what you will need to acquire in the way of track, switches, remote control sections, and the like. So, what's the best way to approach track planning?

The first thing you might do is study some track plans that others have created. These previously published plans will provide some good ideas, and virtually all of them can be modified to some extent to meet your own requirements. You'll find a wide variety of track plans in hobby books and magazines. It really doesn't matter if you're looking at old editions, back issues, or this month's current edition, because track plans are pretty much timeless. There's an advantage to reviewing track plans published in books devoted to O gauge railroading, in particular, because those plans are often published with a list of the track components that will be needed, along with some indication of the actual layout space required. If you've chosen a track plan created for another scale, the component list obviously will not be the same for O gauge as it was for that scale, so you'll have to do a bit of figuring on your own.

Once you have found a track plan that generally suits your interests, you might consider transforming that plan into a life-size version, just to get a better idea of how it will actually look. If you have the necessary track components on hand, you can simply lay them out on the floor, without actually connecting the sections, to gain a better feel for how much space you'll have left to work with on the layout. This can be important if you want to fit a Lionel Coal Loader along a particular siding, or want to locate a freight platform between two parallel tracks. If it helps you to visualize this more completely, you might even form a masking tape "layout perimeter" on the floor so you can see just how close the track will be to the platform edges.

If you prefer to design your own track plan from the ground up, as it were, that's also a great way to gain a better understanding of how a track plan evolves and comes together. All that's really required to create your own track plan is some ruled graph paper, a straightedge, a compass, and a pencil. However, there's even an easier and more enjoyable way to approach this sort of creative track planning, and that involves using a track-planning template. CTT offers just such a template (see Appendix C, page 121). CTT's plastic template for O gauge includes all of the track components in the Lionel O27 and O gauge line, including switches and crossings, and is made in an easy-to-use scale of 1 inch equals 1 foot. The template comes complete with instructions for its use, and one version even comes with graph paper correctly ruled for the scale of the template. However, any ordinary graph paper can also be used.

Lionel railroaders who are familiar with computers may enjoy taking advantage of some of the easy-to-use track planning software that is available for O gauge track planning. "RR-Track" software from R&S Enterprises, and "3D Railroad Concept and Design" from Abracadata, both include sectional track "libraries" of Lionel O27 and O gauge track components so you can design and redesign your Lionel layout. The libraries provided with these software packages also include most Lionel accessories, as well as standard scenic features including trees, bushes, and a variety of other objects. Your computer's mouse does most of the work, and all that's required of you is a bit of imagination and a brief familiarization period to become acquainted with the program. Then it's just a matter of calling-up and placing track sections and other objects; moving them around until you're satisfied with the results; and hitting the "print" button. The result is a properly scaled version of your entire layout, complete with all of the accessories and landscaping features you may care to add. The software even provides a list of the individual track components needed, along with the suggested list prices for each item, and a total for the whole works!

These track planning and layout design programs are available for either PC or Macintosh operating systems. The programs also provide you with a 3-D view of your completed layout design, so you can see how things will look not only from a top view, but also from a lower angle. If you're comfortable with computers, these applications are both easy and fun to use—almost a hobby in themselves! If you're connected to the Internet, you can find information about "RR-Track" from R&S Enterprises at

www.rrtrack.com, and you can learn all about Abracadata's "3D Railroad Concept and Design" software by going to www.abracadata.com.

Regardless of how you choose to draft your track plan, it's useful to review a few additional tips that will assist you in your planning efforts. Try to plant these tips firmly in your mind, because they will also be useful later on when you begin actual construction of your Lionel railroad.

• *Track planning tips*

➤ Try to limit the number of up- and downgrades on your railroad. Where grades are necessary, make them as long and gradual as possible. Many locomotives have a hard time handling steep grades, and just like their real-life counterparts, locomotives tend to speed-up going down a grade. Prototype railroads do their best to avoid grades wherever possible. Model railroaders should generally try to do the same. An acceptable grade on a prototype railroad is between 1 per cent and 2 per cent. In O gauge terms, that would mean a rise (or fall) in elevation amounting to one inch for every 100 inches (about 8 feet).

➤ Avoid using sharp "S" curves on your layout, unless these curves are very broad, and unless the section where the two curved sections meet can be separated by a considerable length of straight track. "S" curves, particularly tight ones, tend to invite derailments. Furthermore, most trains look awkward weaving their way back and forth through such convoluted trackwork.

➤ Place switches where you can most easily get to them. If you're ever going to experience problems with your trackwork and/or derailments, the difficulty will most often occur at or near a switch. Ideally, you should be able to gain access to your switches without ever having to crawl all over the layout to get to them. NEVER place a turnout inside a tunnel or similar enclosed feature—that's just asking for trouble!

➤ Even on a small layout, try to include at least one passing siding. Passing sidings, which require both a left-hand and right-hand switch, make it possible for two or more trains to operate over a single mainline track. When one train approaches or draws too close to the other, the leading train, or the closer of the two approaching trains, can be diverted into the passing siding and held there until the second train passes. After the main route is clear again, the second train exits the passing siding and proceeds to its destination.

➤ If possible, plan to have at least a couple of spurs or sidings on your layout. Spur tracks are dead-end sections of track that divert from the mainline by means of a single switch. The curved, or diverging, section of the switch can face either left or right, depending on where the spur needs to go.

➤ To prevent trains from sideswiping each other or striking objects alongside the track, be sure to provide adequate separation between parallel tracks, and between the track and any trackside signals, tunnel walls, or structures. As a general rule, allow for a 4-inch separation between straight sections of parallel track, when measured from the center rail of one track to the center rail of the adjacent track, and allow for about 6 inches on curves (even more, if you plan to operate very large and long locomotives and cars). Allow for a 1-7/8 inch minimum side clearance between the center rail of a straight section of track and any trackside object, and provide no less than 2-1/2 inches for this clearance on curves.

➤ Be sure to provide adequate vertical clearance between the track and any overhead obstructions, such as tunnel portals, bridge framework, and the like. With most Lionel trains, about 6 inches of vertical clearance, measured from the top of the railheads to the bottom of the overhead obstruction, should be adequate. However, the actual clearance needed should be determined by testing with the tallest locomotive or car you expect to operate on your layout.

➤ Avoid placing switches on or near curves. A switch on a curve is just a problem looking for a place to happen, since any slight discrepancy with point alignment will simply be compounded by the fact that wheel flanges are riding harder against one rail or the other on curved sections. If at all possible, try to have at least one straight section leading into and out of each segment of a switch. This helps to direct locomotive and car wheels along a smooth path through the switch.

➤ Consider employing various scenic features to mask portions of your layout so not all of the track can be seen from any one vantage point. Ideally, a viewer should be required to at least turn his or her head, or even walk around a bit, to take in the complete railroad. Hills, trees, various accessories, and other devices, when properly planned and placed, can help provide the visual break needed to effectively separate one scene from another. This technique will also help to make the layout appear longer and larger, since portions of the trains will disappear, and then reappear, throughout the course of their journey.

➤ When designing your layout, always try to use the widest curves possible, consistent with the area you have available. If you have no choice but to use O27 curves due to space limitations, that's perfectly fine. But if you do have sufficient space for wide and sweeping curves, be sure to employ them wherever possible. Trains always look better negotiating broad curves.

➤ Be sure to devote some additional attention to the layout room. Special attention should be given to the lighting. Incandescent lighting is generally preferred over fluorescent lighting, since the latter type, if not properly filtered for UV radiation, may affect painted objects after prolonged exposure. Track lighting is used by some model railroaders because light can be focused on select scenes and features, but good overhead lighting of any type will do. A comfortable carpet on the floor will also provide some cushion for errant objects that fall off the layout, and will enhance your own comfort during the time that you will be spending with your layout.

Chapter 8

Twenty track plans
for small Lionel layouts

A concern expressed by many first-time hobbyists relates to the amount of space needed for a Lionel layout. The track plans presented here are designed to alleviate that concern, and to demonstrate what can be accomplished in a minimum amount of area.

The track plans in this chapter were created by Rob Adelman, using RR-Track software. All of the plans feature O27 track components, and fifteen of them require a space no larger than a standard 4 feet by 8 feet sheet of plywood. The remaining five layouts might be considered mid-size, and are better suited to a somewhat larger open area, such as unused space in a basement, garage, or finished attic. Keep in mind that these are merely *suggested* track plans, designed to give you some idea of what is possible using O27 track components in a small area. They are intended to stimulate your own thinking and creativity, and all be modified in a number of ways to suit your particular needs and interests.

Each of these track plans was designed to provide good operating potential, and also allow for the continuous running of one or more trains without operator intervention. Some of the plans also feature track configurations—reversing loops or wyes, for example—that would involve a lot of extra wiring and control apparatus on a two-rail model railroad, but which require no special attention in these cases thanks to the Lionel three-rail track system.

The need to employ tight-radius O27 curves on very small layouts does present a few limitations that you should keep in mind. If you plan to eventually operate larger and longer locomotives and rolling stock (near-scale-length streamlined passenger cars and Intermodal well cars, for example), these layouts may not work well for you. Longer locomotives and cars may not be able to clear the switch machines on Lionel O27 switches, and they certainly will not look quite right as they negotiate the very sharp turns associated with O27 track curves. For those reasons, most of the O27 layouts presented here are best suited to the wide range of smaller locomotives and rolling stock normally associated with the Lionel O27 product line.

A few additional points about these track plans:

➤ Switches indicated on the plans may be manually or remote controlled, although remote control would be preferable in hard-to-reach interior portions of the layout.

➤ The grid lines used here represent 1 foot squares. For example, Layout #1 is designed to fit a compact 4 feet by 6 feet platform, and Layout #18 is designed for a 3 feet by 16 feet overall area.

➤ Placement of uncoupling/control and insulated track sections is *not* indicated on these plans. Those special track sections are one-for-one drop-in replacements for one straight section of track, and can be placed wherever the operator prefers.

➤ "Cut straight" in the component list for each plan refers to single straight sections that will need to be cut to length with a hacksaw or model saw. Simply mark the section at the desired length across all three rails; clamp the track into a vise, or use a block of wood and C-clamps to hold it firmly in place (an old towel can be used to protect the rails from being marred); and cut along the line you made. Then use a small file to smooth-off the cut edges of the rails and insert the track pins, as necessary.

Planning for and constructing a functional model railroad in a limited amount of space can be a challenge, but it can also be a whole lot of fun. Don't be afraid to experiment a bit, and to try something different. If you already have a platform available for your layout, go ahead and lay individual sections of track on the board without actually connecting them. You can shuffle things around to your heart's content until you come up with an arrangement that pleases you. Just be sure not to crowd the layout with trackwork, because you'll certainly want to have space left over for some of those fun-filled Lionel accessories!

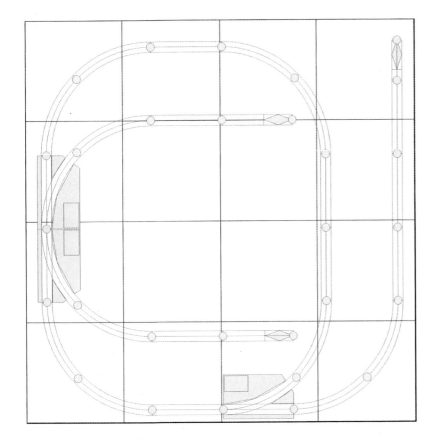

Layout #1:

Overall layout size: 4 feet by 4 feet

This very compact layout manages to pack some good railroading action into a very limited amount of space. Nevertheless, the layout does not appear crowded, and there is ample room for scenery and several Lionel operating accessories. A Magnet Crane would fit nicely on the upper inside siding, and the long outer siding could be used for storing a second train. Small steam or diesel switchers, or Lionel motorized units such as the Rio Grande Snowplow, would look great on this small layout.

O27 track items:

11 ea.	curve
11 ea.	single straight
1 ea.	right-hand turnout
2 ea.	left-hand turnout
1 ea.	half straight
3 ea.	track bumper

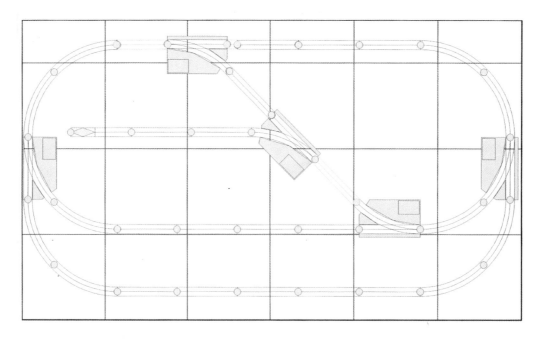

Layout #2:

Overall layout size: 3-1/2 feet by 6 feet

This compact layout features two alternate routes for train operations. If the layout is wired into blocks, one train might occupy the inner loop, while a second train operates along the outside oval. This layout can be extended in any direction to allow for longer runs, and it could easily be expanded to fit a platform made from a standard 4 feet by 8 feet sheet of plywood.

O27 track items:

10 ea.	curve
16 ea.	single straight
3 ea.	right-hand turnout
2 ea.	left-hand turnout
3 ea.	cut straight section
1 ea.	track bumper

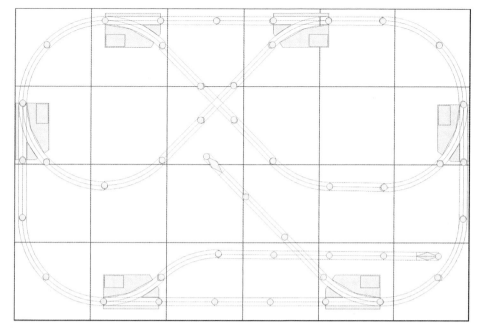

Layout #3:

Overall layout size: 4 feet x 6 feet

This small layout combines a figure eight with an outside oval, allowing for a longer and more varied run. The 45-degree crossing and one of the sidings could easily be eliminated to simplify things, and to provide more open space in the center portion of the layout that might be used for a small town, some hills, or a pond.

O27 track items:

13 ea.	*curve*
18 ea.	*single straight*
3 ea.	*right-hand turnout*
3 ea.	*left-hand turnout*
1 ea.	*90-degree crossing*
1 ea.	*45-degree crossing*
2 ea.	*track bumper*

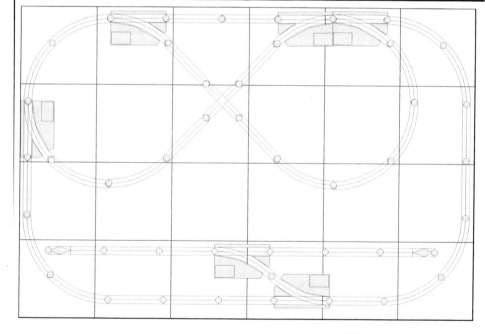

Layout #4:

Overall layout size: 4 feet by 6 feet

A variation of Layout #3, with a slightly smaller figure eight configuration and a center-access siding. This track plan could easily be extended along the right side, expanding it into a 4 feet by 8 feet sheet. This would allow for a somewhat longer siding, or perhaps even an alternate siding. The figure eight might also be extended in a similar manner, as was done with Layout #3.

O27 track items:

14 ea.	*curve*
19 ea.	*single straight*
4 ea.	*right-hand turnout*
2 ea.	*left-hand turnout*
1 ea.	*90-degree crossing*
2 ea.	*track bumper*

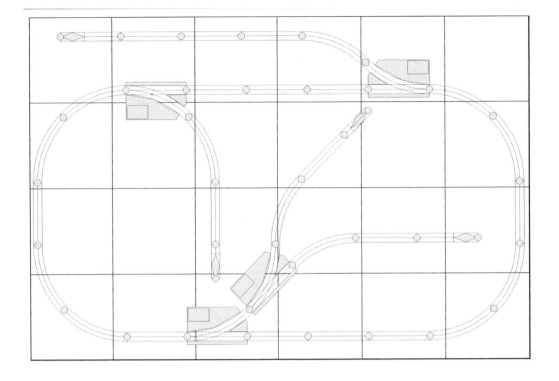

Layout #5:

Overall layout size: 4 feet by 6 feet

Several short sidings inside the oval can be used to serve a variety of industries. Operating accessories such as a barrel loader, magnet crane, and coal loader, would be appropriate featured attractions on this layout. Longer strings of cars, awaiting loading or unloading, could remain on the outside siding until needed. As with several of the other track plans illustrated here, this plan could easily be expanded into a 4 feet by 8 feet sheet by adding to the right-hand side. That simple extension would provide a longer run on an expanded oval, and it would also allow the two parallel horizontal sidings (one inside the oval and one outside the oval) to be extended by several more track sections.

O27 track items:

12 ea.	curve
17 ea.	single straight
2 ea.	right-hand turnout
2 ea.	left-hand turnout
2 ea.	half straight
4 ea.	track bumper

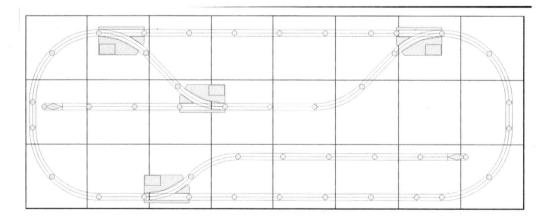

Layout #6:

Overall layout size: 3 feet by 8 feet

A simple track plan for an area where a full layout would be too wide. The long siding provides space for parking a second train, and the passing siding configuration allows for some variation in the route a train will follow. It would be a simple matter to expand this layout into a full 4 feet by 8 feet sheet by adding additional straight sections along the left and right sides.

O27 track items:

10 ea.	curve
22 ea.	single straight
2 ea.	right-hand turnout
2 ea.	left-hand turnout
4 ea.	half straight
1 ea.	cut straight
2 ea.	track bumper

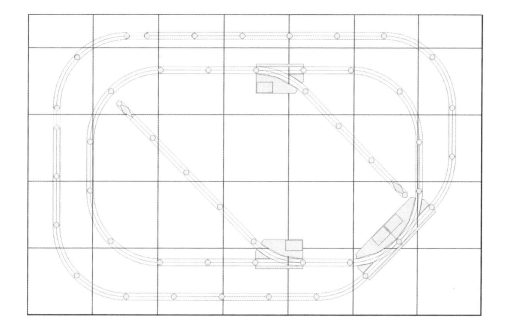

Layout #7:

Overall layout size: 4-1/2 feet by 7 feet

Although the extra half-foot width of this layout would preclude it being constructed from a single sheet of plywood, the 1 foot strip cut from the 8-foot length could be further cut, lengthwise, into two 6-inch-wide strips, thereby providing all of the platform material needed. There's plenty of open area on this layout for operating accessories and a variety of structures. Two trains can be kept running simultaneously, either by careful operator control or by means of automatic stopping devices installed on both sides of the two switches where the mainlines merge.

O27 track items:

14 ea.	curve
27 ea.	single straight
3 ea.	right-hand turnout
1 ea.	left-hand turnout
2 ea.	cut straight
2 ea.	track bumper

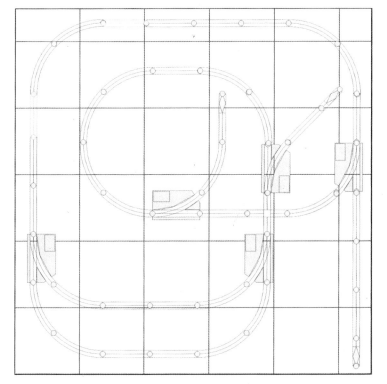

Layout #8:

Overall layout size: 5-1/2 feet by 5-1/2 feet

This layout is designed to provide an extended run for a single train, although a short second train could also be held on the passing siding, awaiting its turn to access the mainline. Two of the three stub sidings are quite short (just a little over a single car length), and either or both of them could be removed, if desired. The third siding is well placed for easy access to trackside operating accessories, such as coal or barrel loaders.

O27 track items:

18 ea.	curve
17 ea.	single straight
3 ea.	right-hand turnout
2 ea.	left-hand turnout
1 ea.	90-degree crossing
2 ea.	half straight
2 ea.	cut straight
3 ea.	track bumper

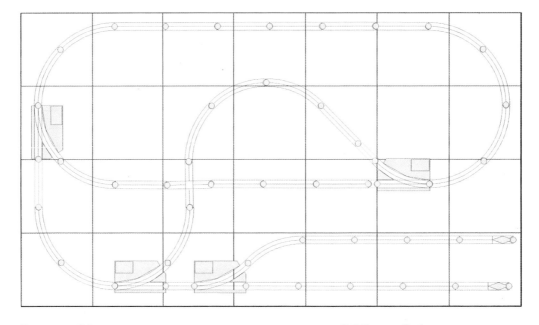

Layout #9:

Overall layout size: 4 feet by 7 feet

This plan features two alternate routes for the train, and two sidings for storage of cars or a second locomotive. There's ample room in the upper right-hand corner for a mountain with a tunnel, and plenty of additional space elsewhere for various types of structures and other accessories.

O27 track items:

14 ea.	curve
20 ea.	single straight
1 ea.	right-hand turnout
3 ea.	left-hand turnout
1 ea.	90-degree crossing
1 ea.	half straight
3 ea.	cut straight
2 ea.	track bumper

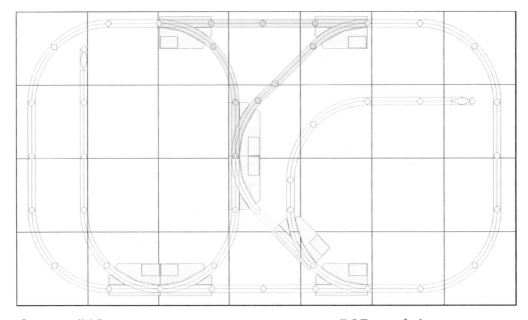

Layout #10:

Overall layout size: 4 feet by 7 feet

Although smaller than a single sheet of plywood, this layout has good operational potential, and features two wye configurations where locomotives can be turned to run in the opposite direction. The layout is complemented with two sidings, with the possibility that a third short siding could be added. Despite its compact size, there is still room on this layout for a number of Lionel accessories.

O27 track items:

13 ea.	curve
17 ea.	single straight
5 ea.	right-hand turnout
3 ea.	left-hand turnout
1 ea.	half straight
2 ea.	cut straight
2 ea.	track bumper

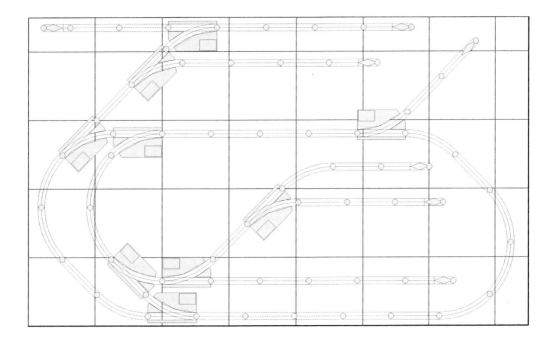

Layout #11:

Overall layout size: 4-1/2 feet by 7-1/2 feet

Railroaders with a fondness for switching operations should enjoy this layout. With a total of six sidings, there's ample opportunity for moving cars around from one line-side industry to another. Slightly wider than a sheet of plywood, the required half-foot extension along the length could easily be ripped from a second sheet, and joined to the supporting framework.

O27 track items:

10 ea.   *curve*
35 ea.   *single straight*
4 ea.   *right-hand turnout*
5 ea.   *left-hand turnout*
1 ea.   *half straight*
7 ea.   *track bumper*

Layout #12:

Overall layout size: 5 feet by 6 feet

A single-train track plan with an extended run, thanks to the addition of a 90-degree crossing. This layout, which can be constructed in a small 5 feet by 6 feet space, could rather easily be expanded by adding to the right-hand side. Depending on the amount of new area gained, it might be possible to complete a full outer loop, and to create a new siding, which would branch off a portion of that newly created section.

O27 track items:

16 ea.   *curve*
17 ea.   *single straight*
1 ea.   *right-hand turnout*
1 ea.   *left-hand turnout*
1 ea.   *90-degree crossing*
4 ea.   *half straight*
3 ea.   *cut straight*
2 ea.   *track bumper*

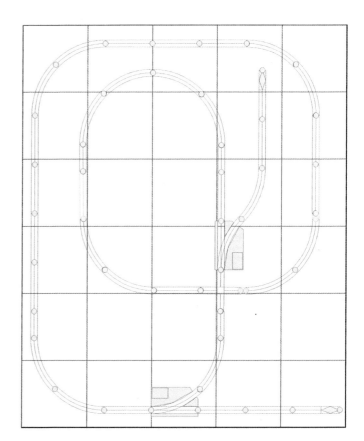

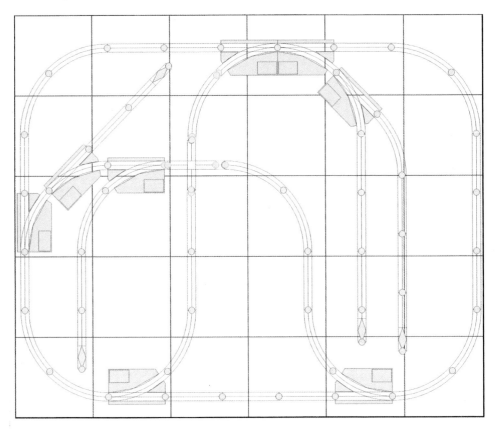

Layout #13:

Overall layout size: 5 feet by 6 feet

Here's a layout that provides a long and varied run, combined with an opportunity for the train to change directions in several different ways. The four sidings on this layout will allow for some interesting switching possibilities, and there's still room left over for a variety of accessories and a bit of attractive scenic treatment. Expansion on the right-hand end of the layout is also an option.

O27 track items:

15 ea. curve
24 ea. single straight
5 ea. right-hand turnout
3 ea. left-hand turnout
1 ea. 90-degree crossing
1 ea. half straight
5 ea. cut straight
4 ea. track bumper

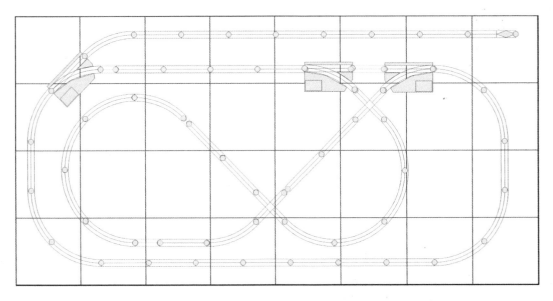

Layout #14:

Overall layout size: 4 feet by 8 feet

A full sheet of plywood will comfortably accommodate this track plan, which features an extensive mainline run and one extra-long siding to handle a complete second train or a good number of cars. Even though there is a lot of trackwork in this plan, the layout still retains an uncluttered look, and there is ample space for more than a few Lionel accessories.

O27 track items:

18 ea. curve
26 ea. single straight
2 ea. right-hand turnout
1 ea. left-hand turnout
2 ea. 90-degree crossing
5 ea. cut straight section
1 ea. track bumper

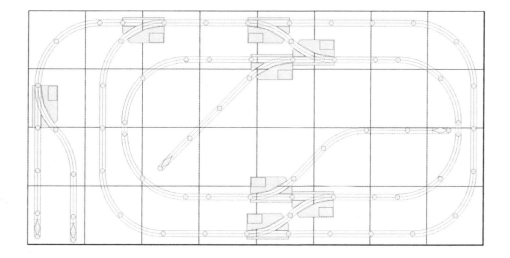

Layout #15:

Overall layout size: 4 feet by 8 feet

Another track plan designed for a full sheet of plywood, and easily expandable into an L-shaped layout by adding a 3 feet by 6 feet or larger sheet to adjoin the lower left corner. The layout could also be expanded lengthwise by adding another 4 feet by 8 feet plywood sheet end-to-end with the right-hand side of this existing plan. This track plan also allows two trains to operate independently of each other.

O27 track items:

19 ea. curve
27 ea. single straight
2 ea. right-hand turnout
6 ea. left-hand turnout
7 ea. half straight
2 ea. cut straight
4 ea. track bumper

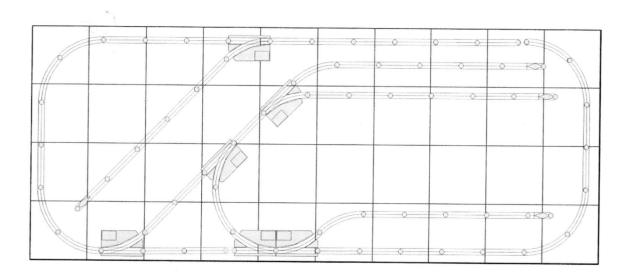

Layout #16:

Overall layout size: 4 feet by 10 feet

A long mainline run and four lengthy sidings are the primary features of this simple but versatile track plan. The wye at the left-front portion of the layout will allow the operator to turn a locomotive to head it off in the opposite direction. The large expanses of open area on this layout can be treated with scenic features, and town, and/or a number of accessories.

O27 track items:

11 ea. curve
43 ea. single straight
2 ea. right-hand turnout
4 ea. left-hand turnout
1 ea. half straight
2 ea. cut straight
4 ea. track bumper

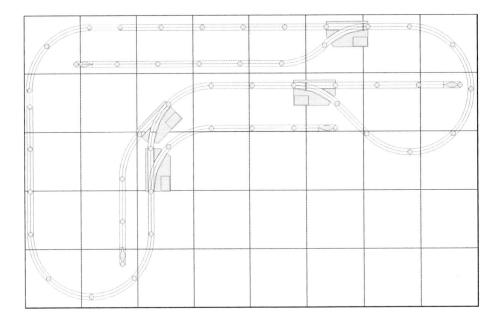

Layout #17:

Overall layout size: 5 feet by 8 feet("L" shaped)
An excellent layout for one corner of a room. This track plan could be constructed atop two 3 feet by 5 feet sheets of plywood placed in the shape of an "L". The relatively narrow width of the layout affords easy operator access to most sections, with the exception of the wider area where the two platforms meet.

O27 track items:

15 ea.	curve
26 ea.	single straight
2 ea.	right-hand turnout
2 ea.	left-hand turnout
2 ea.	cut straight
4 ea.	track bumper

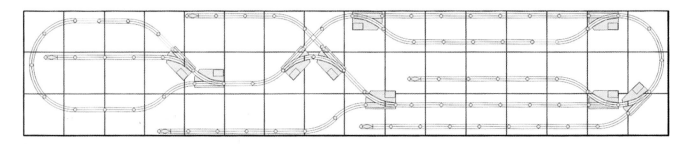

Layout #18:

Overall layout size: 3 feet by 16 feet
A great along-the-wall layout for use in a basement, garage, or family room. Because it is just 3 feet wide, there's easy operator access to the layout along its full length. If an even longer wall space is available, the layout could easily be extended from the left-hand end. The long and varied mainline run, along with a total of 6 sidings, including a passing siding, provide plenty of opportunities for interesting operations. If desired, the siding inside the left-hand reversing loop could be eliminated to allow even more space for scenery or accessories.

O27 track items:

19 ea.	curve
47 ea.	single straight
6 ea.	right-hand turnout
3 ea.	left-hand turnout
1 ea.	90-degree crossing
1 ea.	half straight
5 ea.	cut straight
5 ea.	track bumper

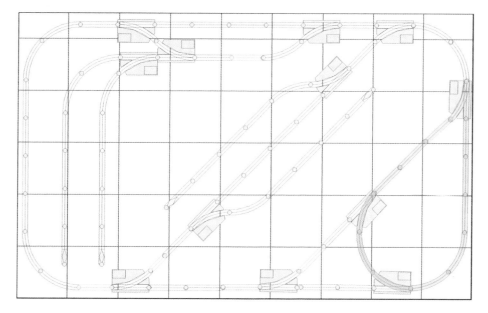

Layout #19:

Overall layout size: 5-1/2 feet by 9 feet

A mid-size layout for the basement, garage, family room, or attic. Features include both a wye and a reversing loop configuration for changing the direction of movement of a locomotive or an entire train heading in either direction, and four sidings of sufficient length to accommodate a number of cars or even a short train.

O27 track items:

15 ea.	curve
44 ea.	single straight
6 ea.	right-hand turnout
6 ea.	left-hand turnout
6 ea.	cut straight
4 ea.	track bumper

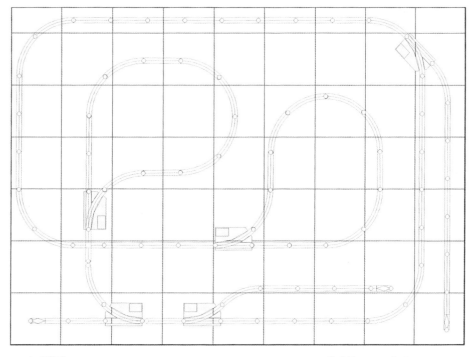

Layout #20:

Overall layout size: 6-1/2 feet by 9 feet

Another track plan designed for a somewhat larger space, and featuring an especially long and varied mainline run, terminating in reversing loops at each end. A layout of this size would best be constructed with access hatches inside the reversing loops so maintenance and scenery work could be accomplished without actually walking or crawling atop the layout.

O27 track items:

24 ea.	curve
43 ea.	single straight
3 ea.	right-hand turnout
2 ea.	left-hand turnout
1 ea.	90-degree crossing
1 ea.	half straight
2 ea.	cut straight
3 ea.	track bumper

Chapter 9

Constructing an action-packed Lionel layout

Aside from the supporting platform, the project layout depicted in this book was largely constructed by 13 year old Ryan Bednarik, with the help of his father, Charles, who is also an avid model railroading enthusiast.

It's time to erect a "stage" for the Lionel trains and accessories in your all-star extravaganza!

Although Lionel trains are large and durable enough to be operated on the floor, they are best presented on a stable and firm platform constructed at a comfortable viewing level. This platform will also provide a suitable area for the placement of various operating accessories and the construction of scenic features such as streams, mountains, roads, and valleys.

If you must operate your trains on the floor, try to avoid deep-pile or shag carpets, because loose fibers may eventually work their way into locomotive gears, wheels, and other moving parts. Lubricants from the gears and axles might

also pose a problem—particularly with your spouse—if the trains are set up directly on costly home carpeting. If there is no alternative to a floor layout, consider placing a sheet of plywood on the floor or carpet. The platform can be painted and given scenery, or covered with a section of green or brown indoor/outdoor carpet, for a more finished look.

Ideally, though, you'll want a more stable supporting platform for your trains, accessories, and scenery. This platform doesn't need to be very elaborate, because most of the supporting structure will eventually be covered with track, scenery, and paint. The platform doesn't even require permanent resident status in your living room, family room, or wherever. It could be constructed with folding or removable legs so you can store the layout elsewhere when the space is needed for another purpose. For that matter, it could be constructed in small, easy-to-transport sections that can be dismantled and stored in a utility closet, basement, or garage.

The project layout depicted in this chapter and the next was made in just such a manner. The platform is comprised of two 4' x 4' plywood sections for fast and easy disassembly into convenient-to-carry and easy-to-store sections. Ordinary carpenter sawhorses, rather than permanent legs, were used to elevate and support the layout, although detachable or folding legs could be used instead.

But this is just one of several possible ways to construct the foundation for a model railroad. There are alternative approaches that will work equally well, and each of the six basic layout construction steps outlined here can also be approached in other ways. The sequence of steps will stay the same, but the materials and methods used can be adapted to individual circumstances. In this chapter, we'll discuss the construction of a model railroad from supporting platform to fully operational layout—a "stage," if you will. The following chapter will describe how to create the "set" and "props" for that stage—those things that make your layout different from all others, and provide it with a distinctive personality.

First, let's get that stage built so our performers—the trains—can go through some dress rehearsals!

• Step #1: Build a firm foundation

The first prerequisite for a permanent or semi-permanent model railroad is a structurally sound supporting base that will provide a firm and level foundation for the trackwork, scenery, and accessories that make up the completed layout. Preferably, this base is also fitted with legs of some type to elevate the layout to a comfortable height for both working and viewing.

Basically, there are two common methods for constructing the foundation for a model railroad of any scale: Platform (or table-top) construction, and open-grid construction.

Platform construction is pretty much described by its name. This type of construction makes use of a solid platform—usually plywood, or plywood topped with a sheet of sound-reducing material—to support the railroad. This is the generally accepted method for constructing a small layout, up to and including a 4 foot by 8 foot plywood board.

The open-grid construction, along with a popular variation known as L-girder construction, is often preferred by hobbyists who are building larger layouts. As the name implies, an open grid layout has an open top, rather than a solid top, with a supporting grid-type framework that is generally comprised of 1 foot by 2 inch and/or 1 foot by 4 inch lumber. With this type of construction, sections of plywood are used only in areas that require a solid, supporting surface—directly under the trackwork, for example, and in places where a rail yard, accessories, or a town might be located. Those portions of the layout that are destined to become mountains, hills, streams, lakes, canyons, and the

like, are left open, and ordinary window screen covered with plaster-soaked cloth or paper towels is used to shape the terrain contours in those areas.

With open-grid construction, the scenery, and even the trackwork itself, can be made to drop below table-top level or, by means of risers attached to the joists, be elevated to any height desired. Another advantage of open-grid construction is that less wood is required overall. The tradeoff is that open-grid framework requires accurate planning and a good amount of cutting. In addition, open-grid construction is not very forgiving if you change your mind later on and decide to reposition some of your trackwork. You can learn more about this type of layout construction by referring to Linn Wescott's excellent book: *How to Build Model Railroad Benchwork*, which is listed in Appendix A.

For a first layout, it's usually best to keep things as simple as possible, and a single sheet of plywood does the job nicely enough. Besides, there's nothing to preclude employing open grid construction later on, as your railroad expands.

In fact, the majority of new hobbyists in nearly all scales from Z through O generally start out with somewhat modest rail empires built on a 4 foot by 8 foot sheet of 1/2-inch or 5/8-inch thick plywood. Thicker sheets, such as 3/4-inch, are also available, but that's going a bit overboard for the structural needs of a small layout. Thinner sheets, such as 1/4-inch plywood, might also be used if weight and transportability are factors, but these thinner sheets will require additional cross-supports underneath to prevent them from sagging and warping.

Photo by Tony McAndrew

A supporting platform for the project layout depicted in this and the subsequent chapter was made of one 4 foot by 8 foot sheet of 1/4-inch plywood, along with 1 foot by 2 inch and 1 foot by 6 inch boards. The 4 foot by 8 foot sheet was cut into two 4 foot by 4 foot sections to make the layout more portable. Pictured here are all of the wood components used for the platform's construction.

Plywood is the preferred platform material simply because it is readily available, relatively inexpensive (a general construction grade with one good side will do nicely), and it provides a good grip for nails or screws driven into its surface. Other common types of composite sheet boards, such as Masonite or particle board, are less acceptable for model railroad applications because they are dense and heavy, tend to sag easily, and often do not take nails, screws, or paint very well.

Some model railroaders prefer to add yet another layer atop the plywood base—a good idea because this adds structural strength to the platform, and helps to deaden sounds. The two most common sheet-type materials used over the plywood are Homasote and extruded Styrofoam—both of which work very well.

Homasote has been around for a good number of years. It is a fairly rigid and relatively soft material with good sound-abating qualities. It also cuts easily with a small saw. The disadvantage of Homasote is that it does not grip screws as tightly as a wood surface. For most model railroad applications this is not a major concern, because few items, including the track itself, really need to be screwed down on a properly finished layout.

Extruded Styrofoam is a more contemporary top-sheet material used on increasing numbers of model railroads. Very light in weight, 4 foot by 8 foot extruded Styrofoam is available in 1-inch, 2-inch, and 4-inch thick sheets (usually blue or pink in color), with the 2-inch-thick sheets being preferred for most O gauge modeling. Extruded Styrofoam is a dense and rigid foam material, but it is easy to cut and carve with an ordinary kitchen knife or, better yet, with an electric hot-wire foam cutter. It can also be very messy, especially if cut with a knife, or carved and shaped with a rasp or sandpaper. Tiny fragments of foam will tend to be attracted to anything and everything in the vicinity. A suction-type hose attachment for your vacuum cleaner or shop vac is a must if you're working with this product.

Be aware that extruded Styrofoam is *not* the same thing as the less-dense, beaded type of foam that is used as packing material, or the type of foam that florists use. The extruded stuff doesn't crumble into tiny beads, and it doesn't break apart easily. It doesn't hold nails or screws well at all, but if you follow the procedures described in this chapter, nails or screws won't be needed on your railroad. If you're planning to build a layout where portability is a consideration, consider using extruded Styrofoam.

Regardless of what you employ as a top layer over your plywood sheet (assuming you intend to use anything at all), the sheets can be glued to the plywood with ordinary white

At the center of the layout, several wood pegs were inserted into pre-drilled holes in one center cross member. The pegs mate with holes in the adjacent center cross member. This provides perfect alignment and additional reinforcement, essentially turning the two 1 foot by 2 inch boards into a more rigid 2 foot by 2 foot.

Window latches were installed at the joints along both sides where the two 4 foot by 4 foot sections come together. This arrangement secures the two joined halves of the layout platform.

glue, carpenter's glue, or Liquid Nails. You do need to be a bit careful in selecting adhesives for foam material, because some types of glue will dissolve the foam, causing it to literally "melt." Some oil-based paints may have the same effect, or may not dry properly, so be sure to use water-based latex paints on foam. In fact, it's a good idea to use water-based paints for all of your layout construction and scenery work, simply because it's easier to dilute, work with, and clean up.

You'll also need a framework to provide additional support to the platform; to give a finished appearance to the layout's perimeter; and to provide a means of anchoring whatever type of legs you decide to use. The most simple type of supporting frame can be made primarily of 1 foot by 4 inch lumber. Here's how to do it:

[NOTE: If you are using power tools in any phase of your layout's construction, ALWAYS wear safety goggles or glasses, and ALWAYS exercise extreme care to use the tools in the way they were designed to be used, and for their intended purposes. Safety first, in all circumstances!]

The frame for the project layout was constructed in two separate sections so the layout could be easily transported.

1. *Purchase five, straight, 8 foot lengths of 1 foot by 4 inch lumber for a 4 foot by 8 foot layout. This will provide enough wood for the entire framework.*

2. *Cut two pieces of 1 foot by 4 inch lumber to the exact 96-inch length needed to fit along each long side of the plywood platform.*

3. *Cut five more pieces of 1 foot by 4 inch lumber to an exact length of 46-1/2 inches. These will be used for the frame ends and cross supports.*

4. *On a flat and level surface (your garage or basement floor should do), set the two 96-inch side pieces so they are parallel, spaced about 46-1/2 inches apart. Set the boards with their narrow sides down, so the four-inch dimension is vertical as you look down on the board.*

5. *Take one of the five 46-1/2 inch boards, and line it up flush with the inside end of one of the 96-inch side pieces. Apply some carpenter's glue to the end of the smaller piece, and butt it up against the inside end of the 96-inch side piece. Use a framing square to assure that you are getting a true 90-degree angle between the end piece and side piece. After the glue has set, countersink two pilot holes from the outside of the 96-inch strip into the glued end of the 46-1/2 inch cross piece. Insert two-inch long, #8 flat head wood or drywall screws into each hole to firmly anchor this joint.*

6. *Repeat Step #4 for the remaining three corners of your frame, being certain to check that all corners are set at 90-degree angles.*

7. *Take the three remaining 46-1/2 inch pieces of 1 foot by 4 inch lumber, and position them crosswise within the framework at about 2-foot intervals. Use glue, and a couple of 2-inch long #8 wood or drywall screws per joint to secure the cross members to the side pieces.*

8. *Lay the plywood sheet on the frame, making sure that all edges line-up evenly; then anchor the plywood to the frame by drilling pilot holes at about 1-foot intervals along all sides and from above the cross members. Again, use flat head wood or drywall screws to secure everything in place. There's no real need to glue the plywood sheet to the frame, but you can if you want to.*

Photo by Tony McAndrew

The completed project layout framework, missing only the 2-inch thick extruded Styrofoam sheet that would later be fitted into the frame.

You now have a completed and very sturdy supporting platform for your layout. The next step is to equip that platform with legs so it will be easy to work on and view. But before we make the legs, there's one important question that begs answering: How high off the floor should the layout be?

Over the years, a floor-to-table-top height in the range of 38 to 42 inches has been something of a standard for O gauge layouts, although you can certainly go lower than that if children will be assisting with building and operating the layout, and you might go higher if you are especially tall, or simply prefer viewing your trains from a more realistic "ground level" perspective. Layout height is largely a matter of personal preference, but there are some practical considerations to keep in mind. You will want the layout to be easy to work on—both from the top and from underneath—because you will be working on both surfaces. Also, you will want to assure that, regardless of what height you choose, all areas of the layout will be within a comfortable arm's reach from the sides. Finally, you will want the layout to be at a comfortable viewing level.

Legs for the platform can be constructed from 2 foot by 4 inch lumber cut to the appropriate length and attached securely at the corners. Be sure to provide corner braces on each leg to prevent them from collapsing. It's also a good idea to cross-brace the legs at each end of the platform by attaching a 1 foot by 4 inch piece of lumber cross member to each set of legs. If you place these cross members a foot or so off the floor, they can serve as supports later on for a below-the-layout shelf that can be used for storage of train boxes, tools, or whatever. A decorative fabric skirt around the perimeter of the layout, and extending nearly to the floor, will conceal this storage area.

In addition to elevating and supporting the layout platform, another function served by legs is to assure that the layout is level. If your floor is perfectly level from side to side and front to back, this will not be a concern. However, if there is any doubt about how level the layout may be in this or some other location, it's a good idea to install carriage bolts, equipped with nuts and washers, to the bottom of all legs so small adjustments can be made.

Platform legs can also be fashioned in a number of other ways, including the use of metal pipes or even the commercially available folding legs sold at most home improvement centers. For a temporary layout, or even for a permanent one, the use of inexpensive carpenter sawhorses provides yet another sturdy alternative.

To give your layout a more finished appearance, add a decorative fascia trim, made of lumber or an appropriate paneling material, along all four sides of the platform. This trim will mask the exposed edges of the wood framework, plywood, and any additional material placed atop the plywood. If ordinary wood is used for the fascia, it can be stained or painted to match or complement the other decor in the room.

Now that we have a platform ready to go, it's time to get on with track-fitting—one step closer to running some trains.

Common wood sawhorses were used to provide temporary legs for the layout platform. These would later be replaced with more permanent legs.

• Step #2: Construct reliable trackwork

If you have followed the advice given in Chapter 7—the layout planning chapter—you have already spent some time developing a theme and track plan for your new railroad. The plan itself could be a simple pencil sketch; something created with a track planning template; or even a detailed rendering completed with the assistance of layout design computer software. The important thing is that you have given a bit of thought to what your railroad will be and how it will operate, and have also considered the possibility of future expansion. Ideally, you have also developed a track plan that can be constructed in easy-to-do, attainable, and affordable phases, with ample space for some Lionel accessories and a bit of scenery.

The project layout depicted in this chapter began as just such a plan. The oval of track that makes up the outer mainline was designed to be quickly constructed with the various track components packaged with a conventional starter set, supplemented with a few additional straight track sections. One or two turnouts could also be added at this early stage, if desired, to provide storage sidings until such time as the inner oval is completed.

The initial track plan for the project layout was created with RR-Track software. The original plan was somewhat modified after actual layout construction began, but having a basic plan to start with greatly simplified and expedited layout building.

The inside oval and the two sets of crossovers that allow a train to move from one loop to the other might be added later, as both time and budget permits. This also applies to the two sidings that run off the inner loop, as well as the various accessories. There's no need to rush anything! The important thing is to get a train up and running smoothly, because this will help to maintain a high level of interest, and you'll learn much about basic layout construction techniques in the process.

Lionel O27 track components were used on the project layout because O27 track is what comes packaged with most starter sets. The assumption was that many who read this book are starting out with just such a set. Another reason for selecting O27 is that the smaller-radius curve sections allow more railroading action to be packed into a relatively small space—an area no larger than a single 4 foot by 8 foot sheet of plywood in this case. With O gauge track, you would not be able to follow this same track plan without making some major modifications.

The project layout team was unable to locate a 2-inch-thick sheet of extruded Styrofoam, so a considerably thinner sheet of Celotex Foam Insulating Sheathing was used instead. With the track plan before him, Ryan Bednarik is test-fitting the track to identify any potential clearance problems along the now-too-high edge trim. After everything appeared to be okay, the track outline was marked (see text) on the foam sheet.

The first step in actual track construction involves matching your paper plan with the "real life" situation on the platform. This can be tested by installing the various track sections on the platform to assure that everything fits according to the printed plan, and that adequate clearances have been provided between adjacent tracks, and along the edges of your layout, so trains will not sideswipe one another or interfere with any trackside items. You'll also use this preliminary "test phase" to mark the location of the track on your layout surface, so roadbed can be installed later.

For this test run, you won't need to install insulating pins, insulated sections, or other special track sections, because all we're doing at this point is checking to make sure everything fits as it should. However, you will still want to make sure that insulating pins are properly installed on any switches that you place on the layout (refer to the instruction manual for a diagram of the pin locations). These pins control the non-derailing feature, which you'll want to have functioning properly, even for a simple test run.

It's also a good idea to place any trackside operating accessories in their respective locations so you can check for proper clearance and mark their location on the platform. This is especially true for such things as coal or log loaders, horse or cattle corrals, and other such devices that will inter-act directly with various cars in your trains. You don't need to attach any wires yet—simply place the accessory where you want it to be.

Once you have all of the track components tightly fit-ted, placed, and aligned, and have positioned all major trackside accessories, take the longest car in your rolling stock inventory and place it on the track. Roll the car by hand, in both directions, past every point on the layout where you suspect that there might be a clearance problem. A car is best for this hand test simply because its wheels turn freely when pushed, while geared locomotive wheels might be damaged if you push them by hand. Once you are reasonably confident that there is adequate side-to-side clearance at all points on the layout, go ahead and attach a Lockon to the track, and then connect your transformer. Now you're ready to confirm your previous test with some actual operation!

Take your longest locomotive, and place it and several cars on the track. Be sure that all wheels are properly seat-ed on the outside rails, and that the locomotive and cars are securely coupled together. Plug the transformer into a wall outlet, and slowly apply power to see if the train begins to move. If the locomotive's light comes on, but the train does not start to move as more power is applied, there's a good chance that the locomotive is in its "neutral" state. In that case, turn the power back to its "off" setting, and then apply power again. At this point, the train should move for-ward or backward (usually forward, since this is the "default" state for most items equipped with electronic reversing mechanisms).

Once the train is moving, run it slowly, backwards and forwards, along all of your trackwork. Then run it at various speeds, again in both directions, to assure that wheels are tracking properly, and that there are no bad rail joints that might cause a derailment. This repeated forward-and-back-ward operation also helps to seat the gears and break-in the motor, if you are operating a new locomotive.

If you have some operating cars, such as the Lionel Operating Milk Car, check to see that the loading platform is positioned so it is parallel with the side of the car. If a remote control section is going to be used to operate the car,

make sure that there is (or will be) at least one additional straight section of track at each end of the remote control section. Adjust the platform's position until it is properly aligned with the remote control track. Follow this procedure with any similar car/accessory combinations where the two items will interact.

After you're satisfied that things will operate smoothly, it's time to move on to the next step: Constructing a roadbed.

• Step #3: Lay the roadbed

Aside from some yard and industrial areas, the track on prototype railroads normally rests atop a raised roadbed made of ballast (small, jagged rocks of various types) that provides a firm and level support for the track, and helps to promote good drainage.

In model railroading, roadbed material made of cork, dense foam, vinyl, rubber, or some other material is most often used to provide the appropriate above-ground eleva-tion to the track. This roadbed is usually sold in 3-foot lengths, or, in some cases, in rolls up to 25-feet in length. Some roadbed is made with a beveled split down the middle so it can be separated along its length and subsequently placed as two sections, with the sloped edge facing out and down to simulate a railroad embankment. The roadbed is, in turn, covered with a top layer of ballast made of very small stones, ground rubber, ground cork, or a variety of other

Photo by Charles Bednarik

Using the previously marked lines as a guide, Ryan is installing Woodland Scenics foam roadbed on the layout. Cork roadbed would be installed in a similar manner. Carpet tacks are used to hold the roadbed in place and to prevent buckling while the glue hardens.

materials to more accurately simulate a real roadbed. Since the roadbed material is applied to the layout before the ballast, we'll initially focus on that process.

Of the various types of roadbed materials used in model railroading, cork is probably the most common. Most cork roadbed is designed to be split into two thin strips, and it's relatively easy to bend the resulting strips so they will conform to tight curves. Here's how you should install cork (or most other) roadbed:

After all of the track and switches are in place, and before you do anything with the roadbed itself, use a pencil or felt-tip marking pen to trace the center line of the track directly on your platform. You will actually make two lines—one drawn on each side of the center rail. Don't worry about any gaps that result where the track ties are located, because you'll just be using these two parallel lines as guides in placing the roadbed. If the roadbed you're using comes as one wide strip, trace the outside edges instead. When you come to a switch, outline the entire outside perimeter of the switch and its switch machine; there's no need to worry about the track centerline at that location. After you're done, follow these simple steps:

1. *Remove all track and accessories (you can keep relatively long sections of track intact, if you so desire), and place them aside where they won't get damaged.*

2. *Round up a box of upholstery tacks—the ones that look like large thumbtacks with decorative heads—and a small hammer. You'll use these tacks to temporarily anchor the roadbed in place while the glue dries.*

3. *Working in sections about three or 4 feet long, apply a continuous bead of white glue approximately 1/4-inch outside either one of the two center lines you have drawn on the platform. It doesn't really matter whether you start with the inside line or the outside line.*

3. *Separate a 3-foot length of roadbed into two strips. Take one of the strips and, making sure that the beveled edge is facing to the outside and sloping down, start to lay the roadbed strip in place using the approximate center between the two lines you have drawn as a guide. In other words, the inside (flat) edge of the roadbed strip should be positioned between the two lines you drew. Placement doesn't need to be exact, but try to be as precise as possible.*

4. *As you work your way along, tap an upholstery tack through the roadbed and into the platform top to hold the roadbed in place. It is particularly important to do this on curves, because the roadbed will tend to move out of position and/or buckle as you lay it. A tack placed every couple of feet or so as you go along is fine on straight sections, but in curved areas the tacks should be placed every 4 to 6 inches or so. There's no need to push or hammer the tacks all the way down, because their sole purpose is to prevent the roadbed*

material from shifting out of alignment. In any case, these tacks will be removed after the glue sets. If you find that the roadbed still tends to buckle on tight curves, use bricks or a heavy books to weigh it down until the glue dries.

5. *Continue working along the same side of the track outline until you have completed one side of the roadbed for the entire layout. By the time you have finished, the first section that you worked on will be dry enough so you can extract the tacks and place them nearby so they can be used for the adjacent roadbed strip.*

6. *Follow the same procedure for laying the adjacent roadbed strips. Apply a bead of white glue, then position the strip in place by butting its vertical inside edge up against the strip you laid earlier. Here's a useful tip: Stagger the ends of the strips by several inches or so, rather then lining them up evenly with the previously laid strips. This will result in a more uniform appearance to the roadbed, especially on the curves.*

7. *When you come to a switch, just run the roadbed through the switch in the direction the track would normally follow. Use a hobby knife or utility knife to cut the ends of the roadbed, where necessary. Also glue some strips of roadbed, with the beveled edge facing out, along, and slightly outside of, the previously drawn perimeter outline of the switch machine and switch platform. Again, a sharp hobby knife will allow you to easily cut the pieces to fit.*

That's all there is to it! Once the glue has dried, go back and remove any upholstery tacks and/or weights used to hold things in place.

Another tip: Roadbed material can also be used to create streets on your layout. Since roads are generally wider than track roadbed, you can use multiple strips to form any width of road that you desire. The roads can be painted a dark gray color later on, or even covered with very fine N scale ballast or ground foam "dirt" to simulate a gravel or unpaved road.

At this point, it's a good idea to give the entire layout platform, including the just-laid roadbed and any streets that you may have laid, a heavy coat of inexpensive interior flat latex paint to seal the wood surfaces and to blend the roadbed into the rest of the still-flat topography. An earth-color paint is best—preferably a medium shade of brown. Later, when scenery and accessories are added, this paint will be covered by groundcover and other features. But for now, at least, the painted surface gives a much more finished look to the entire layout.

Now it's time to reinstall all of the track and switches. If your track plan calls for insulated or remote control sections, or if you still need to place insulating pins on any other section of track (to form insulated blocks, for example), this is the time to make sure that *all* of these items are properly installed in the correct location.

If you are using Lockons to feed power to the track, or to activate any operating accessories, they should also be attached now. It will be much more difficult to install Lockons later on, after the trackwork has been ballasted. The track itself should be pretty well-centered on the roadbed at this point, and there should be no large gaps between the ends of any of the roadbed sections. If there are gaps, fill them with small wedges of roadbed material cut to size and glued in place.

When you are satisfied with the appearance and fit of the track, you may wish to screw it down to keep it from shifting position or working loose at the joints. Always use screws, and not nails, because any attempt to remove nails later on will risk damaging the track. Use small (#4 or #5 x 3/4-inch) round head screws, which can be inserted through the existing holes in the track ties. On long, straight stretches of track, one screw every three track sections or so will be more than adequate. On curves, you may want to use one screw per section. Don't tighten the screws down too tightly or you'll risk bending the tie and possibly forcing one of the rails out of alignment! When the screw is properly installed, you should be still be able to see a slight bit of up-and-down movement if you push down firmly on the top of the track.

Keep in mind that weight-activated contactors provided with certain accessories such as trackside signals will not operate properly if the track is screwed down or ballasted, because there will no longer be any up-and-down movement of the track. You'll need to replace these pressure-sensitive contactors with insulated track sections, and you'll certainly want to attend to that before you add the ballast.

You may also want to enhance the realism of your track by placing additional ties under the rails, between the metal ties. These ties can be made from balsa or stripwood that has been stained or painted an appropriate shade of grayish-brown, or you can purchase ready-made ties made of wood, rubber, or plastic. Slip the additional ties into position before you tighten down the track screws, and certainly *before* you ballast the track. You won't be able to add ties— at least not easily—after the ballast is applied.

• *Step #4: Ballast the track*

Ballasting track takes a bit of time, but it is easy enough to do, and it certainly gives the entire layout a much more realistic look.

Model railroad ballast is made in a variety of sizes and colors to represent the rock and cinder materials used on real-life railroads. You'll want to select ballast that is sized for O gauge track, and your hobby dealer can help you make the right selection. Black, gray, brown, beige, and red ballast is readily available. You can also mix two or more colors, but do try to avoid the salt-and-pepper effect that results from blending a dark ballast with a light or contrasting-color ballast. Follow these steps to apply and affix ballast to your roadbed:

1. *If you're planning to mix two or more colors of ballast, pour the ballast into a large plastic bowl or small bucket and thoroughly blend the various colors. Make note of the exact quantities of each color you have used, because you'll need that information later if you need to blend a matching batch.*

2. *Fill a small paper cup with ballast, and crimp the sides of the cup with your fingers to form a sort of spout. Then, carefully pour ballast down each side of the center rail, and along the outside edges of the track and embankment until it reaches tie-top level and covers the sloped outer edges of the roadbed. Use your finger in a plow-like fashion between the center rail and outside rails to bulldoze and pack the ballast to a level at or near the top of the ties.*

3. *Because it is difficult to distribute ballast evenly when it is poured from a cup and moved about with your fingers, a small paintbrush can be used to prod the ballast into place, and to clear any ballast off the ties or lower edges of the rails. On the outside edges of the roadbed, use a scrap of cardboard to push stray ballast pieces into alignment, at the same time using the paintbrush to even things out along the slope. Again, the ballast should come up to the top of the ends of the ties, and it should completely cover the sloped edge. Avoid placing ballast on or near switch machines and, in particular, on or near the movable parts of switches where particles of ballast might foul the points.*

When you are satisfied with the appearance of your freshly laid ballast, it's time to glue everything into place. Although some modelers prefer to leave the ballast

---

Ballasting materials and supplies:

- Stone (preferred), ground rubber, or other ballast material—about 5 pounds of stone ballast will be needed for every 20 feet of track.
- Small (1/4- to 1/2-inch or so) artist's paintbrush.
- Small spray bottle capable of producing a fine mist.
- Small squeeze bottle with a spout (an empty mustard or ketchup squeeze bottle will do), or an eye dropper, ear syringe, or small basting syringe for dispensing the glue mixture.

- Elmer's white glue (or matte medium).
- Liquid dishwashing detergent.
- Covered glass or plastic container for mixing and holding the glue mixture.
- Plastic bowl for holding and mixing the ballast material.
- Several small paper cups to use as ballast dispensers.
- Scrap rags or paper towels for cleanup.
- Water.

loose, this is not a very good idea. Movement of the trains will eventually cause ballast granules to shift out of place, and they might possibly work their way into switch points or other areas where they can cause problems. Moreover, loose ballast is certainly not the way to go if you have any intention of moving or storing the layout elsewhere at some point.

With ballasting materials close at hand, Ryan applies and affixes ballast to the roadbed. The routine is: Apply and shape the ballast; mist thoroughly with a "wet water" mixture (see text); and then apply the glue mix with a dispensing bottle, basting syringe, or eyedropper.

4. *Prepare a pre-soaking solution of "wet water" by filling your spray bottle with water. Then add about 4 drops of liquid dishwashing detergent. The detergent is what makes the water "wetter" so it will penetrate the spaces between ballast granules and not glob-up on top.*

5. *Prepare the glue mixture that will be used to cement your ballast in place. A basic formula for the mix is one part Elmer's white glue or matte medium; two parts water; and 3 or 4 drops of liquid dishwashing detergent. Mix thoroughly, and store the mixture in a covered container.*

6. *With the misting/spray bottle, gently soak and saturate about four feet of the track and ballast. The idea is to get the ballast as wet as possible with this "wet water"*

without disturbing the small ballast stones. Don't worry about water harming the track (it won't), but do temporarily remove any trains or accessories from the area to prevent them from getting misted.

7. *Fill the squeeze bottle, eye dropper, syringe, or other device with your pre-mixed glue mixture, and then carefully dispense the glue onto the wet ballast along both sides of the center rail. Continue adding glue until the area is thoroughly saturated (you will observe the glue rising to the top of the ballast and no longer soaking in). Then go back and add glue to the outside embankments until the entire ballasted area is saturated and glue begins to flow out the bottom of the roadbed embankment. Things will look like quite a mess at this point, but don't worry about that!*

8. *After you have applied glue over about 4 feet of track, a scrap of clean cloth or a paper towel can be used to wipe the railheads clean of any glue. Don't worry about the sides or bottom of the rails, because it's only important that the top portion of each rail be clear, clean, and dry. Then, move on to the next area down the line and repeat the above procedure: Mist first; apply the glue mixture; then wipe off the railheads.*

Allow everything to dry overnight, and by the next day you'll find that all traces of that yucky white glue mixture have magically disappeared! Best of all, when you run your finger along the newly ballasted track, which still appears to be covered with loose stones, you'll find that everything is, in fact, firmly and permanently bonded. As if by magic, you have created very realistic roadbed!

If you previously screwed-down the track, you can now go back and remove the screws. Properly glued ballast will hold your track firmly in place, and removing the screws will also help to quiet the noise made by trains operating on your layout. If you ever need to remove the track—say to realign it or to install a new switch—simply add some hot water to the area to be worked on. This will soften the glue sufficiently so the track can be gently pried free.

Now it's time to move on to some simple electrical work!

• Step #5: Wire the layout

The basics of wiring a Lionel layout were also discussed in Chapters 4 and 6, so it might be a good idea to review those two chapters at this point. Also, locate and read the instruction manuals that came with your operating accessories so you'll be able to determine the type of wire that should be used, how much wire will be needed, and where and how the wires need to be placed and connected.

All you need do now is drill holes through the top of the layout for the wires that will connect the accessory to your track or transformer. The connecting wires should be stapled, fed through eyebolts, or otherwise neatly bundled and anchored to the cross supports on the underside of your layout to keep everything neat and tidy. It's also a good idea to color code wires used for different purposes, and/or to label each wire with a small tag so specific wires can be readily identified whenever you're working beneath the layout. You might, for example, use red wire for all of your power leads; black for all of your "common" grounds; and green for accessory wiring. You could even go a step further and use one color of wire for low voltage accessories and yet another color for higher voltage items, or use a different color of wire for each independent loop of track. Just remember which color is used for what purpose—a small card taped to the bottom of the layout would make that information readily available.

It's generally best to use stranded wire for your layout's electrical connections, rather than solid wire. Stranded wire is more flexible, and tends to hold up better when bent or twisted repeatedly. It's also best to use the heaviest gauge (thickness) of wire possible, consistent with the requirement that it be flexible enough to work with. For O gauge model railroads, wire in 14, 18, or 20 gauges will generally be fine (the *smaller* the number, the heavier the gauge). Plan to use the heavier gauge wire for power connections from your transformer to the track, and for any additional feeders installed to distribute power to other sections or to independent blocks. The lighter gauge wire (20 gauge, for example) can be used to connect trackside signals and other accessories in situations where no great distances are involved between the accessory and its power source.

Some Lionel railroaders prefer to solder wires to the track rather than use Lockons. That is fine, but if you're not familiar with soldering techniques, it's best to practice with a scrap section of track first so you can become familiar with the process.

Photo by Charles Bednarik

Ryan is in the process of wiring accessory controllers on the project layout. In order to keep the layout as light and portable as possible, the control panel is made from a kitchen shelf rack, of the type available at most home improvement centers. With a small layout like this, the rack will be used to hold the two transformers, while accessory controllers, toggle switches for insulated blocks, and switch machines will be mounted to the side trim board.

Soldering technique:

Items needed include a Brite Boy® pad or emery cloth; soldering iron or gun (the gun-type works best for wire-to-track soldering); rosin flux; rosin-core solder.

1. *Use the Brite Boy or emery cloth to clean and shine the surface to be soldered.*
2. *Apply liquid or paste rosin-core flux to both surfaces to be joined (track joint and the tip of the wire, for example).*
3. *Be sure the surfaces to be joined are in firm contact with each other (an alligator clamp can help hold things so you'll have both hands free).*
4. *Tin the tip of a hot soldering gun with a bit of solder (it should flow onto the tip).*
5. *Touch the tip of the hot soldering iron to the area to be soldered, and flow solder onto the joint by placing the solder in brief contact with the joined pieces, not with the tip of the soldering iron. The solder should flow freely and instantly. Remove the tip quickly, and the resulting soldered joint should be bright and shiny. After everything cools, apply a firm tug to the joint to make sure it is secure.*

If you decided in advance of track-laying to solder your track connections, the soldering can be done at your workbench. You can solder wires to the bottom of the rails, where the joint will be invisible. If you elect to solder wires after all the track is in place and ballasted, you should solder to the lower edge on either side of the center rail, and to the lower outside edge of one or the other of the outside rails. That way, soldered joints will not interfere with the movement of wheel flanges. Soldered joints can subsequently be painted, or covered with ballast, to disguise them.

Beneath your layout, the total amount of wire used can be greatly reduced if you install what is known as a "bus wire" to link all of the common grounds. A bus wire is nothing more than a length of heavy (#12 gauge or heavier), bare, copper wire that is attached to the bottom of your layout platform. Eyebolts can be used to shape and hold the wire to the various cross members on your layout frame. You might run the bus wire lengthwise down the center of a small layout, or you may want to configure it in an oval or even an "S" or "Z" shape for a larger layout. Ground wires from all of the various accessories can be connected to the bus wire at the most convenient point, and that single bus will provide a common return to the transformer.

If you are adding block control to your layout—to independently control power to a passing siding or an industrial spur, for example—you should have already inserted fiber insulating pins in the center rails at the desired locations to mark the beginning and end of each block (as noted in Step

#3). If you haven't done that, or decide later that you want to add a new block to track that is already ballasted, you can insulate the center rail by carefully cutting through the center rail track pin with a motor tool equipped with a cutting wheel or disk.

[Be sure to wear eye protection and, preferably, gloves and a tight-fitting long sleeve shirt, because cutting disks can shatter, and fragments of whatever you are cutting can also fly anywhere. If the sleeves on your shirt are loose, use rubber bands to hold the fabric snugly to your arm.]

After you have cut through the center rail pin, a small plastic shim can be glued into the gap that has been created. Then cut or sand off any excess plastic that protrudes around the railhead. This tiny plastic buffer will prevent the gap from working itself closed at some point, which would result in a short circuit.

In its most basic form, every insulated block on your layout will receive power by means of an off/on single-pole toggle switch installed along the power wire leading from your transformer. The toggle switch can be mounted on a control panel, or it could be mounted to the side trim board anywhere along the layout's perimeter, but preferably near the transformer. When the toggle is in the "on" position, current will flow to that block. When it's in the "off" position, nothing within or connected to that block will operate or move. If you want the same block to be controlled by two separate transformers, use a double-pole, double-throw (DPDT), center-off toggle switch, which will allow you to route power from one transformer or the other.

The many interesting things that can be accomplished with creative electrical wiring are far too numerous to detail in a basic book such as this. For more information on wiring techniques, you would be well advised to consult a reference devoted to the topic, such as the three-volume series, *Wiring Your Lionel Layout*, written by Dr. Peter Riddle. Volume One in that series covers basic techniques; Volume Two deals with intermediate wiring techniques; and Volume Three describes more advanced applications. You'll find these and other wiring, electrical, and electronics books listed in Appendix A.

• *Step #6: Place and connect operating accessories*

No Lionel layout is truly complete without at least a few of the renowned Lionel operating cars and accessories—items that over the years have distinguished Lionel trains. If you have browsed through some Lionel catalogs, or visited a hobby shop or two since acquiring your first Lionel set, the chances are good that you have already purchased at least a couple of these items to add action, interest, and operating fun to your layout.

Because Lionel has produced such a great variety of operating accessories over the years, it would be virtually impossible to provide instructions relating to the proper

Photo by Fred M. Dole, Editor, O Gauge Railroading magazine

Surrounded by Lionel illuminated and operating accessories, a Western Maryland switcher leaves the engine shed and slowly moves onto a transfer table in preparation for its daily run on Don Horn's layout. Don's passion for Lionel accessories is obvious when viewing his layout from any angle.

wiring procedures for every accessory. That information is detailed and illustrated in the instructional material that comes packaged with every accessory. If the instructions have been misplaced, there are a number of good technical references, usually covering specific eras of Lionel production, that will show you how to wire, operate, and maintain virtually every Lionel accessory ever made. You'll find these manuals listed in Appendix A.

What we can do in this section is provide a few useful guidelines and tips that generally apply to all operating accessories, no matter what they do or where they may be located on your layout. The following are a few considerations to keep in mind.

➤ If you have elevated your track on roadbed, you'll want to similarly elevate any trackside accessory whose proper operation requires that it be at a certain level and/or distance from the track. Such accessories include milk, horse, and cattle platforms; log, lumber, coal, culvert, and barrel loaders and unloaders; and certain other accessories where a trackside component interacts with an item of rolling stock. Perhaps the easiest way to elevate the trackside item is to provide it with a base made of the same roadbed material you used for the track. That way, both the accessory and its related car will be at exactly the same height. You don't need to construct a full base support for the accessory—a supporting perimeter made up of roadbed strips, and constructed so it extends slightly beyond the outside perimeter of the accessory's base on all sides, will do fine.

➤ It's important that any trackside accessories associated with operating cars be located along a straight stretch of track so there is at least one full straight section (and ideally more than one) extending beyond each end of the remote control or uncoupling section. This will assure that the car and its related accessory are in parallel alignment for operation. These types of accessories are not

Some Lionel loading and unloading accessories require precise placement if they are to perform properly. Good examples are the #456 Coal Ramp with its 3456 Operating Hopper Car (upper left) and the #397 Coal Loader seen in the center foreground. These two accessories work well together if they are correctly positioned.

The #342 Culvert Loader and #345 Culvert Unloading Station provide yet another example of two Lionel accessories working in concert with each other. Both of these accessories should be located along a relatively long stretch of straight track, with at least one full straight section extending beyond each end of the accessory(s).

intended to be placed adjacent to switches, and they should not be placed along a straight section of track leading into or out of a curve, where the accessory itself may be sideswiped by the overhang of a long locomotive or car as it rounds the bend.

➤ Track-to-accessory clearances are also important for items such as block signals, semaphores, signal bridges, operating water tanks, diesel fueling stations, bridges, tunnel portals, and other similar devices. Test for adequate clearance, both side-to-side and top-to-bottom, by moving or running your longest and largest locomotive or cars back-and-forth past the accessory.

➤ Consider powering your operating accessories with one or more small transformers that are independent of the transformer(s) being used to power your trains. For example, you might consider using one small transformer to control all of the lighted accessories on the layout, such as street lamps, light towers, and lamps installed in structures. You can then use the variable voltage control on the transformer to adjust illumination to a

pleasing level, and this will also help to extend bulb life. You can run two parallel bus wires, of the type described earlier, down the center of your layout, and connect all light-only accessories to those two bus wires by tapping in at the nearest location. This is known as a "parallel" electrical connection, and it will save a lot of wire. Also, if one bulb burns out along the line, the others will remain lighted. A second small transformer might be used to power accessories that require more voltage, such as log and coal loaders, gantry cranes, and the like—in other words, the accessories that "do something" in addition to simply being lighted.

So now you have a proper "stage," along with the featured "performers" in your cast, and everything is working as it should because you've conducted a "rehearsal." Now it's time to devote some attention to "set design," which, in the case of our model railroad production, implies scenery and the sundry little details that truly make your layout one-of-a-kind. These features will be covered next. Meantime, have some fun operating your Lionel trains and accessories!

Chapter 10

Personalizing your layout with scenery and details

Photo by Charles Bednarik

Ryan Bednarik, Construction Foreman and Chief Engineer for this book's project layout, attends to some track cleaning on the nearly completed pike. Much of the construction work was done outdoors in the family's back yard, and designing the layout in two separate 4x4 sections made it easily transportable. The seam dividing the two sections is visible across the road near the front corner of the station.

Throughout this book, a model railroad has been likened to a theatrical production, with the trains considered as the performing cast. If you followed the layout construction techniques described in the previous chapter, you now have a stage for your cast—a level platform topped with some nice trackwork and a few operating accessories. What's needed next is a set to adorn that stage. In a typical theatrical performance, on-stage sets are used to establish a time reference and location for the action, and to help convince the audience to suspend its link with everyday reality, even if for a brief period. Ideally, your new Lionel layout will ultimately feature a "set" that serves much the same purpose.

Creating an attractive, appropriate, and convincing scenic environment for your trains is a lot easier than you might imagine. Moreover, once you get started, you'll also find that it can be a whole lot of fun. Best of all, scenery building is a very forgiving process. If you don't like the look of something you've done, just cover it up with new scenery, or rip it out and start over. You certainly don't need to be a trained or accomplished artist to create scenic effects that will greatly enhance the look of your miniature empire.

Granted, there won't be a whole lot of space on a 4 foot by 8 foot Lionel layout to provide majestic features such as towering mountains, deep canyons, and wide rivers or lakes. Nevertheless, there is enough room to at least try your hand at creating such features on a more modest scale, and this can be a great educational experience in scenery construction that will serve you well as your railroad expands.

As you read through this chapter, keep in mind that scenery building, like most other phases of layout construction, is replete with viable alternatives in terms of materials and techniques that might be used. Coffee grounds, for example, are often used to simulate rich soil. Real dirt and sand is often used to represent . . . well . . . real dirt and sand. Dyed sawdust has become "grass" on countless numbers of model railroads over the years. Mountains can be formed with papier mache, various types of plaster, extruded Styrofoam, joint compound, wood putty, expandable foam products, and numerous other materials.

Scenery is most effective when it represents a specific geographic location, and even a particular season of the year, so you may want to give some thought to both of these considerations before investing in a load of scenery supplies. For example, the region you propose to model will often determine what type of trees are most appropriate, what type of rock faces are most prevalent, and the general topography of the land.

The season of the year represented on your layout will also need to be considered before you begin shopping for scenery materials. By far the two most commonly modeled seasons are summer and fall—probably because summer appears to present less of a challenge to most hobbyists, and because autumn is such a colorful season in many parts of the nation. Spring rarely blossoms on most model railroads, and aside from some artificial snow sprinkled on a Christmas layout, winter seems to be a season that most choose to avoid, both in real life and in modeled form. But, if you really want your layout to stand out from the rest, you might seriously consider trying a springtime or winter theme. The starkness of a winter landscape, for example, is an ideal way to highlight the colorful trains and accessories. Several of the scenery references listed in Appendix A will tell you how to effectively model the different seasons, and they will also expand on alternative ways of scenery building that are not covered here.

So now it's time to put aside any trepidation you may have; gather up the necessary materials; unleash those diverse and unrealized artistic talents that you possess; and get on with some creative expression of your unique personality.

• Groundcover treatments

It's easiest to start our landscaping efforts with a treatment that will turn that uniformly brown, painted layout top into something more closely resembling the natural environment you see you when look around your own neighborhood. What you most often will see, in addition to structures and roads, is grass (and weeds), dirt, shrubbery, and trees.

Since grass, weeds, and dirt generally constitute what we might consider the primary layer of groundcover, we'll begin by modeling those features.

Model railroaders today are blessed with a large and ever-expanding variety of excellent products that can be used to accurately simulate nearly every conceivable feature in the natural environment. Firms such as Woodland Scenics, Scenic Express, and Noch, for example, offer an extensive assortment of ground foam rubber products that are used by architectural model builders, as well as model railroaders, to represent soil, various colors of grass and weeds, trees and bushes of all types, and even flowers, fruits, and vegetables. These lightweight foam products are versatile, affordable, and very easy to work with, and they are highly recommended for either the novice or the more experienced hobbyist.

If you elect to go with foam-based products for most of your scenic treatments, here is what you will need for creating dirt, grass, and weed-covered areas:

1. *An assortment of packages or containers of ground foam soil, grass, and weeds in a variety of colors and shades, and in fine, coarse, and extra-coarse textures.*

2. *Elmer's white glue.*

3. *Several medium-size plastic or glass bottles (with caps or lids), for blending, storing, and dispensing your grass and soil. Mason jars are a convenient size, but any similar bottle or jar will do just fine. Ready-made "scenic material shakers" are also available.*

4. *A large jar, with lid, for mixing and storing your glue mixture.*

5. *An inexpensive, 2- or 3-inch wide paint brush for applying the glue to your layout.*

6. *A vacuum cleaner with a suction hose attachment (or a shop vac), for reclaiming any loose foam after everything has been bonded in place. If you start with a clean bag in the vacuum cleaner, the reclaimed foam pieces can be used again.*

Once you have all of your supplies and materials at hand, start by pouring some of the fine-grade foam soils into one or more of your mixing bottles. If you decide to blend two or more soil colors together, that's fine, but do try to avoid a salt-and-pepper effect. In other words, avoid mixing light colors with dark colors.

Take the lids or caps of your dispensing jar(s), and punch a series of small randomly spaced holes in the lids. What you're doing is creating a sort of large saltshaker that can be used to dispense foam onto the layout. Don't make the holes so big that foam bits pass through too easily. You can also buy foam shaker bottles ready made, if you don't mind spending the extra money.

With the jars of foam prepared, go ahead and mix the

glue solution that will be used to affix everything to the layout. A mixture of about one part white glue to three parts water should be about right.

Now, select an area of your layout to landscape. It's best to work in fairly small sections of several square feet. Since your trackwork is already in place, you might choose to start in a corner, or perhaps with one of the internal areas that is bordered by roadbed on all sides. You should also temporarily remove any trains and accessories from the immediate vicinity.

Apply a liberal coating of the glue mixture, and spread it as evenly as possible with the paintbrush. Avoid getting any glue on the already-ballasted roadbed.

After the area has been well covered with glue, take your shaker bottle(s) and begin sprinkling on your base coating of groundcover. If you have several bottles mixed with different colors or shades, apply the foam in a thoroughly random manner. Natural landscapes are rarely uniform in color, so just go at it with splotches of one shade here, and sprinkles of another shade there. Don't worry about loose foam that falls on the track and roadbed, since you can easily remove it with your vacuum cleaner hose later on.

Completely cover the area with foam, and let everything sit undisturbed until the glue is completely dry. Then use your vacuum cleaner hose to suck up any loose foam that was not bonded by the glue. Now step back and take a look.

Ryan applies various colors of ground foam turf to the project layout with a Woodland Scenics shaker. This process can be repeated over and over again, until you are satisfied with the results in a given area.

You may notice some spots where you didn't apply enough glue, and you may see other areas where you're simply not happy with the overall effect. Not a problem! Just go back and repeat the glue-sprinkle-vacuum procedure on top of the original layer. You can actually repeat this process as many times as it takes to provide the effect you're seeking. In fact, you will be repeating this process in any event, because once you are satisfied with the soil layer, you will then go back and apply grass, weeds, and ground-hugging

bushes and vines (made with coarse turf materials) in exactly the same way. In all cases, start this layering technique with the finer materials, and then build up to the more coarse foam products.

Keep in mind that, except for golf course putting greens, grass in a real-life environment is rarely a uniform shade of green. Even the best-kept residential lawns show some variation in coloring, depending on how different areas have been exposed to the effects of light and water. You will want your modeled grass to reflect similar variations, and that effect is easy enough to achieve with pre-blended "grass" products, or with grass mixtures that you blend yourself, just as you did with various soil colors.

After the soil is in place and some "grass" has been planted, begin adding small vines, low-clinging bushes, and other undergrowth to select areas around the layout. This type of vegetation can be formed with coarse turf, clump foliage materials, and/or foliage fiber. The application procedure is pretty much the same, except you can apply dabs of undiluted white glue directly to select spots where you will be attaching small bushes or similar forms of vegetation.

To add a splash of color here and there throughout the layout, and particularly on bushes and other low growth, sparingly sprinkle on some brightly colored "flower" foam. The flowers (or vegetables) can be fixed in place with a mist of diluted white glue, applied with the same spray bottle that you previously used for misting your ballast with "wet water," or with inexpensive hair styling spray. Be sure to cover any trackwork in the immediate area, and thoroughly rinse the sprayer in warm water after use to prevent it from becoming clogged with dried glue.

After you've completed the basic groundcover, step back and take a good, long look at your layout. See what a difference the various colors and textures make to the overall appearance!

About the only thing missing at this point is some sense of vertical depth—some variation in the contouring of the landscape. You still have what is essentially flat terrain. So, we'll now turn our attention to doing something about that.

• Trees for the layout

Trees on your layout will help to impart a greater sense of dimension and elevation. Artificial trees—both deciduous and conifer—can be purchased ready-made, or you can make them yourself out of a variety of materials, including twigs, weeds, twisted-wire armatures, bottle brushes, and any number of other items.

The foliage used for model trees most often consists of a web-like net of ground foam, but clumps of lichen—a spongy natural product that can be pickled and preserved to retain its flexibility—is also sometimes used. Over time, however, lichen has a tendency to dry out and crumble if it is disturbed. For that reason, ground-foam foliage netting is the preferred way to go.

Foam foliage material is very easy to work with, and the results are very realistic. Simply cut off a chunk of the material with a scissors (a circle or oval a couple of inches in diameter will do as a starting point). Then use your fingers to pull and stretch the piece in all directions until you achieve a thin, lacy, web-like structure, which you can then affix to the tree branches with dabs of glue applied to the branch tips. For some trees, a single piece of foliage netting will do, while for larger trees you'll want to apply several small pieces.

Ryan plants a completed Woodland Scenics tree on the project layout. The under-construction mountain and tunnel are in the background.

Ryan spray paints a Woodland Scenics metal tree armature in brown and gray tones before attaching the foam foliage.

Most ready-made trees are equipped with either plastic or metal trunk and branch armatures. Some of these trees are sold with the foliage already attached, while others may have the armatures and foliage packaged separately. Ready-to-plant trees are certainly fine for those who want to install a lot of trees in a short period of time, but the build-them-yourself variety is usually preferred by those who enjoy customizing their trees for an even more realistic effect. You might even consider placing some custom-made trees in the foreground areas, and locating ready-made types in background areas to create larger groves and forests.

It's a good idea to purchase trees in a variety of different sizes, types, and shapes to enhance the visual impact of a scene. You'll want to select trees that will work well with O gauge trains, of course, but some can be quite small and others may be quite large, just as in the real world. If you want your layout to appear larger than it actually is, place larger and more detailed trees in the foreground areas, with progressively smaller trees further back in the scene.

You can improve the appearance of pre-made model trees by applying a wash of diluted gray hobby paint to the trunk and, if they are accessible, the branches. Most plastic tree trunks are molded or painted in a uniform brown color, but few real trees have brown trunks, and fewer still are uniformly colored. In most cases, the trunks and branches are really much closer to a brownish-gray color.

When you're placing trees on the layout, be sure to group them into odd-number clusters comprised of various sizes and shapes. Groves made up of odd numbers of various-size trees will appear far more realistic than an isolated single tree, or a small grouping made up of even numbers of equal-size trees.

If you have purchased an assortment of ready-made trees for your layout, you'll find that many of them come with a wide base so they can be made to stand on their own. The trees will look far more realistic if you remove that base and plant the tree directly into the layout. Just drill a hole to the appropriate size and glue the trunk in place (if you used a foam sheet atop your layout, you won't even need a drill). If you have access to a hot glue gun, use that instead of white glue. Place a dab of hot glue in the hole you made, and then plant the tree. Hot glue sets up very quickly, so you won't have to worry about your tree leaning while the glue hardens.

One final tip about trees: In real life, we often see trees that tend to lean one way or another, perhaps from being partially blown over in a storm. On a model railroad, however, it's best if you plant all of your trees, except for fallen ones, so they are as close to vertical as possible. For some reason, leaning model trees on a layout tend to look like leaning model trees, which isn't the effect we're striving for.

Even on a small layout, it's almost impossible to have too many trees, unless, of course, you're modeling a desert or industrial scene. The fact is, most model railroads don't have nearly enough trees, and they often don't display enough variety. Of course, the cost of a forest of trees can quickly add up if you purchase the ready-made types. But, as was noted earlier, trees can be made from a variety of materials, including twigs taken from real trees. Don't hesitate to be inventive and creative in your horticultural efforts, or in any of your modeling approaches. That's part of what makes this hobby so much fun!

• Hills, mountains, and rock formations

If, even after the addition of soil, grass, and trees, you're still not satisfied with the overall development of your "set," perhaps what's needed is a more varied topography. Features such as hills, mountains, gulches, and valleys will certainly make your layout appear to be anything but flat, and these features are easy enough to add at virtually any point in the construction of a tabletop layout, assuming there is sufficient space available.

Construction of certain of these features—those that will fall below track level, in particular—will be much easier if you initially placed a 2-inch-thick sheet of extruded Styrofoam on top of your plywood base. But even if you didn't, the careful use of a saber saw can remedy that situation. The above-layout features can be added at any time, regardless of the composition of the platform, since no modification to the table top is required. Even on a 4 foot by 8 foot layout, there's almost always some space for at least a few minor topographical features such as ditches, small hills, and perhaps even a mountain with, of course, the obligatory tunnel.

Ditches can be created in spaces between adjacent tracks, and in other areas where one of your larger accessories simply will not fit. These features can be made by carving out the foam, or even by cutting through the plywood, if necessary, and then using a section of window screen to form a convex surface for a few layers of plaster-impregnated paper towels and a finishing coat of plaster, SculptaMold, or some other material. The modified area can be completed with groundcover, as was used on the rest of the layout, with more attention given to soil and yellow weeds rather than green grass. Puddles of "water" might even be added to the ditch (see the water features section of this chapter).

Aboveground features can be constructed in a number of ways, depending on their height. Small hills and embankments can be created with wadded up newspapers, shaped to the general size and configuration of the formation, then held in place with masking tape. This supporting structure can then be covered with several layers of plaster-soaked paper towels, followed by a finishing layer of plaster or SculptaMold.

If you want to include a rock face as part of an embankment or hill, they can be cast in latex rock molds filled with plaster, or you can purchase ready-made foam rock faces that can be cut to fit; blended into the surrounding landform with plaster; and then painted with washes of diluted artist acrylics or water soluble hobby paint in colors that most closely represent the composition of the rock you are duplicating. Highly diluted India Ink can be used to add dimension to rock cracks and crevices, and this treatment is followed with applications of diluted washes of artists colors such as burnt umber, raw sienna, burnt sienna, and yellow oxide, among others. Refer to photographs of real rock formations as a color guide, and always use highly diluted washes of paint so they will blend together. After the first coat has been applied, allow everything to dry before applying any additional coats. It's a whole lot easier to darken an area of rockwork than it is to lighten it. Also, before applying paint to a cast plaster rock face, be sure to mist the surface with water so colors will bleed together in an imperceptible and realistic manner.

It seems that almost no model railroad with a significant mountain is considered truly complete unless there's also a tunnel for the trains. This mountain-and-tunnel combination will require some careful thought in the layout planning stage because it will occupy a considerable amount of space on the layout, and the tunnel portion will need to be constructed with adequate clearances for the trains.

On a small layout, the customary location for a mountain and tunnel is at one of the corners, or along one end of the layout. If the corner or end selected for the mountain is close to a wall on one or more sides, this works to your advantage because the back (not visible) side of the tunnel can be left open so you can easily perform track mainte-

Photo by Charles Bednarik

The mountain and tunnels on the project layout occupied one end of the platform. A grid-type framework for the mountain was made with lengths of coat hanger wire, held together at intersecting points with twist-ties. Plastic screening material was then draped over the framework, and Crayola® "Model Magic Modeling Compound" was subsequently applied over the screening to form a durable shell. Charles Bednarik spotted the Crayola® material at a crafts store, and decided to give it a try. Charles and Ryan found it to be lightweight, easy to work with, and structurally solid when dry.

nance chores later on. Whatever you do, always make sure that you will have easy access to the full length of any tunnel. If problems are going to develop with your trains and/or track anywhere on the layout, you can be pretty sure the glitch will occur inside a tunnel, where it's hardest to get to.

As with virtually every other aspect of model railroad construction, there are a number of ways to construct major landforms such as mountains, including mountains with tunnels. The method outlined below represents just one of several viable options. Nevertheless, this technique is preferred because it results in a durable but lightweight mountain and tunnel that can be easily removed if the layout itself needs to be transported or stored.

To start with, you'll need at least one 4 foot by 8 foot sheet of 2-inch-thick (preferably) extruded Styrofoam, of the same type that you may have used atop your plywood platform. If your mountain is going to be a long one, you may even need an additional sheet.

Create a cardboard or paper draft template that defines the full base area of your mountain, including the tunnel. Then, lay the draft template on the layout in the area where you plan for your mountain to be, and continue to work with the template until you have it cut to the desired size and shape. If track is entering and exiting a proposed tunnel at any point on the template, you may want to mark and cut those entry and exit points so they are at a 90-degree angle (perpendicular) to the track. The width of these faces should total about 6 inches (three inches on each side of the center rail, where it meets the Styrofoam). Just envision that your tunnel portals will eventually be installed along these faces.

Now, transfer the outline of the template to one corner of your sheet of Styrofoam (assuming that your mountain is being placed in a corner of the layout, and thus will have one or more straight sides); mark the template's outline on the foam sheet with a marking pen; and then cut the base section of your mountain from the Styrofoam.

Photo by Charles Bednarik

A view of the screening material used to form the project layout mountain's basic shape, seen here covered with a partially completed shell of Crayola modeling compound. This modeling compound approach differs from the foam-sheet construction technique described in the text, but either of these methods, plus a number of others, will work equally well.

Then, cut additional Styrofoam layers for your mountain in the same manner. If you are making the mountain out of 2-inch-thick Styrofoam, you'll want to prepare about five sections—and perhaps one or two more if you really want some elevation to your mountain. With relatively small mountains, you should have no trouble getting all the sections you need out of a single 4 foot by 8 foot sheet of the Styrofoam. There are two ways to handle cutting these additional sections:

You could use your first cut foam section as a template, and cut four (or more) identical sections of the same size and shape. This will result in a straight-sided mountain that can later be carved, cut, and otherwise shaped to add the less-than vertical sloped faces.

Or, you could cut each successive layer slightly smaller than the preceding layer, but still conforming to the general shape of that previous layer, to develop a sort of wedding cake tiered mountain (similar to what is seen on a contour map).

If your mountain is going to include a tunnel, the first method is probably easier to work with, because you want to make sure that the tunnel will be completely enclosed in the mountain—at least to start with.

What you have now is a stack, five or more layers high, of cut Styrofoam pieces that are roughly the shape of your mountain, as far as the base perimeter is concerned.

The next step is to place all of the cut sections, one on top of the other, so they are oriented correctly all around, forming a giant sandwich, of sorts. Use carpenter's glue or Liquid Nails to glue the sections together. You don't need to spread the glue over the full top area of any piece. Just run a bead of glue around the top, several inches in from the edge. If the outside edges are left unglued, this will make it somewhat easier to cut and shape the foam later on.

Allow at least a full day for the foam "sandwich" to dry, and then place it in its proper position over the layout and track (if any). Once you have the mountain in perfect alignment with the side and end edges of your layout platform (if applicable), use both hands to apply some downward pressure from the top of your mountain. This will cause the track to make some indentations in the bottom layer of foam, thereby providing you with a convenient map of the exact shape of your tunnel.

Turn the mountain upside down on the floor, and draw one line about 3 inches outside the indentation made by the center rail, and draw another line about 3 inches inside the indentation made by the center rail (both lines will be parallel to the two outside rails). These lines will define the inside walls of the tunnel. You'll want to cut straight down along both lines to a depth of at least 6 inches. If you use a kitchen knife with a 6-inch blade, that makes things easy, because you'll simply cut along both lines down to handle depth.

After both cuts for the tunnel wall have been made, go back and begin cutting away the foam between the two cuts. Work carefully when you get near the six-inch depth, because you probably won't want, or need, to go any deeper than that with your tunnel roof. Use a rasp and/or a

The nearly completed project layout mountain and tunnel structure. Although not part of the original plan, a stream and waterfall was added to the mountain for color and variety.

sanding block to clean up the tunnel roof and the tunnel's inside walls.

When you have the tunnel completely hollowed out, place the mountain back into position, and run your longest locomotive or car slowly through the tunnel to check for proper clearance on the top and both sides. If more cutting, shaping, or sanding is needed, it's a very simple matter to attend to this now, before moving on.

Once the tunnel is complete, sand the walls and roof smooth one final time. Use your vacuum to remove any foam dust, and then paint the entire inside of the tunnel—roof and walls—with a flat black latex paint.

You're now ready to glue the mountain to your layout platform. There's no need to apply glue to every inch of the bottom—just a drop in four of five spots will do—because you may want to remove the mountain later on. In fact, you may want to simply install a few wood or metal pins in the top of the layout, and push the mountain down onto those pins so it can be easily removed in the future.

Ryan applies a final coat of paint to the completed mountain and tunnel structure. The four tunnel portals were also lightly spray painted to relieve the plastic sheen, and to blend them into the surrounding landscape.

Obviously, you still have a pretty unrealistic looking mountain at this point because the sides are either vertical or step-like, and the top is perfectly flat. You'll correct that with a knife, rasp, sandpaper, or hot wire foam cutter, or any combination of these tools. Just carve, cut, and smooth the mountain into whatever shape pleases you. If you cut too much away at some spot, just glue a scrap of foam to that area, and try again. The final shape your mountain takes is entirely up to you, but it's helpful to examine photos in a few hobby books and magazines to gain some useful ideas.

You may want to add some cast plaster or foam rock faces to the sheer portions of your mountain. Simply dig into the foam to create a shallow hole for these formations; glue them into place; and fill in any gaps with plaster.

You might also consider leaving a small area on the top of the mountain perfectly flat, so you can install a Lionel Rotating Beacon there to warn approaching aircraft. That accessory is particularly well suited to a mountain top location, as is the Lionel Microwave Tower and the Rotating Radar Antenna.

Once you are fully satisfied with the shape and appearance of your mountain, mix a batch of plaster, Hydrocal, SculptaMold, Durham's Wood Putty, or whatever finishing shell material you care to use, and apply a liberal coating to the entire outer surface, blending rock faces and all other such features into one unified mass. You can then paint and landscape the mountain in the same way, and with the same materials, that were used for painting and landscaping the rest of the layout. If you want to apply foam turf, weeds, or grass to small ledges and near-vertical surfaces on your mountain, just apply glue to the area; fold an index card; fill the fold with some foam material; and use a soda straw to gently blow the foam onto the glue.

Finally, add the tunnel portals. Cut away some of the foam so they'll fit perpendicular to the track, and use a bit of plaster to fill in any gaps. The idea is to have the portals appear as if they were actually built into the side of the mountain.

• *Water features*

Strange but true: About the *least* realistic and most troublesome way to model water on your layout is to use real water! For one thing, real water just doesn't look all that "real" on a scaled-down model railroad. Also, real water requires some extreme measures to keep it contained where you want it to be, and to keep it continually flowing and clean. If you've ever had an aquarium in your home, you already know what you're up against.

Most model railroaders prefer to rely on artificial water which, when properly done, can actually look more real than the real thing. Some of the products commonly used over the years to simulate water on model railroads include various types of resins, gloss medium, plastic films or sheets, glass, varnish, glossy paint, and pellets that can be melted and poured. Of these various options, one of the most popular is a two-part epoxy resin sold in craft stores under the brand name EnviroTex. This product is commonly used for decoupage and other craft projects. EnviroTex is easy to mix and work with, has little odor, gives off little or no heat during curing, and provides a flat, hard surface that is resistant to scratches and easy to clean. If you decide to give EnviroTex a try, the steps outlined below will guide you in creating a small pond for your layout. EnviroTex will also work well for other water features, including steams, rivers, waterfalls, and larger lakes, but you're better off starting out with something small and manageable until you gain some feel for how the product works.

Before we begin pouring water, we'll assume that you previously topped your plywood layout platform with some other sheeting, such as Homasote or a 2-inch thick (or thicker) layer of extruded Styrofoam. If so, it's relatively simple matter to carve out or cut the top layer to provide some depth for your pond or stream. Then, once you have created an appropriately sized and shaped hole, go back and give the pond bottom and all parts of the embankment a solid coat of plaster or SculptaMold to *completely* seal everything. It is *very* important that the sides and bottom of the water feature be completely sealed and watertight! If they aren't, you're liable to end up with an epoxy resin lake on your carpet or floor because EnviroTex liquid will seek out even the smallest hole in your pond bottom. When you are satisfied that the plaster coating is complete, go ahead and paint everything with the same earth-colored latex paint that you earlier used for the rest of the layout.

If you're working with just a flat plywood tabletop, you'll need to cut a hole in the same manner as you did when making a ditch or other depression, as noted earlier. If the pond is going to be a large one, it would be a good idea to provide a plywood support for the bottom, which can be anchored to the underside of your layout with 1 foot by 2 inch strips of wood.

After you have completed the site preparation procedure, you're ready to make a pond!

The first step is to give your pond some basic underlying color. You may be thinking that a pleasing shade of blue will do nicely for this, but you would be wrong! Water only appears blue because we're normally seeing an angled reflection of the sky on that water. Real water is, of course, colorless, or very nearly so. What color it does present usually depends on the bottom material under the water, how deep the water is, how much movement there is in the water, and what particles might be suspended in it.

For our purposes, it's best to strive for a bluish-black color to represent the deepest water; a greenish-brown color to represent more shallow areas; and a yellowish gray-brown color nearer the shoreline. Actually, none of these areas should be well defined—they should all tend to blend together in a sort of continuum from shallow shoreline to deep mid-section of the pond. To achieve this effect, start with water-soluble latex hobby paints or artist acrylics in shades approximating those basic colors.

Have a small bowl of water nearby as you apply the paints, to keep the brush wet and to help to blend and feather the colors together as you apply them. Start with the darkest color first—the bluish-black—and apply that color

to areas representing deep water. Then brush on some greens and browns around that area; followed with gray, yellow, and brown as you approach the shoreline. Apply these colors in a thoroughly random pattern, wetting the brush frequently and swirling the paints together so everything tends to run together. When dry, the darkest colors in the middle of your pond should gradually and almost imperceptibly change to lighter shades near the shore.

If you have made the pond deep enough, you may want to add a few objects along the sides and bottom to provide additional visual interest. For example, you could have a fallen tree on the embankment, with some of its branches submerged in the water. Or, you might have a discarded tire or other "stuff" lying on the bottom of the pond. A few rocks here and there will also help to provide a sense of depth to the scene. These, and any other objects you care to place in or under the water should be held in place with a dab of white glue.

After everything has had several days to dry, it's time to add the water. If you're using EnviroTex, just follow these simple steps:

1. *Mix equal parts of EnviroTex resin and hardener in a disposable plastic cup. The quantity of each liquid used will depend on the size of your pond, but the general idea is to prepare enough solution to cover the entire bottom of the pond no deeper than 1/4-inch deep. Use a wood coffee stirrer to thoroughly mix the two liquids together. Mix gently, to avoid creating air bubbles. You must mix exact quantities of the two liquids for the epoxy to harden properly. Otherwise, you could end up with a surface that feels slightly tacky to the touch, even after many weeks. If the first layer does not fully harden, your best bet is to add another thin layer on top of it (you may be doing this anyhow, depending on how deep your pond is).*

2. *Optional: You can also add a couple of drops of transparent dye to the mix, if desired. EnviroTex offers transparent dyes (for river water) in blue, green, amber and pearl, and they offer opaque dyes (for deep or muddy water, and for ice) in white, blue, green, and brown. Just a couple of drops per 10 ounces of mixture will be adequate. Use even fewer drops, or none at all, as you add successive layers.*

3. *Pour the EnviroTex into the middle of your pond. You can use your stirrer to spread it out a bit, but if you leave it alone it will pretty much spread by itself and seek a level throughout the pond.*

4. *Check to see if there are any air bubbles in the layer you just poured. If you find any, blow on the surface gently and repeatedly to dissipate the bubbles (the carbon dioxide in your breath does the trick).*

5. *If left undisturbed, EnviroTex will cure and harden to a perfectly flat surface. Even if you move it around twenty*

minutes or so after the pour, the liquid will still level itself. If you want to add a ripple or wave effect to the surface (particularly in the final layer that you pour), you'll need to catch the epoxy at just the right time in the curing process. This is largely a matter of guesswork and experience, but the right point is usually reached about an hour after the pour. Use a roofing nail, dental pick, or a similar device to pick at, lift, prod, and twirl the entire surface. You'll notice that the epoxy will still try to level itself, but if you keep at it for a while, it will eventually reach a state where most of the waves and ripples will pretty much stay in place.

6. *If your have poured your pond in an area of your home that is subject to airborne dust, it's a good idea to place a piece of heavy cardboard over the entire pond area to keep the surface dust free while the mix cures and hardens. Do not allow the temporary cover to contact the surface at any point.*

7. *After the initial layer of EnviroTex has hardened—usually a period of several days—you can pour one or more additional layers to add more depth to the pond. Repeat the procedures described above, using progressively less tinting dye, if you added dyes to earlier layers. Also, when you get to the final layer, be sure to refer back to Step 5 if you want to create ripples or waves.*

Once you're comfortable with the technique for modeling water, you may want to add a stream to your newly created pond to justify the addition of a culvert or small bridge going under the track at some point. The procedure for modeling a stream is about the same as for a larger water feature, but if the stream is to exit the layout at some point along the perimeter, you'll need to construct a temporary "dam" to prevent the liquid epoxy from dripping onto the floor. A temporary barrier can be made from a piece of styrene sheeting that is temporarily glued into place, bottom and sides, with flexible silicone caulking or aquarium sealer, then reinforced from the outside with duct tape. The caulking and styrene dam can be peeled away after the stream has cured and hardened.

To learn more about constructing various types of water features for model railroads, including waterfalls and rapids, refer to one of the scenery books listed in Appendix A. Especially useful in this regard is *How to Build Realistic Model Railroad Scenery*, 2nd Edition, by Dave Frary.

• Details that make a difference

Details definitely do make a difference on a model railroad, and the more small details you add to individual scenes on your layout, the more lifelike and believable it will appear to those who partake of your handiwork.

To start with, plan to detail your layout in small segments, creating dis-

This view of the scrap yard on Roy Everett's Little Lakes Lines nicely illustrates how careful attention to even the smallest details can truly bring a scene to life.

tinctive little vignettes here and there that will attract and hold a viewer's attention. You can spend a great many fun-filled hours just adding all sorts of details to an area no larger than a couple of square feet, and you'll quickly find that this is a very creative and rewarding activity. You'll know you've attained the status of "master detailer" when you start looking at everyday household items and asking yourself, "Gee! How could I use this on the layout?"

Some basic detailing principles apply to whatever scene you are creating. For example, you'll want to pay close attention to the scale of the accessories and detail items that you choose for your railroad. Human figures used on a Lionel layout should be at or near O scale (1:48) size. A 6-foot-tall figure, as represented in O scale, would measure about 1-1/2 inches tall. You can use that as a guide in selecting larger or smaller figures. A good number of manufacturers offer ready-made O scale figures, so you should have no trouble populating your towns and other scenes.

The scale of structures and vehicles used on your layout's streets and highways should also closely match the 1:48 proportions of O scale. A number of manufacturers offer O scale buildings, both in built-up form and as easy-to-assemble kits. A large variety of inexpensive die-cast cars and trucks are manufactured in 1:43 scale, and this is certainly close enough for our purposes.

Another point about vehicles: Try to select cars and trucks that are appropriate to the era you are modeling. If the parking lot of your station is full of vintage automobiles from the 1940s, visitors will just naturally assume that you are modeling that earlier period in history. Interestingly, people are quite adept at dating automobiles, whereas most would be hard pressed to come within 30 or 40 years of determining when a particular locomotive or piece of rolling stock was built.

A list of detailing tips for model railroads could easily fill a volume several times the size of this book, but the following examples should get you headed in the right direction. Many of these tips were provided by members of *O Gauge Railroading* magazine's on-line forum, in response to the posted topic: "What detailing tips would you like to share?"

➤ A dead tree here or there adds a realistic touch to any model railroad. You might even consider adding a fallen tree to some scene on the layout.

➤ Although you may not want to alter your treasured Lionel operating accessories, do consider repainting other plastic accessories and structures to give them a distinctive look, and to relieve the sheen that is common with most plastic items. Use flat hobby latex paints, applied with a good quality brush or, if they are still in kit form or can be masked, with an airbrush.

Photo by Fred M. Dole, Editor, O Gauge Railroading magazine

The small details that help to bring a layout to life are clearly evident in this overview photo of Bill and Pat Wasik's spectacular Lionel layout. A multitude of human and animal figures, vehicles, telephone poles, and a variety of other miniature representations of real-life objects all help to unify the layout, and give the railroad purpose.

A night scene on Liz and Paul Edgar's Lionel layout. Traffic lights, construction barrels, and lane stripes on the street all add to the realism of this scene.

Photo courtesy of Paul Edgar

➤ You can reduce the sheen on pre-painted plastic structures and figures by spraying them Dullcoat, or a similar dulling spray. Spray cans of clear dulling finishes are available wherever hobby paints are sold.

➤ Consider adding lights to as many of your structures as possible. If you buy a structure in kit form, paint the inside of the structure's walls black before you assemble the kit. The black paint will prevent interior lights from glowing through the walls. If the structure is pre-built, adding some black cardboard or construction paper to the interior walls will also help.

➤ Apply window treatments to the buildings on your layout. Window shades and drapes can be cut from construction paper of various colors, and glued or taped from the inside.

➤ Houses and other structures can be provided with a "concrete" foundation by elevating the base on a scrap of wood that has been cut to size and painted a concrete gray.

➤ Place your structures in logical groupings. For example, if you have several houses available, group them into a residential neighborhood that's separate from your downtown area, and somewhat removed from any industrial scenes.

➤ Freshly-washed clothes hanging on a back yard clothes line behind one of your model homes adds a nice touch. The clothing items can be cut from paper or made from scraps of cloth, and the clothes line might be a length of fishing leader, string, or wire strung between a couple of wooden dowels, or even between two trees.

➤ If you have a residential area on your layout, consider creating a garage sale scene in the front yard and driveway of one of the homes.

➤ Good fences make good neighbors, so think about adding some fences between the various properties on your layout. They can be purchased ready-made in a variety of styles, or hand-made out of a number of common, everyday items. A chain link fence, for example, can be made with posts and crosspieces cut from a metal clothes hanger, and with fine mesh window screen, cut on an angle, for the fencing. A coat of a silver or aluminum paint will provide the finishing touch.

➤ The same ground foam material that's used for ground-cover and foliage can also be used to form vines on the sides of structures and bridges.

➤ You can almost always find a good selection of inexpensive 1:43 scale die-cast vehicles in the toy department of major discount store chains. Paint 'em, bang 'em up a bit if you so desire, and make use of those streets, parking lots, and highways.

➤ Add a junked or wrecked car or two to your layout. Strip the doors and wheels off a cheap die-cast car; add some rust-colored paint to select portions of the vehicle, and place it in an empty field or a junkyard. The wheels and tires can be used as detail items around your local gas station.

➤ Highway dividing lines can be made with auto pinstriping, or with ChartPak tape that can be found at most graphic arts supply stores.

➤ Place some traffic lights and stop signs at the major intersections on your layout. If you've neglected to do so, and an accident occurs, go ahead and create an accident scene with a damaged car or two, a police car, fire truck, ambulance, and some assorted passersby who have paused to observe the action.

This small scene on Jim Richardson's layout features enough details to keep a viewer's eyes busy for quite some time. Notice the small pond, with a picnic table nearby; the activity around Andrew's Garage; and the window adornments and signs that are a part of Big Jim's Grocery.

Photo courtesy of Jim Richardson

➤ Be sure to install some telephone poles along your streets. These inexpensive accessories can be given a more realistic look if you paint them a grayish-brown, and then add a bit of glossy light green paint to each of the insulators on the cross-arms.

➤ Don't forget to place some lamp posts at appropriate locations—at or near intersections, and around parking lots, for example—so the residents of your town can see where they're going at night.

➤ A variety of crates, barrels, and boxes will really dress up a freight platform loading dock. You can find many appropriate items at a dollhouse store.

➤ Signs, signs, and more signs! Signs help to bring a layout to life, and define the era being modeled. From roadside billboards to advertising signs on the sides of buildings and in shop windows, the real world displays an abundance of signs, and your modeled world should do likewise. Signs are certainly easy enough to make. Many of them can be found on the pages of magazines, and even on the printed packaging for a variety of food items. If you can't find what you want, fire-up the computer and make 'em yourself!

➤ Lots of litter is a good thing on a model railroad! Bits and pieces of just about anything can be scattered along the base of your roadbed embankment, along your streets, and in empty lots to give things a more true-to-life appearance.

➤ Load your freight cars! This is especially true for open-top cars, such as hoppers, gondolas, and flat cars. Give them something to haul, such as pipes, metal scrap, coal, ore, lumber, or some other commodity. Most of these loads can be made with common everyday items and a little imagination. Plastic soda straws, for example,

might be cut and painted to represent metal pipe loads. These pipes would also look good placed alongside your highway in random fashion, to represent water mains that have not yet been installed.

➤ The next time you attend a train show or a yard sale, look for a couple of old, beat-up freight cars that can be repainted and turned into great detail items. A caboose, with its wheels removed, can become a lineside office. A battered old boxcar can be made into a storage shed. Remove the tank from a tank car; elevate it on a wood support structure painted to represent concrete; add a ladder and perhaps a soda-straw pipe or two; and you now have a dandy fuel storage tank.

➤ Cardboard tubes of various diameters can be cut and painted to represent culverts, large pipes, fuel storage tanks, and a variety of other objects.

➤ If you're not satisfied with the appearance of ready-made human or animal figures that you buy, simply repaint them to your liking. Start with an overall base coat in the flesh color you want, and then work from the largest areas on the figure to the smallest, using very fine artist brushes. There's no need to bother painting detailed faces with eyes and lips, because these features will generally be too small to be readily noticed.

➤ Improve the appearance of many ready-to-use plastic figures by carefully cutting off the molded-on plastic base that allows the figures to stand upright. Use a small file and a bit of model paint to touch up the feet or shoes, and then use rubber cement to affix the figure in place. If you decide to move the figure at some future point, rubber cement is easily removed, with no damage or residue, by simply rolling it with your finger until it comes loose.

Chapter 11

Great Lionel layouts from the pages of *O Gauge Railroading* magazine

Over a number of years, Fred M. Dole, editor and resident photographer of *O Gauge Railroading* magazine, has visited and documented many of the finest Lionel layouts in the United States. He graciously shares a few example of his work here in the hope that others will recognize the virtually unlimited potential of model railroading with Lionel trains, and will then be inspired to achieve similar excellence in their own modeling efforts.

Many of these photographs originally appeared in *O Gauge Railroading* magazine — a leading publication for operators of O gauge (3-rail) and O scale (2 rail) electric trains. Thanks to Myron J. Biggar, publisher, and Barbara Saslo, vice president and chief operating officer, for their assistance. Very special thanks also go to each of the dedicated and talented hobbyists whose fine craftsmanship with Lionel trains is displayed here.

Photo by Fred M. Dole, Editor, *O Gauge Railroading* magazine

Roy Everett's Little Lakes Lines
Lionel postwar and LTI-era Hudson steam locomotives prepare to depart Podunk City terminal on Roy Everett's Little Lakes Lines. Steam power ranks as Roy's favorite, and only a few early-generation diesels can be seen operating on the LLL. Roy treats his layout as theater, with the trains themselves performing as "actors" on the layout "stage." Many of the scenes on Roy's layout are so meticulously detailed, and so lifelike, that a first-time viewer of photos of his work may find it hard to determine if what is being observed is real or modeled.

Photo by Fred M. Dole, Editor, *O Gauge Railroading magazine*

The Hicks Family Layout

A gleaming Santa Fe freight winds its way along the middle of three long mainlines on the Hicks family layout. The layout features more than 650 feet of O gauge track, 35 feet of O27 track, and 64 feet of American Flyer track. Up to eight trains can operate on the layout at the same time. Model railroading is truly a family affair in the Hicks household, where John, his wife, Linda, and all five children share an interest in Lionel trains. All have assisted, at one time or another, with construction and detailing of the 27 feet by 24 feet empire in the basement of their home.

Photo by Fred M. Dole, Editor, *O Gauge Railroading magazine*

Don Horn's Layout

A pair of Lehigh Valley diesels depart the passenger terminal area on the 11 feet by 17 feet center section of Don Horn's 23 feet by 25 feet layout. The main terminal building, visible in the far distance, is elevated above track level, with station tracks running below in a manner similar to the practice followed by many prototype railroads. Replete with colorful trains, shiny three-rail track, and examples of just about every operating accessory Lionel has ever made, this is an inspiring rail empire sure to warm the heart of any train enthusiast.

Photo by Fred M. Dole, Editor, O Gauge Railroading magazine

Harry Sklar's Bridge Creek Railroad

Although diesel power rules on Harry Sklar's Bridge Creek Railroad, some steam power, such as the Lionel circus train on the upper level in the background, still makes an occasional appearance. Harry's layout began as a dream back when Harry was just five years old. That dream was finally realized years later, in December 1993, when a golden spike ceremony was held to celebrate the completion of Harry's 45 feet by 38 feet multi-level Lionel layout.

Bill and Pat Wasik's Layout

Two of the most colorful Lionel passenger trains ever made— the Texas Special, and the Southern Pacific Daylight—meet at a grade crossing on Bill and Pat Wasik's layout. Again, note the myriad of small details that bring this scene to life, including the motorcycle cop lurking behind the billboard, awaiting an errant motorist who may have been momentarily distracted by the passing of those gorgeous diesels. One of Bill's goals was to make the layout more scale-like in terms of the scenery, details, and operations—the concept known as "Hi-Rail" model railroading—and Pat, who built structures and detailed the many small scenic vignettes, ably assisted in accomplishing that goal.

Photo by Fred M. Dole, Editor, O Gauge Railroading magazine

Photo by Fred M. Dole, Editor, O Gauge Railroading magazine

Jeff James' Lionel Layout

Jeff James can operate six trains simultaneously on his 14 feet by 19 feet U-shaped layout, which also features an independent trolley line. Most of Jeff's layout is fitted with Lionel O gauge track, but two elevated sections, sitting atop 88 handmade wooden pillars, are done in O27 gauge track with O42 and O54 curves. Since there's always room for something a bit whimsical on any Lionel layout, you'll note that in this scene Daffy Duck and Bugs Bunny are engaged in track maintenance chores on the upper-level line.

Photo by Fred M. Dole, Editor, O Gauge Railroading magazine

The Webster Family Layout

Two types of electric-outline locomotives—an EP-5 and a Rectifier, both in New Haven livery—work their loads in the foreground, while a Lackawanna Trainmaster diesel plies the rails on the elevated section of the layout constructed by Ken Webster and his father, Wes. This layout provides another excellent example of Hi-Rail model railroading at its best, with attractive scenery and finely detailed scenes complementing the trains and placing them in a credible context.

Photo by Fred M. Dole, Editor, O Gauge Railroading magazine

Carnegie Science Museum Miniature Railroad and Village

The beautiful O gauge layout at the Carnegie Science Museum in Pittsburgh, Pennsylvania, is a sight sure to delight every lover of Lionel trains. The huge 30 feet by 80 feet layout displays, in miniature, the essence of life in and around the Pittsburgh area in the late nineteenth and early twentieth centuries, when the steel-making industry reigned supreme in the region. Ample evidence of the layout's size and splendor is provided by this scene, which includes an enormous model of the Sharon Steel Mill. Built from the prototype mill's blueprint, the model covers a 12 feet by 18 feet area, and it took four years to construct. The Southern Railway locomotive seen in the foreground—a Lionel model—gives some idea of the mill's overall size.

The Children's Museum of Virginia Lionel Layout

There are many Lionel layouts across the nation that you can visit to watch the trains run, enjoy some superb modeling, and pick up a few inspirational ideas for your own layout. Among these facilities is the Lancaster Train & Toy Collection at the Children's Museum of Virginia, located in Portsmouth, Virginia. The O gauge layout at the museum is one of four layouts in several scales that form the centerpiece for an extensive collection of toy trains donated to the museum by the late A.J. "Junie" Lancaster and his wife, Millie. Originally built by the Lancasters for their Mike's Trainland retail store in Portsmouth, the layout was dismantled and moved to the Children's Museum where it has since been enjoyed by thousands of youngsters, their parents, and visiting train enthusiasts from all parts of the country. The Lancaster train collection is displayed in cases surrounding the layout exhibit area.

Bill Heron's Alamoosook Junction

Bill Heron wanted bridges and trestles on his dream layout, and bridges and trestles is what he got! Such imposing structures are a hallmark of Clarke Dunham's craftsmanship. Dunham, a custom layout designer and builder, first constructed Bill's 19 feet by 9 feet Alamoosook Junction in his workshop, and then disassembled it and shipped it to Maine, where Bill's dream became a reality. The imposing chasm seen here, which drops all the way to floor level, is a centerpiece on the Alamoosook Junction.

Chapter 12

Maintenance tips for Lionel trains

Photo courtesy of Lionel LLC

The locomotive servicing facilities on the Lionel Visitor Center layout include a "washing" unit to keep a Lionel railroad's diesels looking sharp. You'll want to keep your locomotives, rolling stock, and operating accessories in equally good condition, and all the requires is a bit of regular maintenance. Lionel trains are made to last a lifetime, and they will if they're given the proper care.

When you purchase a new Lionel set, locomotive, operating car, or accessory, you'll find an operator's sheet or booklet enclosed in the box that specifies routine maintenance procedures for that item. Be sure to read that information completely *before* operating your Lionel train. If you follow the simple maintenance instructions printed there, and continue to do so according to the recommended schedule, your train will perform properly for a good many years.

If you acquire an older Lionel item that no longer has its original packaging or operator's manual, it's a good idea to purchase one the several Lionel train maintenance and repair manuals that are offered by several publishers. In most cases, these books feature reprints of the original

instruction and service sheets issued by Lionel for items manufactured in a specific time frame, such as the 1945-1969 postwar period. You'll find these books listed in Appendix A (page 116).

Although this chapter deals with the maintenance of Lionel trains and accessories, it does not cover the level of servicing involved in repairing a specific product. If you're interested in repairing Lionel trains, there are a number of good service manuals published by independent sources. If you don't feel comfortable performing your own repairs, you can always take the item to your local Authorized Lionel Service Center.

• Maintenance tools and supplies

Every maintenance job requires the right tools and equipment if it's to be accomplished with a minimum of fuss and bother. Here's a list of basic items that you'll likely want to include in your Lionel train maintenance kit. You might even consider purchasing a small toolbox to keep these items together in one place, so they'll be close at-hand when you need them.

Basic tools and supplies:

➢ Lionel 6-62927 Lubrication/Maintenance Set (includes gear lube, oil applicator, track-cleaning fluid, track-cleaning eraser, and cleaning instructions).
➢ Pliers
➢ Needle nose pliers
➢ Diagonal-cutting pliers
➢ Set of flat-blade screwdrivers
➢ Set of Phillips screwdrivers
➢ Set of jeweler's screwdrivers
➢ Hobby knife
➢ Tweezers
➢ Supply of cotton swabs
➢ Scraps of clean cloth—cut-up old T-shirts work well for this purpose.
➢ Small paint brush with relatively stiff bristles
➢ Small bowl to hold screws/small parts removed from the item

Optional tools and supplies:

➢ Voltmeter, with three-foot test leads and alligator clips, for testing circuits.
➢ Small transformer, such as the one that may have come with your starter set. Equipped with test leads (see below) this transformer can be placed on your workbench for conveniently testing equipment there instead of on the layout.
➢ Foam- or cloth-lined U-shaped locomotive cradle, so you can invert your locomotives to work on them without causing damage to detail parts, or scratching the paint.
➢ Pencil-type soldering iron, with resin-core solder. (Never use acid-core solder for work on toy train electrical equipment.)
➢ Motor tool for light drilling, sanding, polishing, cutting, and the like.

• Locomotive and rolling stock maintenance tips and procedures

Because Lionel has manufactured so many different sizes and types of locomotives over the years, it's really not possible to include all of the models in an introductory book such as this. Still, there are some general maintenance and lubrication tips that pretty much apply to all Lionel locomotives and rolling stock items, regardless of when the item was originally made.

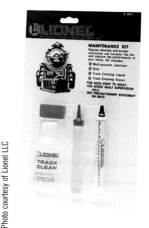

Photo courtesy of Lionel LLC

The Lionel Maintenance Kit includes everything you need to keep your trains in tiptop running condition. You'll also want to have a good supply of Lionel Smoke Fluid on hand if you're running steam locomotives on your pike (and certain diesels, as well).

First and foremost, it's worth repeating the importance of following the lubrication instructions that came packaged with your set, locomotive, car, or accessory. Although all Lionel locomotives are lubricated at the factory before being shipped, it's still a good idea to follow the recommended lubrication procedures before you run the item, since it may have been sitting in a warehouse, or on a dealer's shelf, for some time before it ever reached your hands. The same advice applies to locomotives that you have stored away for extended periods. In the case of older items that you purchase, a pre-operation check and lubrication is a must.

General locomotive maintenance tips:

➢ Remember that *oil* should be applied to surfaces that are subject to friction—parts that slide or roll against each other, for example—and *grease (lubricant)* is normally used on toothed gears and on heavy friction areas, such as truck pivots and pickup roller tension springs.

➢ Too much oil is as bad as, or worse than, too little. Excess oil or grease can work its way down the wheels and onto the track, or it may be splattered onto parts of the motor, such as brushes and commutators, where it will interfere with electrical contact. One drop will do fine in most every instance. Blot or wipe off any excess with a cotton swab or a clean scrap of cloth.

➢ When working with either steam or diesel locomotives, both of which require lubrication on the underside of the unit, it's a good idea to rest the locomotive, upside down, on a thick, soft towel to prevent damaging the paint or any detail parts. You could also buy or construct a simple U-shaped, foam- or cloth-lined cradle to safely and securely hold your locomotive. The wood structure, which can be glued, nailed, or screwed together, should be lined on the inside with a soft, heavy towel, or one or more pieces of soft, flexible foam—the "egg carton" type often used in packing electronic equipment is ideal. This cradle will permit you to work with both hands free, and you won't have to worry about the locomotive toppling over. The soft cushioning will protect fragile parts such as horns, bells, handrails, and the like, from being damaged.

➤ If you have a locomotive cradle, you can "test run" some locomotives (see below) after lubrication by placing it upside-down in the cradle and connecting it to a small transformer conveniently located at your workbench. Make two wire leads out of 3-foot lengths of wire. Strip the insulation off both ends, and attach small alligator clips to one end of each wire. Attach the bare ends of the wires to the two transformer posts normally used for supplying track power. Then attach one alligator clip to the clip that holds one of the locomotive's pickup rollers, and attach the other clip to an area of the locomotive's metal frame where it won't mar any painted finish. Turn up the power to a relatively low level, and allow the locomotive to run for a few minutes to work any lubricants into the mechanism, and to spin-off any excess. It's better to have excess oil or grease spin off at your workbench rather than on your layout, where it might end up on your trackwork and switches. A note of caution: You should not perform this cradle test run with articulated steam locomotives, which should always be operated right side up to prevent their valve gear from binding or jamming.

➤ If your locomotive runs fine, but the horn or whistle doesn't sound, and the locomotive won't change directions when you press the direction button on your transformer, the problem may not be with the locomotive. Check the connections from your transformer to the track. The wires must be properly connected to the track output posts for these controls to function. Try switching the connections at either the transformer or the track end, and see if that corrects the problem.

➤ If your locomotive tends to slow down at the far end of the track (the point furthest away from the point were the transformer is connected to the track), you may be experiencing voltage loss in the track, and not an internal problem with the locomotive. Installing additional power feeds to points furthest away from the transformer's location should help to solve this problem.

➤ As your roster of locomotives grows, consider setting up an index card file to keep track of the maintenance you have performed on each item. The file can be arranged by month, or in whatever way you prefer, to assure that every item receives the attention it deserves at predetermined intervals.

Steam locomotive maintenance tips:

➤ Routine operator maintenance of a Lionel steam locomotive does not normally require major disassembly of the locomotive itself. The parts that require oil or grease on a regular schedule are all easily reached from the bottom and sides of the locomotive.

➤ Apply *grease/lubricant* to toothed gears inside the drive wheels, and to front and rear truck pivot points, as well as to the frame-mounted springs that maintain pressure between the pickup rollers and the track.

➤ Apply *oil* to side rod and valve linkage pivot points (the areas where the various rods turn or slide against each other when the locomotive is in motion). Use just one drop of oil, and wipe off any excess. A single drop of oil should also be applied to the ends of axles (inside the wheels) and to wheel bearings on the main driving wheels.

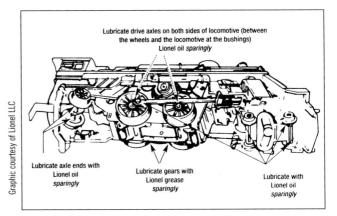

Lubrication points on a typical small Lionel steam locomotive. Be sure to consult the owner's manual that came with your locomotive for specific information relating to lubrication of that item.

➤ Steam locomotives with open-frame motors have parts that do require attention from time to time. Most often, a cleaning or change of the two carbon brushes is all that's required. Your operator's manual will show you where the brushes are located, and tell you how to clean or replace them.

➤ Steam locomotives equipped with can-type motors require no operator maintenance on the motor itself.

Diesel and electric-"outline" locomotive maintenance tips:

➤ Routine operator maintenance of a Lionel diesel or electric-outline locomotive does not normally require any major disassembly of the locomotive. The parts that need oil or grease on a regular schedule are all easily reached from the outside bottom of the locomotive.

➤ Apply a small dab of *grease/lubricant* to the toothed gears of the drive train. These gears are visible on the inside edge of one side of the drive wheels. There's no need to apply lubricant to each of the visible gears. Just a small dab placed on one of them will be distributed to the others if you turn the wheels by hand (not possible with all models) or if you place the locomotive on the track and then slowly run it back and forth in both directions a few times. After you've done this, take a swatch of clean cloth and wipe the locomotive wheels and the railheads free of any excess lubricant that may have dropped down.

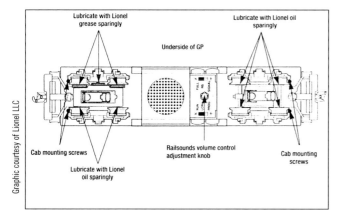

Lubrication points on a typical Lionel diesel locomotive. Be sure to consult the owner's manual that came with your locomotive for specific information relating to lubrication of that item.

➤ Use a toothpick or a needle oiler (which looks almost like a needle) to apply a single drop of *oil* to the ends of each axle.

➤ Open-frame motors may require brush cleaning or replacement from time to time. Your operator's manual will tell you how to perform these procedures.

➤ Diesel and electric-outline locomotives equipped with can motors require no operator maintenance to the motor itself.

• Rolling stock maintenance tips:

➤ Most rolling stock requires very little operator maintenance. A drop of oil applied at the axle ends (where the axle joins the sideframe of the truck) will take care of any squeaks that may develop.

➤ On lighted and/or operating cars with electrical pickup rollers, be sure to inspect the roller assemblies from time to time to make certain that the springs are providing sufficient tension to make good contact between the roller and the track. A dab of lubricant on the spring will often help, as will a tiny drop of oil applied to each end of the pickup roller. Be careful not to get any oil on the roller itself!

➤ Plastic rolling stock items that are grimy or dirty can be cleaned by removing the body from the frame, and then immersing the plastic body in a mild, lukewarm solution of a mild dishwashing detergent and warm water. If any scrubbing is necessary, use a soft-bristle toothbrush and scrub *very* gently and with great care. Avoid scrubbing any of the graphics, such as decals or heat-stamped logos and lettering, if at all possible. If they must be scrubbed, do this very carefully and very gently. A bit of Old English Lemon Cream Wax, sparingly applied to the car's plastic surface, will help to restore the original luster.

• *Track and switch maintenance tips:*

Lionel track that has been tightly fitted, properly installed, and secured in position on a layout will normally remain trouble-free for a very long time. About all that is required is a regular wipe-down with a clean cloth to remove any oil, grime, or other deposits. If done before or after each operating session, a piece of clean, dry cloth will do the job quite nicely. If your track-cleaning sessions are more infrequent, you may want to add a bit of track cleaning fluid to the rag; apply that to the track, and then wipe the rails dry with a clean piece of cloth.

Switches do require periodic inspection, and perhaps even a bit of maintenance, although this is usually a preventative type of maintenance rather than a corrective type. The following are a few steps that can be taken to improve the reliability of both your trackwork and your switches.

➤ Never use steel wool or sandpaper to clean or shine the rails. Caked-on grime can best be removed with a rubber track-cleaning eraser, of the type provided in the Lionel Lubrication/Maintenance Set, or with a Brite Boy pad. Steel wool and sandpaper will leave tiny deposits on the track that will eventually find their way into locomotive gears and motors, possibly ruining them. Also, these abrasive materials leave fine scratches in the metal rails, which simply invite more and faster buildup of unwanted deposits.

➤ Once your layout becomes large enough, you might consider soldering the track joints to increase electrical conductivity. Over time, track pins have a tendency to become slightly loose, resulting in a small voltage loss at each connecting point. Over the expanse of a large layout, this can quickly add up.

➤ The most common problem with switch operation relates to unobstructed movement of the points, which guide locomotive and rolling stock wheel flanges into the proper route. Switch points must move freely, and they must fully close against the stock rails. This requires periodic inspection to make sure that no pieces of ballast, scenery material, or other material has managed to work its way into any area traversed by the points. A small, new, and inexpensive paintbrush can be used to keep these areas clear of debris.

• *Operating accessory maintenance tips:*

➤ All Lionel operating accessories are packaged with a set

of instructions relating to their set-up, operation, and maintenance. Since different types of mechanisms and motors are used in various accessories, it's not possible to detail all of the maintenance procedures in this book. Individual instruction sheets should be retained and consulted for the information relevant to setting-up, operating, and maintaining specific accessories. It's a good idea to create a separate file folder for all of these sheets that can be located somewhere near your workbench so maintenance procedures are readily available. This is especially true in the case of items that are not being stored in their original boxes, and which are actually being used on the layout.

➤ Exercise care when disassembling older Lionel accessories. Some of these items are fitted with metal tabs, which must be straightened to remove the cover or housing. These tabs are easily broken off, especially if they have been bent back and forth several times over a period of time. If you feel that there is a risk of breaking off one of the tabs, just re-assemble the accessory with the tab in its straight position. The accessory will still stay together, as long as you don't lift it by that component, and it will be easy to get to if additional maintenance is needed.

➤ Bulbs are easily replaced in most accessories. Consider replacing a burnt-out bulb with a similar bulb that carries a higher voltage rating. For example, you might replace a 12-volt bulb with one designated as 14 or even 18 volts. These bulbs will last longer, burn cooler, and provide a more realistic and pleasing glow to the accessory.

➤ The solenoids and vibrator mechanisms used in some accessories are prone to occasionally sticking. A small bit of Teflon powder (available at most hobby shops) applied sparingly to the flexible "fingers" of the mechanism may help to enhance operations.

• Miscellaneous troubleshooting tips

➤ If you move the throttle lever on your transformer, and nothing happens—no lights and the trains don't run—the first thing to check is to make sure that the transformer is plugged in to the wall outlet or terminal strip. Then check to make sure that the outlet itself is receiving power (it may be one that is controlled by an on/off switch elsewhere in the room). If the transformer is equipped with a manually operated circuit breaker reset switch, also check to make sure that switch is properly set.

➤ If the transformer's circuit breaker trips when power is first applied, you likely have a short circuit somewhere on your layout. First, re-check the wires running from the transformer to the track. If all is well there, check for obvious causes for the short along the trackwork—such things as some metal object laying across the center rail

and an outside rail at some point, derailed wheels on a locomotive or car, and that sort of thing. If this isn't the cause of the problem, you may need to disconnect all other wires that you have running to the layout, and then reconnect them one at a time, checking to see that all is working well after each connection is made. This is another very good reason for starting small, and expanding your layout in phases!

➤ If your trains and accessories seem to operate properly some of the time, but the circuit breaker trips with some regularity, it's possible that you are at or near the limit of that transformer's capacity. Disconnect a couple of accessories, and see if that improves things. If so, consider using a small starter set type transformer to power some or all of the accessories on your layout; reserving the larger transformer for train operations.

➤ If the headlight on your locomotive is lit, but the locomotive doesn't change direction when the direction button on the transformer is pushed, the first thing to check is the position of the reversing unit switch. This switch allows the operator to lock-out the reversing mechanism of the locomotive so it will run in one direction only, or simply stand in neutral with its headlight glowing. Older Lionel locomotives were equipped with a reversing lever that protruded from the top, bottom, or one side of the locomotive. This lever connected to the Lionel "E-unit," which is the actual reversing mechanism for the motor. More recent Lionel locomotives may have a sliding switch beneath the locomotive that controls a more contemporary electronic reversing mechanism. In any event, apply a small amount of power to the track and, holding the locomotive in place with one hand, move the reversing unit switch through its various positions to see if this makes a difference.

• The Lionel LLC Customer Service Center in Michigan and the Authorized Lionel Service Center Network

The Lionel network of Authorized Service Centers is unique in the model railroading industry. These Service Stations, all of which are staffed by one or more skilled repair persons, are located in virtually every major city and region of the nation. They are equipped with the right tools and equipment to handle any type of repair to Lionel trains and accessories, ranging from simple lubrication to complex repairs of motors and electrical components.

You can call **1-800-4LIONEL** to obtain the name and address of an Authorized Service Center nearest you. Or, you can visit the Lionel web site at *www.lionel.com*. An item that is still under warranty can also be sent to the main Lionel Service Center in Michigan. The warranty information included with your set or item describes the procedure to be followed in returning an item directly to Lionel.

• Protecting and preserving your Lionel trains

It's worth devoting some attention to preserving the external appearance of your Lionel trains and accessories. If you collect these items—and most folks do begin building a "collection" once they start to acquire additional locomotives, cars, and accessories—appearance is as important as operation. Besides, Lionel trains and accessories are beautifully decorated, nicely detailed, and colorful objects, so you'll want to maintain them in as close to their pristine original condition as possible, consistent with the most important part of Lionel railroading: Having fun, and running them! Here are a few tips to help you care for the overall appearance of your trains:

➤ Between operating sessions on your layout, consider using a sheet of inexpensive clear plastic drop cloth—the type used by painters—to cover either the entire layout or at least select areas of it where you normally park your locomotives and rolling stock. This step will save a lot of time dusting items in the future, and it even helps to keep dust off the track and accessories.

➤ If you remove a locomotive or car from your layout to replace it in its original box, or in some other packaging, it's a good idea to remove excess oil and grease from the wheels before storing the item. Here's a tip that works well for diesel and electric-outline locomotives, in particular: Saturate a scrap of clean cloth with track cleaning fluid, and place it across the track under one set of the locomotive's powered wheels. Then, holding the locomotive in place with one hand, apply just enough power to make the wheels spin slowly. This will clean the oily residue off the wheels. You may need to use a couple of thumbtacks or small nails to hold the cloth in place, since it will tend to bunch up under the rotating wheels. Repeat the process for the other powered truck. For rolling stock, you can use the same technique by just rolling the car back and forth over the cloth; first one end, and then the other.

➤ If you're preparing your trains for storage, and no longer have the original packaging, do *not* wrap them in news-papers. The ink from newspapers may leave marks on the finish of the locomotive or car. Instead, wrap the item in wrapping tissue, of the type used for gift packaging, and then roll the item in a long sheet of plastic bubble wrap to provide a protective outer cushion. Be sure to use wrapping tissue as a first layer, however, because some bubble wrap may, over time, leave marks on the item's finish.

➤ Always store your trains in a cool and dry area of your home—a walk-in closet is probably ideal, although even the area under your bed, or some other unused storage area, will suffice. Do *not* store train items in a non-insulated attic or a damp basement. If possible, place some silica gel packets (of the type provided with many trains, cameras, and electronic components) in the outer storage box, and then seal and label the box so you'll know what's in it the next time you go looking for things.

➤ You can use a small, new, soft-bristle paintbrush to dust-off your locomotives, cars, and accessories without risking damage to any of the detail parts. A 1-inch wide or so brush should do just fine. Keep this brush separate from any others that you might use to sweep ballast particles out of switches, or the like, because that switch-cleaning brush is likely to pick up some oil or grease, and you sure don't want to deposit that on the finish of your locomotives and cars.

➤ Never use any harsh chemical cleaners or polishes on the painted and decorated surfaces of your train items. A very gentle cleaning with a soft cloth dipped in a mild solution of dishwashing liquid and warm water should be enough to remove any fingerprints or smudges left by routine handling over time.

Just keep in mind that today's Lionel trains, like their predecessors, have been built to last for many years. Properly maintained and cared for, they certainly have the potential to become treasured heirlooms that will bring smiles to the faces of your family members, and your descendants, for many generations to come.

Appendix A

References for Lionel operators and collectors

Magazines and periodicals:

Classic Toy Trains Magazine
Kalmbach Publishing Co.
21027 Crossroads Circle
P.O. Box 1612
Waukesha, WI 53187-1612
Phone: 800-446-5489
www.classtrain.com

The Lion Roars
Lionel Collectors Club of America (LCCA)
P.O. Box 479
La Salle, IL 61301-0479
e-mail: lcca@cpointcc.com
www.lionelcollectors.org

The Switcher
Lionel Operating Train Society (LOTS)
6364 West Fork Road
Cincinnati, OH 45247-5704
Phone: 513-598-8240
e-mail: businessoffice@lots-trains.com
www.lots-trains.org

O Gauge Railroading Magazine
P.O. Box 239
Nazareth, PA 18064-0239
Phone: 610-759-0406
Fax: 610-759-0223
e-mail: OGaugeRwy@aol.com
http://members.aol.com/OGaugeRwy/ogr.html
www.ogaugerr.com

The HiRailers Buzz
Journal of HiRailers Unlimited and Independent HiRailers
10433 Shadyside Lane
Cincinnati, OH 45249-3649
Phone: 513-683-5740
Fax: 513-683-6023
e-mail: Fequalls@aol.com
www.hirailers.com

TCA Quarterly
Train Collector's Association (TCA)
300 Paradise Lane
Ronks, PA 17572-9537
Phone: 717-687-8623
Fax: 717-687-0742
www.traincollectors.org

TTOS Bulletin
Toy Train Operating Society (TTOS)
25 W. Walnut St., Suite 308
Pasadena, CA 91103
Phone: 626-578-0673
Fax: 626-578-0750
e-mail: ttos@ttos.org
www.ttos.org

Books:
Layout Planning, Construction, and Operations:

Beginner's Guide to Toy Train Collecting and Operating
Kalmbach Publishing Co.
21027 Crossroads Circle
P.O. Box 1612
Waukesha, WI 53187-1612
Catalog/orders: 800-533-6644
http://db.kalmbach.com/catalog/catalog.html

Classic Lionel Display Layouts You Can Build
Author: Roger Carp
Kalmbach Publishing Co.
21027 Crossroads Circle
P.O. Box 1612
Waukesha, WI 53187-1612
Catalog/orders: 800-533-6644
http://db.kalmbach.com/catalog/catalog.html

Easy Lionel Layouts You Can Build
Author: Peter H. Riddle
Kalmbach Publishing Co.
21027 Crossroads Circle
P.O. Box 1612
Waukesha, WI 53187-1612
Catalog/orders: 800-533-6644
http://db.kalmbach.com/catalog/catalog.html

Fun with Toy Trains
Author: Robert Schleicher
Krause Publications
700 E. State St.
Iola, WI 54990-0001
Catalog/orders: 800-258-0929
www.krause.com/Books

How to Build Model Railroad Benchwork, 2nd edition
Author: Linn H. Wescott
Kalmbach Publishing Co.
21027 Crossroads Circle
P.O. Box 1612
Waukesha, WI 53187-1612
Catalog/orders: 800-533-6644
http://db.kalmbach.com/catalog/catalog.html

How to Build Your First Lionel Layout
Author: Stanley W. Trzoniec
Kalmbach Publishing Co.
21027 Crossroads Circle
P.O. Box 1612
Waukesha, WI 53187-1612
Catalog/orders: 800-533-6644
http://db.kalmbach.com/catalog/catalog.html

Layout Plans for Toy Trains
Kalmbach Publishing Co.
21027 Crossroads Circle
P.O. Box 1612
Waukesha, WI 53187-1612
Catalog/orders: 800-533-6644
http://db.kalmbach.com/catalog/catalog.html

Realistic Railroading with Toy Trains
Authors: Joe Lesser and Pete Youngblood
Kalmbach Publishing Co.
21027 Crossroads Circle
P.O. Box 1612
Waukesha, WI 53187-1612
Catalog/orders: 800-533-6644
http://db.kalmbach.com/catalog/catalog.html

Realistic Track Plans for O Gauge Trains
Author: Martin McGuirk
Kalmbach Publishing Co.
21027 Crossroads Circle
P.O. Box 1612
Waukesha, WI 53187-1612
Catalog/orders: 800-533-6644
http://db.kalmbach.com/catalog/catalog.html

The O Gauge Railroading Primer, 3rd Edition
Myron Biggar Group
P.O. Box 239
Nazareth, PA 18064-0239
Phone: 610-759-0406
Fax: 610-759-0223
E-mail: customerservice@ogaugerr.com
www.ogaugerr.com

Toy Train Collecting and Operating: An Introduction to the Hobby
Author: John Grams
Kalmbach Publishing Co.
21027 Crossroads Circle
P.O. Box 1612
Waukesha, WI 53187-1612
Catalog/orders: 800-533-6644
http://db.kalmbach.com/catalog/catalog.html

Track Planning for Realistic Operation, 3rd Edition
Kalmbach Publishing Co.
21027 Crossroads Circle
P.O. Box 1612
Waukesha, WI 53187-1612
Catalog/orders: 800-533-6644
http://db.kalmbach.com/catalog/catalog.html

Track Plans for Toy Trains
Kalmbach Publishing Co.
21027 Crossroads Circle
P.O. Box 1612
Waukesha, WI 53187-1612
Catalog/orders: 800-533-6644
http://db.kalmbach.com/catalog/catalog.html

Your First O Gauge Layout
Author: Mike Ashey
Kalmbach Publishing Co.
21027 Crossroads Circle
P.O. Box 1612
Waukesha, WI 53187-1612
Catalog/orders: 800-533-6644
http://db.kalmbach.com/catalog/catalog.html

Scenery and Structures:

How to Build Realistic Model Railroad Scenery, 2nd Edition
Author: Dave Frary
Kalmbach Publishing Co.
21027 Crossroads Circle
P.O. Box 1612
Waukesha, WI 53187-1612
Catalog/orders: 800-533-6644
http://db.kalmbach.com/catalog/catalog.html

Realistic Plastic Structures for Toy Train Layouts
Author: Art Curren
Kalmbach Publishing Co.
21027 Crossroads Circle
P.O. Box 1612
Waukesha, WI 53187-1612
Catalog/orders: 800-533-6644
http://db.kalmbach.com/catalog/catalog.html

Realistic Scenery for Toy Train Layouts
Kalmbach Publishing Co.
21027 Crossroads Circle
P.O. Box 1612
Waukesha, WI 53187-1612
Catalog/orders: 800-533-6644
http://db.kalmbach.com/catalog/catalog.html

The Scenery Manual
Woodland Scenics
P.O. Box 98
Linn Creek, MO 65052
phone: 573-346-5555
E-mail (information): webmaster@woodland-scenics.com
www.woodlandscenics.com

Wiring, Electrical, and Electronics:

Animations for Your Layout
Author: Roy Everett
Myron Biggar Group
P.O. Box 239
Nazareth, PA 18064-0239
Phone: 610-759-0406
Fax: 610-759-0223
E-mail: OGaugeRwy@aol.com
www.ogaugerr.com

Easy Electronics Projects for Toy Trains
Author: David E. Greenwald
Kalmbach Publishing Co.
21027 Crossroads Circle
P.O. Box 1612
Waukesha, WI 53187-1612
Catalog/orders: 800-533-6644
http://db.kalmbach.com/catalog/catalog.html

Greenberg's Wiring Your Lionel Layout (Vols. 1-3)
Author: Peter Riddle
Kalmbach Publishing Co.
21027 Crossroads Circle
P.O. Box 1612
Waukesha, WI 53187-1612
Catalog/orders: 800-533-6644
http://db.kalmbach.com/catalog/catalog.html

Repair & Maintenance:

Beginner's Guide to Repairing Lionel Trains
Author: Ray L. Plummer
Kalmbach Publishing Co.
21027 Crossroads Circle
P.O. Box 1612
Waukesha, WI 53187-1612
Catalog/orders: 800-533-6644
http://db.kalmbach.com/catalog/catalog.html

Dr. Tinker Repairs Toy Trains (Vols. 1 and 2)
Myron Biggar Group
P.O. Box 239
Nazareth, PA 18064-0239
Phone: 610-759-0406
Fax: 610-759-0223
E-mail: OGaugeRwy@aol.com
www.ogaugerr.com

Greenberg's Guide to Lionel Prewar Parts and Instruction Sheets
Author: Robert Osterhoff, ed.
Kalmbach Publishing Co.
21027 Crossroads Circle
P.O. Box 1612
Waukesha, WI 53187-1612
Catalog/orders: 800-533-6644
http://db.kalmbach.com/catalog/catalog.html

Greenberg's Repair and Operating Manual: Prewar Lionel Trains
Author: John G. Hubbard
Kalmbach Publishing Co.
21027 Crossroads Circle
P.O. Box 1612
Waukesha, WI 53187-1612
Catalog/orders: 800-533-6644
http://db.kalmbach.com/catalog/catalog.html

Greenberg's Repair and Operating Manual for Lionel Trains, 1945-1969 (7th Edition)
Kalmbach Publishing Co.
21027 Crossroads Circle
P.O. Box 1612
Waukesha, WI 53187-1612
Catalog/orders: 800-533-6644
http://db.kalmbach.com/catalog/catalog.html

Tips & Tricks for Toy Train Operators (2nd Edition)
Author: Peter Riddle
Kalmbach Publishing Co.
21027 Crossroads Circle
P.O. Box 1612
Waukesha, WI 53187-1612
Catalog/orders: 800-533-6644
http://db.kalmbach.com/catalog/catalog.html

Toy Train Repair Made Easy
Author: Ray L. Plummer
Kalmbach Publishing Co.
21027 Crossroads Circle
P.O. Box 1612
Waukesha, WI 53187-1612
Catalog/orders: 800-533-6644
http://db.kalmbach.com/catalog/catalog.html

Prewar Lionel References and Guides (1900-1942):

America's Standard Gauge Electric Trains
Author: Peter Riddle
Antique Trader Books/Krause Publications
700 E. State St.
Iola, WI 54990-0001
Catalog/orders: 800-258-0929
www.krause.com/Books

Greenberg's Guide to Lionel Trains, 1901-1942: O Gauge
Author: Bruce C. Greenberg
Kalmbach Publishing Co.
21027 Crossroads Circle
P.O. Box 1612
Waukesha, WI 53187-1612
Catalog/orders: 800-533-6644
http://db.kalmbach.com/catalog/catalog.html

Greenberg's Guide to Lionel Trains, 1901-1942, Vol. III: Accessories
Author: Peter Riddle
Kalmbach Publishing Co.
21027 Crossroads Circle
P.O. Box 1612
Waukesha, WI 53187-1612
Catalog/orders: 800-533-6644
http://db.kalmbach.com/catalog/catalog.html

Greenberg's Guide to Lionel Trains, 1901-1942, Vol. IV: Prewar Sets
Author: Dave McEntarfer
Greenberg/Kalmbach Books
Kalmbach Publishing Co.
21027 Crossroads Circle
P.O. Box 1612
Waukesha, WI 53187-1612
Catalog/orders: 800-533-6644
http://db.kalmbach.com/catalog/catalog.html

Lionel Standard Gauge Era
Carstens Publications
108 Phil Harden Rd., Fredon Township
P.O. Box 700
Newton, NJ 07860-0700
Information/orders: 800-474-6995
www.rrmodelcraftsman.com

Lionel Trains: Standard of the World, 1900-1943 (2nd Edition)
Train Collectors Association
P.O. Box 248
Strasburg, PA 17579
Information/orders: 717-687-8623
www.traincollectors.org

Trains From Grandfather's Attic
Author: Peter Riddle
Greenberg/Kalmbach Books
Kalmbach Publishing Co.
21027 Crossroads Circle
P.O. Box 1612
Waukesha, WI 53187-1612
Catalog/orders: 800-533-6644
http://db.kalmbach.com/catalog/catalog.html

Postwar Lionel References and Guides (1945-1969):

Greenberg's Guide to Lionel Trains, 1945-1969, Vol. 1: Motive Power and Rolling Stock (Centennial Edition)
Author: Paul V. Ambrose
Kalmbach Publishing Co.
21027 Crossroads Circle
P.O. Box 1612
Waukesha, WI 53187-1612
Catalog/orders: 800-533-6644
http://db.kalmbach.com/catalog/catalog.html

Greenberg's Guide to Lionel Trains, 1945-1969, Vol. III: Cataloged Sets (2nd Edition)
Author: Paul V. Ambrose
Kalmbach Publishing Co.
21027 Crossroads Circle
P.O. Box 1612
Waukesha, WI 53187-1612
Catalog/orders: 800-533-6644
http://db.kalmbach.com/catalog/catalog.html

Greenberg's Guide to Lionel Trains, 1945-1969, Vol. IV: Uncatalogued Sets
Authors: Paul V. Ambrose and Joseph P. Algozzini
Kalmbach Publishing Co.
21027 Crossroads Circle
P.O. Box 1612
Waukesha, WI 53187-1612
Catalog/orders: 800-533-6644
http://db.kalmbach.com/catalog/catalog.html

Greenberg's Guide to Lionel Trains, 1945-1969, Vol. V: Rare and Unusual
Author: Paul V. Ambrose
Kalmbach Publishing Co.
21027 Crossroads Circle
P.O. Box 1612
Waukesha, WI 53187-1612
Catalog/orders: 800-533-6644
http://db.kalmbach.com/catalog/catalog.html

Greenberg's Guide to Lionel Trains, 1945-1969, Vol. VI: Accessories
Author: Alan Stewart
Kalmbach Publishing Co.
21027 Crossroads Circle
P.O. Box 1612
Waukesha, WI 53187-1612
Catalog/orders: 800-533-6644
http://db.kalmbach.com/catalog/catalog.html

Greenberg's Guide to Lionel Trains, 1945-1969, Vol. VII: Selected Variations
Authors: Paul V. Ambrose and Harold J. Lovelock
Kalmbach Publishing Co.
21027 Crossroads Circle
P.O. Box 1612
Waukesha, WI 53187-1612
Catalog/orders: 800-533-6644
http://db.kalmbach.com/catalog/catalog.html

Lionel's Postwar F3's
Author: Joe Algozzini
Kalmbach Publishing Co.
21027 Crossroads Circle
P.O. Box 1612
Waukesha, WI 53187-1612
Catalog/orders: 800-533-6644
http://db.kalmbach.com/catalog/catalog.html

Lionel's Postwar Space and Military Trains
Author: Joe Algozzini
Kalmbach Publishing Co.
21027 Crossroads Circle
P.O. Box 1612
Waukesha, WI 53187-1612
Catalog/orders: 800-533-6644
http://db.kalmbach.com/catalog/catalog.html

Modern Era Lionel References and Guides (1970-present):

Greenberg's Guide to Lionel Trains, 1970-1991, Vol. II: Promotions, Sets, Boxes, etc.
Authors: Roland E. LaVoie, Michael A. Solly, and Louis Bohn
Kalmbach Publishing Co.
21027 Crossroads Circle
P.O. Box 1612
Waukesha, WI 53187-1612
Catalog/orders: 800-533-6644
http://db.kalmbach.com/catalog/catalog.html

Greenberg's Guide to Lionel Trains, 1970-1997, Vol. III: Accessories
Author: Roland E. LaVoie
Kalmbach Publishing Co.
21027 Crossroads Circle
P.O. Box 1612
Waukesha, WI 53187-1612
Catalog/orders: 800-533-6644
http://db.kalmbach.com/catalog/catalog.html

Greenberg's Pocket Price Guide to Lionel Trains, 1900-2000
Kalmbach Publishing Co.
21027 Crossroads Circle
P.O. Box 1612
Waukesha, WI 53187-1612
Catalog/orders: 800-533-6644
http://db.kalmbach.com/catalog/catalog.html

Lionel 1900-2000 Illustrated Price & Rarity Guide, Vol. 2: 1970-2000
TM Books & Video
Box 279
New Buffalo, MI 49117
Phone: 800-892-2822
Fax: 219-879-7909
E-mail: tmbooks@aol.com
www.tmbooks-video.com

Multiple-Era References and Guides:

Collecting Toy Trains—Identification & Value Guide, 4th Edition
Krause Publications
700 E. State St.
Iola, WI 54990-0001
Catalog/orders: 800-258-0929
www.krause.com/Books

Greenberg's Guide to Lionel Paper and Collectibles
Author: Bob Osterhoff
Kalmbach Publishing Co.
21027 Crossroads Circle
P.O. Box 1612
Waukesha, WI 53187-1612
Catalog/orders: 800-533-6644
http://db.kalmbach.com/catalog/catalog.html

Greenberg's Roadname Guide to O Gauge Trains
Kalmbach Publishing Co.
21027 Crossroads Circle
P.O. Box 1612
Waukesha, WI 53187-1612
Catalog/orders: 800-533-6644
http://db.kalmbach.com/catalog/catalog.html

Lionel 1900-2000 Illustrated Price & Rarity Guide, Vol. 1: 1901-1969
TM Books & Video
Box 279
New Buffalo, MI 49117
Phone: 800-892-2822
Fax: 219-879-7909
E-mail: tmbooks@aol.com
www.tmbooks-video.com

Lionel Trains History:

A Century of Lionel Timeless Toy Trains
Author: Dan Ponzol
Friedman/Fairfax Publishers
15 West 26th Street
New York, NY 10010
Phone: 212-685-6610
Fax: 212-685-1307
www.metrobooks.com

**All Aboard! The Story of Joshua Lionel
Cowen and His Lionel Train Company
(2nd Edition)**
Author: Ron Hollander
Workman Publishing
708 Broadway
New York, NY 10003-9555
www.workman.com

It Comes from Within: The Frank Pettit Story
Author: Chris Ritchie
Myron Biggar Group
P.O. Box 239
Nazareth, PA 18064-0239
Phone: 610-759-0406
Fax: 610-759-0223
E-mail: OGaugeRwy@aol.com
www.ogaugerr.com

**Lionel: A Collector's Guide and History (six
volumes)**
TM Books & Video
Box 279
New Buffalo, MI 49117
Phone: 800-892-2822
Fax: 219-879-7909
E-mail: tmbooks@aol.com
www.tmbooks-video.com

Lionel: America's Favorite Toy Trains
Authors: Gerry and Janet Souter
MBI Publishing Company
729 Prospect Avenue
Osceola, WI 54020
www.motorbooks.com

**Lionel's Model Builder: The Magazine that
Shaped the Toy Train Hobby**
Author: Terry Thompson and Roger Carp
Kalmbach Publishing Co.
21027 Crossroads Circle
P.O. Box 1612
Waukesha, WI 53187-1612
Catalog/orders: 800-533-6644
http://db.kalmbach.com/catalog/catalog.html

The World's Greatest Toy Train Maker
Author: Roger Carp
Kalmbach Publishing Co.
21027 Crossroads Circle
P.O. Box 1612
Waukesha, WI 53187-1612
Catalog/orders: 800-533-6644
http://db.kalmbach.com/catalog/catalog.html

Toy Trains of Yesteryear
Carstens Publications
108 Phil Harden Rd., Fredon Township
P.O. Box 700
Newton, NJ 07860-0700
Information/orders: 800-474-6995
www.rrmodelcraftsman.com

150 Years of Train Models
Carstens Publications
108 Phil Harden Rd., Fredon Township
P.O. Box 700
Newton, NJ 07860-0700
Information/orders: 800-474-6995
www.rrmodelcraftsman.co

Videos:

The following videos are available from:
TM Books & Video
Box 279
New Buffalo, MI 49117
Phone: 800-892-2822
Fax: 219-879-7909
E-mail: tmbooks@aol.com
www.tmbooks-video.com

A Century of Lionel Trains

Christmas Videos

Great Lionel Layouts (Vols. 1 and 2)

Great Toy Train Layouts of America

How to Build a Toy Train Layout

I Love Lionel

I Love Toy Trains (Vols. 1-9)

I Love Christmas

**Lionel Legends 1: The Making of the Lionel
Scale Hudson**

Lionel Legends 2: The Hudson

Lionel: The Movie (Vols. 1-3)

The History of Lionel Trains

The Magic of Lionel Trains (Vols. 1-4)

**The Making of the New Lionel Showroom
Layout**

**The Re-Making of the 1949 Lionel Showroom
Layout**

Toy Train Accessories (Parts 1 and 2)

Toy Train Revue (Vols. 1-12)

The following videos are available from:
Myron Biggar Group
P.O. Box 239
Nazareth, PA 18064-0239
Phone: 610-759-0406
Fax: 610-759-0223
E-mail: OGaugeRwy@aol.com
www.ogaugerr.com

Great Train Layouts You Can Visit

Jim Barrett in the Backshop (Vols. 1-6)

O Gauge Railroading: The Video (Vols. 1-16)

**OGR Video Guide to the Lionel TrainMaster
Command System (Vols. 1 and 2)**

Appendix B
Lionel Trains On-line

The Internet, and its associated World Wide Web (www or simply "Web"), offers a treasure trove of valuable information for the Lionel enthusiast. You'll find just about everything you could possibly imagine on the Internet, ranging from current Lionel and after-market supplier catalogs to Lionel dealer sites, club sites, and sites established by individual hobbyists.

The listings presented here provide known addresses for key Web sites of particular interest to the Lionel hobbyist. Many of these sites also provide direct "links" to related sites containing information that will enhance your enjoyment of Lionel trains. All of these sites, regardless of where they may be located in the world, are as close as a simple click of your computer's mouse button.

Keep in mind that Web site addresses do change from time to time as businesses expand or as groups and individuals move from one location to another. In most cases, keying in the old address will bring up a screen that will automatically link you to the new site, or tell you how to locate the new address.

www.lionel.com
Lionel LLC Web site

www.classtrain.com
Classic Toy Trains magazine Web site; part of trains.com web site

www.coilcouplers.com
("Clyde Coil's" site for comprehensive information about products and new developments in Lionel electronic control and sound systems for O gauge trains)

www.ehobbies.com
(Model railroad discussion groups and general interest train topics)

www.hirailers.com
(HiRailers Unlimited and Independent HiRailers Group site)

www.hobbyretailer.com
(On-line hobby dealer locator)

www.lionelcollectors.org
Lionel Collectors Club of America (LCCA) Web site

www.lots-trains.org
Lionel Operating Train Society (LOTS) Web site

www.modelshopper.com
(On-line hobby dealer and product locator)

www.napanet.net/~jlbaker
The O Gauge Toy Train Page
(On-line links to a large number of O gauge Web sites.)

www.delphi.com/railroad
Delphi Railroading Forum
(Site for general railroad/railfan/model railroad topics.)

www.ogaugerr.com
O Gauge Railroading magazine web site
(Includes the leading discussion forum for O gauge enthusiasts)

www.railserve.com
RailServe Home Page
(On-line directory to rail-related content on the Internet.)

www.tcastation.org
Train Collectors Association (TCA) Web site

www.tmbooks-video.com
TM Books & Videos Web site
Toy Train Revue On-Line
(News and information from the world of toy trains.)

www.trainclub.com
(Model railroad forums and information relating to all scales.)

www.traincom.com
(Provides supporting software for the Lionel TrainMaster Command Control system.)

www.trains.com
Kalmbach Publishing Company's model and prototype railroading Web site

www.trainfinder.com
(On-line directory to toy and model train Web sites.)

www.ttos.org
Toy Train Operating Society (TTOS) Web site

http://thortrains.hypermart.net
All-Gauge Model Railroading Home Page (emphasis on O/O27 trains, with a variety of topics).

http://members.tripod.com/ToyTrains1/
(Web site of Toy Trains 1)

Appendix C
Collector and operator clubs and associations

Some model railroaders prefer to pursue their hobby alone – a kind of "escape" from the real world, if you will. Others enjoy the bonding that occurs when the hobby is shared with family members. Still others enjoy the fellowship and creative learning experience that group membership often provides. And, of course, some folks simply don't have enough space in their home to enjoy the type of railroading activity that interests them most. If you fall into either or both of these latter two categories, in particular, membership in a local or national club may be just the thing for you.

Following is a list of national associations of special interest to the Lionel enthusiast. Nearly all of these organizations welcome new members with open arms and with modest membership fees, so don't hesitate to contact them if the social aspects of club membership and sharing the hobby with others appeals to you. Web site and/or e-mail addresses are also listed so you can check on-line to learn more about each orgainization before applying for membership.

You can also learn about any Lionel or three-rail operating clubs in your local area by contacting an area hobby shop. Most hobby retailers have flyers available that will tell you what the club is all about, when they meet, the dates of any operating sessions open to the general public, and the name of the individual to contact regarding membership. If there are no clubs in your area, other folks you meet during your visits to your Lionel Authorized Dealer may be interested in joining with you to form one.

HiRailers Unlimited
10433 Shadyside Lane
Cincinnati, OH 45249-3649
513-683-5740
fax: 513-683-6023
www.hirailers.com

Lionel Collectors Club of America (LCCA)
P.O. Box 479
LaSalle, IL 61301
www.lionelcollectors.org

Lionel Railroaders Club (LRRC)
(sponsored by Lionel LLC)
50625 Richard W. Blvd.
Chesterfield, MI 48051-2493
810-940-4100
e-mail: talktous@lionel.com
www.lionel.com

Lionel Operating Train Society (LOTS)
6364 West Fork Road
Cincinnati, OH 45247-5704
www.lots-trains.org

National Model Railroad Association (NMRA)
4121 Cromwell Rd.
Chattanooga, TN 37421
423-892-2846
fax: 423-899-4869
www.nmra.org

Toy Train Operating Society (TTOS)
25 W. Walnut St., Suite 308
Pasadena, CA 91103
626-578-0673
www.ttos.org

Train Collectors Association (TCA)
National Business Office
P.O. Box 248
Dept. 10
Strasburg, PA 17579
www.traincollectors.org

Appendix D
Suppliers of equipment and accessories for Lionel railroaders

The firms listed here supply a wide variety of products designed to enhance your Lionel layout and collection. Complete mailing, e-mail, and Web site addresses are provided, where known. The phone number listed is the firm's information number. Be advised that phone numbers (including area codes), e-mail addresses, and Web site addresses often change, but the information presented here was current as of this book's publication date. If a web site address is listed, and assuming you have access to a computer that can connect to the Internet, your best bet is to check that site first, since many firms publish their most current complete catalog, along with pricing and contact information, on these sites.

Lionel LLC
50625 Richard W. Blvd.
Chesterfield, MI 48051
Phone: 810-949-4100
Dealer/service center locator: 1-800-4LIONEL
E-mail: talktous@lionel.com
www.lionel.com

Abracadata
P.O. Box 2440
Eugene, OR 97402-9808
Phone: 1-800-451-4871
E-mail: abracadata@POBoxes.com
www.abracadata.com
(Software for layout track planning and design)

Arduk Engineering
P.O. Box 734
Pekin, IL 61555
Phone: 309-346-9607
E-mail: ardukinc@aol.com
(O gauge test benches)

Arttista Accessories
105 Woodring Lane
Newark, DE 19702
Phone: 302-455-0195
Fax: 302-455-0197
(O scale figures, animals, etc.)

Aztec Mfg. Company
2701 Conestoga Dr., #113
Carson City, NV 89706
Phone: 775-883-3327
Fax: 775-883-3357
E-mail: aztecmfg@usa.net
www.aztectrains.com
(Track cleaning car)

BackDrop Warehouse
P.O. Box 27877
Salt Lake City, UT 84127-0877
888-542-5277
Fax: 801-962-4238
E-mail: backdrop@backdropwarehouse.com
www.backdropwarehouse.com
(Scenic murals and backdrops)

Bowser Manufacturing Co., Inc.
1302 Jordan Ave.
P.O. Box 322
Montoursville, PA 17754
Phone: 570-368-2379
Fax: 570-368-5046
E-mail: bowser@mail.csrlink.net
www.bowser-trains.com
(Turntables, trolleys, and other accessories for O gauge)

Brennan's Model Railroading
1600 Arlington Ave.
Independence, MO 64052
Phone: 816-252-4605
http://members.primary.net/~brensan
(O scale track ballast)

Burns Manufacturing
P.O. Box 5301
Rocky Point, NY 11778
Phone: 516-821-1644
(Electronic train detectors, flashers, station stoppers, controllers)

Centerline Products, Inc.
18409 Harmony Road
Marengo, IL 60152
www.centerline-products.com
(Track-cleaning cars)

Charles C. Wood & Co.
P.O. Box 179
Hartford, OH 44424
Phone: 330-772-5177
E-mail: chas 327@aol.com
(Train enamel for collectible toy trains)

Classic Case Company
P.O. Box 395
Rolling Prairie, IN 46371
Phone: 800-897-3374
E-mail: classic@ccase.com
www.ccase.com
(Display cases for O gauge trains)

CTT/Collectible Trains & Toys
109 Medallion Center
Dallas, TX 75214
Phone: 214-373-9469
www.trainsandtoys.com
(Track planning templates for O gauge)

Dallee Electronics, Inc.
246 W. Main St.
Leola, PA 17540
Phone: 717-661-7041
www.dallee.com
(Digitized sound and detection systems, throttles, flashers, etc.)

Die-Cast Direct, Inc.
1009 Twilight Trail, Dept. CT9911
Frankfort, KY 40601-8432
Phone: 502-227-8697
www.diecastdirect.com
(Die-cast vehicles for O gauge layouts)

Douglas Brooks Creative Models
307 MacKay Ave.
Ventura, CA 93004
(Model palm trees)

GarGraves Trackage Corporation
8967 Ridge Rd.
North Rose, NY 14516-9793
Phone: 315-483-6577
Fax: 315-483-2425
www.GarGraves.com
(Track and switches)

Glenn Snyder Display Systems
260 Oak Street
Buffalo, NY 14203
Phone: 716-852-4676/716-648-5817
Fax: 716-852-4677
E-Mail: glenn@gsds.com
www.gsds.com
(Wall-mounted train display shelves)

Hobby Innovations (Vinylbed)
1789 Campbell Rd.
Mountain City, TN 37683
Phone: 423-727-8000
(Vinyl roadbed)

The Ink Well
P.O. Box 3053
York, PA 17402
Phone: 800-946-5935
(Miniatures for O gauge layouts)

Johnny "O"
11016 Burbank Road
Burbank, OH 44214
Phone: 330-624-0942
www.johnnyogauge.com
(Assembled wood structures for O gauge)

Laster Hobbies
P.O. Box 51253
Philadelphia, PA 51253
Phone: 888-469-0404
(Layout accessories and tinplate tools)

McDonald Models
895 Prospect Blvd.
Waterloo, IA 50701
Phone: 319-233-0545
(Custom-painted rolling stock)

Model Building Services
264 Marrett Rd.
Lexington, MA 02421-7024
Phone: 781-860-0554
http://home.att.net/~aarnannstu/mbs.html
(Structure kit assembly services)

Rail Rax
786 Seely Ave.
Aromas, CA 95004
Phone: 800-830-2843
(Wall-mounted display shelves for O gauge trains)

R. Bishop Model Crafters
P.O. Box 82
Grafton, VT 05146
Phone: 802-843-1012
E-mail: info@modelcrafters.com
www.modelcrafters.com
(Military train models in O gauge)

Retro Displays
P.O. Box 992
Park Ridge, IL 60068
(Display layouts)

Rick Johnson
19333 Sturgess Drive
Torrance, CA 90503
Phone: 310-371-9668
(Molded rubber roadbed products)

Ross Custom Switches
P.O. Box 110
North Stonington, CT 06355
Phone: 800-331-1395
Fax: 860-536-5108
(Custom switches and three-rail track)

RR-Track/R&S Enterprises
P.O. Box 643
Jonestown, PA 17038
Phone: 717-865-3444
www.rrtrack.com
(Sectional track layout planning software)

Scale Models, Arts & Technologies, Inc.
P.O. Box 600505
N. Miami Beach, FL 33160
Phone: 305-949-1706
Fax: 305-947-7458
www.smarttinc.com
(Custom model railroad layout builders)

Scenic Express
1001 Lowry Avenue
Jeannette, PA 15644-2671
Phone: 800-234-9995
E-mail: scenery@ibm.net
www.scenicexpress.com
(Scenery materials of all types for model railroads)

Schrader Enterprises, Inc.
230 S. Abbe Road
Fairview, MI 48621
Phone: 517-848-2225
E-mail: support@railroadcatalog.com
www.railroadcatalog.com
(Decorations and accessories for the train room)

Stoney Express
P.O. Box 526
Tecumseh, MI 49286
Phone: 517-423-5980
Fax: 517-423-5980
E-mail: stoneyex@ini.net
www.stoneyexpress.com
(Finely detailed ceramic structure reproductions)

Toys of Steel
Pat J. Fusco
2028 East 27th Street
Brooklyn, NY 11229-5002
Phone: 718-769-7430
E-mail: trigtrax@aol.com
www.steeltoys.com
(Catenary, elevated track systems, bridges, and structures for O gauge)

T-Tracker
Dept. 2
3735 N.E. Shaver St.
Portland, OR 97212
(Track assembly/tightening device; track accessories)

Valley Model Trains
P.O. Box 1251
Wappingers Falls, NY 12590
Phone: 845-297-3866
Fax: 845-298-7746
E-mail: vmt@idsi.net
www.valleymodeltrains.com
(Big-Buck-Buildings and other kits in O scale)

Wm. K. Walthers Inc.
5601 W. Florist Avenue
Milwaukee, WI 53218
Phone: 1-800-4-TRAINS
E-mail: custserv@walthers.com
www.walthers.com
(Structures and accessories for O gauge)

Woodland Scenics
P.O. Box 98
Linn Creek, MO 65052
Phone: 573-346-5555
E-mail: webmaster@woodlandscenics.com
www.woodlandscenics.com
(Scenery materials of all types for model railroads)

Glossary for Lionel Railroaders

This glossary is presented in two sections. The first section contains common electrical terms and definitions used in model railroading, The second section contains common model and prototype railroading terms that new hobbyists should become familiar with, since they are often used in books and magazine articles relating to Lionel railroading.

If, in the course of reading about prototype or model railroading, you come across a term that is not found here (and there are a great many more terms used in the hobby), be sure to visit the Lionel Web site at **www.lionel.com** where you will find a far more comprehensive glossary of railroading terms.

Electrical terms used in model railroading:

AC (Alternating Current)—Electric current, which repeatedly alternates (cycles) from positive to negative a specified number of times per second (usually 60 cycles in the U.S.). Toy train transformers typically operate on, and output, AC current to run the trains. See also, DC.

Ampere—A unit of measure for determining the strength of electrical flow in a circuit. Most often abbreviated as Amps. The higher the amperage, the greater the quantity of current passing through the circuit. Technically, the amount of current produced by the force of one volt acting through one ohm of resistance.

Block—In prototype railroading, a section of track through which rail traffic is controlled as a unit. In model railroading, commonly the designation for a length of track with an independently controlled power supply, constructed so two or more trains may operate independently on, for example, a simple oval of track.

Cab Control—A system for switching control of a series of blocks on a model railroad so that two or more throttles are capable of controlling operation in those blocks, depending on which locomotive is to use the blocks at any given time.

Circuit Breaker—A device which interrupts an electrical circuit if a short or overload occurs.

Coil—In model railroading, a tightly wound "spool" of thin wire which is a component of electrical devices such as solenoids and electromagnets.

Cold Joint—In electrical work, a soldered connection in which the materials being joined were insufficiently heated to melt the solder and cause it to flow and bond.

Common Ground—In model railroading, the use of a single wire to complete a circuit for numerous track sections or accessories. Eliminates the need for a large number of "ground" wires, one for each accessory or track.

Commutator—The rotating part of an electric motor that contacts stationary carbon brushes to complete the electrical circuit.

Contactor—In model railroading, a switch-like device that fits beneath a section of toy train track, and is activated by the weight of a train passing over it.

Control Rail—In model railroading, any rail fitted with auxiliary electrical connections that allow it to perform special electrical functions, such as the two extra rails in Lionel remote-control track sections. Also, *Insulated* Control Rail: wherein one of the outer, or running, rails of a section of three-rail toy train track is isolated electrically and then connected by wire to an accessory. When the metal wheels of a passing train contact this rail, an electric circuit is completed which causes the accessory to operate.

Convertor—Electrical device for changing Direct Current (DC) into Alternating Current (AC).

Current—The movement or flow of electricity.

Cycles—In electricity, the alternation of the direction of current flow, generally expressed as cycles per second. In the U.S., most household current alternates at 60 cycles per second. Also known as "hertz."

DC (Direct Current)—Electric current that flows in only one direction. Model railroad power packs for two-rail trains typically input AC (household) current, and convert (rectify) it for output as low-voltage DC current to run the trains.

E-Unit—An electrically-activated mechanical reversing device on some model locomotives, especially those made prior to 1990. Most recent model locomotives are equipped with solid-state electronic reversing units.

Electromagnet—A device made of a core of iron or steel wrapped in a wire coil, which attracts other ferrous metals when current is passed through the wire.

Feeder—In model railroading, a power connection from the transformer or power pack to the track, and then on to another portion of the trackwork. Also a short branch road feeding traffic to a main line.

Fixed Voltage Post—In model railroading, a terminal post on a transformer or power pack, which is permanently configured to provide a set amount of voltage at all times. Generally used to power accessories and lamps.

Frog—The portion of a turnout grooved for the wheel flanges; so-named for its resemblance to a frog.

Gauge (wire)—In electricity, a measure of the thickness of electrical wire, generally expressed as a number. The higher the number, the thinner the wire; e.g., 18 gauge is finer than 14 gauge.

Ground—One of the two poles of a battery, transformer, or power pack, which, in conjunction with the "hot" wire from the other pole, completes an electrical circuit.

Hertz—See "Cycles."

Hot Wire—A wire connected to one of the two primary poles of a battery, transformer, or power pack, which provides power to an electrical device (in conjunction with the Ground). A model train transformer may have several "Hot" poles—each providing a different voltage.

Induction—In electricity, the process of creating an electrical field or electrical current in a body that is in proximity to, but not connected with, the generating force; the principal behind voltage reduction in a toy train transformer.

Insulating Track Pin—In model railroading, a small track-connecting pin made of a non-conductive material that substitutes for the metal pin(s) normally used to connect two track sections. Prevents the flow of electricity from one section to the next section.

Insulated Track Section—In model railroading, a modified section of toy train track in which one of the outside running rails is insulated from the metal track ties by fiber strips or some other non-conductive material, and which is further insulated from adjacent rails by insulating track pins; commonly used to operate accessories.

Lock-On—A device used to connect wiring to tracks, especially on a three-rail model railroad. Allows the operator to directly connect wires from the transformer to the outside (ground) rail and inside (power) rail.

Ohm—In electricity, the fundamental unit of electrical resistance. It is a measurement that describes the resistance of a circuit to the flow of electricity passing through it. A greater number of Ohms indicates a higher resistance, or impediment, to current flow.

Parallel Circuit—In electricity, a single electrical circuit serving several electrical devices (such as lamps), each of which is connected directly to both poles of the power source. All devices in the circuit will receive the full amount of electrical voltage available from the two poles. (See also Series Circuit).

Phase or **Phasing**—In model railroading, the connection of two or more transformers in such a way that the continuous movement of alternating current (AC) in all of the transformers from positive to negative is identical. Two transformers that are "Out of Phase" can be corrected by rotating the wall plug of *only one* of them 180-degrees.

Pickup Roller—A device mounted on the underside of a toy train car or locomotive, which contacts the third (center) rail to supply electrical power to the motor(s) or lamp(s).

Polarity—In electricity, the condition of either positive or negative magnetic or electrical attraction, which cause current to flow.

Pole—In electricity, each of the two opposing parts of a battery or other power source, which exhibit attraction for each other, thus inducing a flow of electric current.

Power Pack—In model railroading, normally a train control device configured to convert household AC current to low-voltage DC current that is used for the operation of most model trains that run on two-rail track.

Primary Coil—The lighter wire winding in the core of a toy train transformer that connects directly to the household electrical supply by means of a wall plug. See also, Secondary.

RCS (Remote Control Section)—A special type of Lionel track used for uncoupling and unloading cars through activation of an electromagnet by remote control; replaced by the designation "UCS."

Rectifier—In electricity, a device used to transform alternating current (AC) into direct current (DC). May be used with an AC-type transformer to power equipment, which requires DC current. See also, Power Pack.

Relay—In electricity, an electrically-powered switch which, in turn, effects a change (activates other switches) in some other electrical circuit or circuits.

Resistor—In electricity, a device that impedes current flow, thereby reducing the voltage passing through a circuit; resistance is measured in ohms.

Rheostat—In electricity, a device for adjusting the amount of resistance in an electrical circuit, thereby varying the amount of voltage produced in that circuit.

Secondary Coil—In electricity, the heavier wire winding within the core of a transformer that produces reduced voltage and which connects directly (in model railroading) to the track and accessories. See also, Primary.

Series Circuit—In electricity, an electrical circuit serving several devices (such as lamps) wherein the current passes from one pole of the power source through each device in succession before reaching the other pole. In this type of circuit, each lamp receives only a portion of the total voltage available at the source. For example, if there are two lamps, each receives half the power; if there are three lamps, each receives one-third the power; etc. See also, Parallel.

Third Rail—The center rail on Lionel-type toy train track. On prototype electric, subway, and even some scale model railroads, a third rail for electric current pickup may be located outside one of the running rails.

Throttle—The speed control on a locomotive. In model railroading, a rheostat generally functions as the throttle by controlling the voltage, which reaches the track.

Track Pin—In model railroading, a short metal electrically-conductive rod that is inserted into the ends of toy train track to connect adjacent sections.

Transformer—A device for changing (transforming) high-voltage Alternating Current (AC) into low-voltage AC.

Uncoupling Track—Special section of track in tinplate railroading used to activate couplers by means of a brief electromagnetic charge sent from the transformer.

Variable Voltage Post—In model railroading, the terminal post on a transformer that is connected internally to a rheostat, and provides different amounts of voltage output according to the positioning of a movable control handle.

Volt—A unit of electrical measurement, which determines the level of force or pressure behind an electrical current to force it through a circuit. The greater the voltage, the more powerful the current. Specifically, it is the amount of pressure that will cause one ampere of current to flow through one ohm of resistance.

Watt—The unit of electrical energy expended in powering a device. Wattage is the product of multiplying volts times amps. This term is used to illustrate the top power capacity of an electrical device such as a transformer or light bulb.

Prototype and model railroad terms and definitions:

Articulated Locomotive—A steam-powered locomotive with two separate sets of wheels and cylinders—each of which pivots on separate frames. Certain types of electrically-powered locomotives may also be articulated.

Automatic Coupler—Couplers which couple and uncouple automatically through the use of uncoupling ramps, and permanent or electro-magnets; permits remote operation of couplers instead of manual coupler operation.

Ballast—Cinders, crushed rock, or gravel placed on the roadbed to hold track ties in place and to promote uniform drainage.

Balloon Stack—A widely-flared steam locomotive smokestack designed to prevent sparks from escaping; commonly used on 19th Century locomotives.

Bascule Bridge—A counter-balanced lift bridge, generally used where relatively low-lying railroad tracks pass over narrow waterway channels which must be used by waterborne traffic.

Big Boy—Common name for the largest steam locomotive: a 4-8-8-4 Union Pacific.

Birney—A short, single-truck (4-wheel) trolley car designed for use in congested urban areas where tight track curves are required.

Blind Drivers—Driving wheels without flanges, permitting locomotives to negotiate sharper curves than the wheel arrangement would normally allow; widely used on narrow gauge locomotives. Blind drivers are also used on some model locomotives for the same reason.

Block Signals—A signal or series of signals, usually automatic, which control a block.

Box Cab—Electric or diesel locomotive with a cab shaped like a box.

Branch Line—Secondary line of a railroad.

Bumper—A device for stopping railroad cars at the end of a spur track.

Brill—A type of two-truck, eight-wheel trolley car used primarily in urban areas.

Cab-Forward—A type of steam locomotive (most commonly used by the Southern Pacific) built so the cab portion is at the front for added visibility and safety from smoke and fumes in tunnels and snow sheds.

Caboose—Car for the brakeman and other crew; office for the conductor at the rear of a freight train.

Camelback—A steam locomotive with the cab set astride the boiler. The fireman on this type of locomotive rides under a hood at the rear. Also called a "Mother Hubbard."

Catenary—A system of overhead wires suspended over the track to provide power for electric-type locomotives.

Classification Lamps—Lights (or flags) mounted on the front of a locomotive to indicate the status of the train. White lamps (or flags) indicate an "Extra," while green indicates all sections but the final one of multi-section trains.

Clerestory Roof—Raised center portion along the length of a roof of certain passenger cars featuring "clerestory windows" along the sides to allow natural light into the car.

Climax—A type of geared steam locomotive used primarily by logging railroads. The locomotive's twin cylinders drive a crank-shaft aligned parallel with the axles; power is transmitted to the trucks through an arrangement of bevel gears and a drive shaft; rods couple the axles on each truck.

Consist—The full set of cars which make up a train, usually used in reference to a freight train.

Counterweight—In the context of a steam locomotive, the solid weights on the drive wheels which offset the weight of the engine's crank pins and drive rods.

Coupler—A device at the ends of a car or locomotive used to connect that car to other cars or locomotives.

Crossing—An intersection between two tracks on the same level.

Crossing at Grade (also Grade Crossing)—An intersection between a road or highway and railroad tracks on the same level.

Crossover—Combination of track and switches enabling trains to cross from one parallel track to another.

Culvert—A passageway under tracks for the drainage of water.

Cupola—A small cabin atop the caboose where the brakeman can scan ahead over the roofs of freight cars in a train.

Depot—A station for passengers and freight; term usually applied to a rather small facility in a town or village.

Diamond Stack—A diamond-shaped smoke stack, usually associated with 19th Century locomotives. See also, "Balloon Stack."

Division—That portion of a railroad managed by a superintendent.

Double-header—A train pulled by two locomotives, each with its own crew.

Double Stack (or Stacks)—Intermodal service characterized by shipping containers that are stacked two-high on railcars.

Drawbar—The bar that connects (couples) a steam engine to its tender.

EMD—Electro-Motive Division of General Motors. Manufacturer of diesel-electric and electric-outline locomotives.

ETD—End-of-train device. A box-like apparatus equipped with a flashing warning beacon, and often train status detectors, which is mounted on the end of the last car in a freight train. On most contemporary railroads, an ETD replaces the caboose.

Facing Switch—A turnout (switch) situated with the points facing traffic.

Flange—A protruding lip on a grinder or wheel; the inside edge of a railroad car wheel which guides the wheel and keeps the wheelset on the track.

FM—Fairbanks-Morse. Manufacturer of diesel-electric locomotives, especially opposed-piston types.

Gandy Dancer—Member of a track section gang—so-called because the movements and chants of early track-laying crews resembled orchestrated dancing.

G Scale—Model railroading in a scale of 1:22.5; often erroneously applied to other scales in large scale model railroading such as 1:13.7, 1:20.3, 1:24, 1:29, and 1:32—all of which also operate on #1 gauge (45mm track). See also "Large Scale."

Gauge (track)—The distance measured between the inside top edges of the running rails.

Geep—Slang for a series of Electro-Motive Division (General Motors) road switchers designated as GP-7, GP-9, etc. (GP stands for General Purpose).

Grade—The degree of inclined elevation of the track's surface over a given distance, usually expressed as a percentage.

Heisler—Type of geared steam locomotive used by logging railroads. It has two cylinders arranged in a "V" connected to a drive shaft which, in turn, is connected to the trucks. See also, "Climax" and "Shay."

Helper—The second or added locomotive on a double-header, or a locomotive cut-in to the consist or pushing on the end to assist the train up a grade.

Highball—To run at speed, or a sign to go ahead; so-called from old railroad ball signals, which were hoisted on a pole.

Hi-Rail or **Hi-Railer**—Term commonly applied to toy train operators who prefer prototypical operations and a realistic operating environment on their model railroad—often including scale-proportioned and detailed locomotives, rolling stock, and accessories—even though the track itself may have three rails or an unrealistically high profile.

HO Scale—Model railroad scale in the proportion of 1:87. Pronounced "aich-oh." Roughly half the size of O Scale, or Half-O. The most popular model railroading scale in use today.

Interchange—Junction of two railroads where cars may be transferred from one line to the other.

Intermodal—An inter-mixing of non-rail transportation equipment such as highway truck trailers and overseas shipping containers on railcars—often called "Piggyback" service.

Interurban—A streetcar/trolley-style car used for passenger service (sometimes including light freight and mail service, and often in multiple units) between cities and towns, as opposed to local streetcar service. The term applied to such transportation systems and service in general.

Kit-bash—A term used to denote the making of a model railroad structure, car, etc., from parts of two or more ready-to-assemble kits.

Knuckle Coupler—Couplers on the ends of railroad cars and locomotives (standard in the U.S.) which, when viewed from above, resemble two hands with the fingers bent to grip one another.

Large Scale—Term commonly used to designate all model railroading scales in the nominal proportions of 1:13.7, 1:20.3, 1:22.5, 1:24, 1:29, and 1:32, all of which operate on #1 Gauge (45mm) track. Also, the trade name applied to a line of such model train products produced by Lionel trains. See also, "G Scale."

Layout—In model railroading, the term applied to an arrangement of tracks on a table or platform; also commonly applied to the complete assembly of tracks, accessories, and scenery. See also, "Pike."

Lichen—A moss-like plant which, when dried, preserved with glycerin, and dyed, is commonly used as a scenic decoration to simulate foliage, brush and undergrowth on model railroad layouts.

Main Line (Mainline, Main Iron, Main Stream, etc.)—Through trackage; governed by rules and restricted to travel only by scheduled trains or trains operating with train orders.

Mallet—An articulated steam locomotive named for the designer. The term is generally applied to any articulated steam locomotive. Correctly pronounced "ma-lay."

Modular Layout/Modular Railroading—A type of model railroad layout in which the layout itself is comprised of portable modules constructed to specifications that permit each module to be joined to others, thereby creating a large layout limited only by space and number of modules available.

N Scale—Model railroad scale in the proportion of 1:160. The second most popular (after HO Scale) of the model railroad scales in use today.

Narrow Gauge—Term designating railroad track having a rail spacing (gauge) of less than the North American standard of 4 feet, 8-1/2 inches—typically mining, industrial, and scenic railways which most commonly have rail spacing of either 3 feet or 2 feet. In model railroading, narrow gauge is designated by the modeling scale, followed by an "n" (narrow gauge), and then the modeled track gauge—for example, On3 or HOn2.

O Scale/O Gauge—Model railroad scale in the proportion of 1:48 (nominally, 1/4 inch = 1 foot); includes O scale, O gauge, O27 gauge, and On30, On3, and On2 scale model trains and equipment. The standard track gauge for O/O27 measures 1-1/4 inches between the running rails.

Open-top or **Open-Grid Layout**—A type of layout design which uses a wooden frame with joists, thereby allowing the roadbed to rise and fall beneath the top level of the frame by means of cross members and strips of wood called stringers.

O27 Gauge—Toy train track which has the same distance between the outside running rails as O Gauge (1-1/4 inches), but is lighter in weight, has a lower profile, and measures only 27 inches over the diameter of a full circle. Also, the term applied to O27 trains, which generally are shorter or somewhat smaller than their true O Gauge counterparts—made so to negotiate the smaller-radius curves.

Pantograph—The collapsible, adjustable, "floating" structure which provides electrical contact with overhead wires on an electric locomotive, so-called for its pivoting capability.

Passing Siding—A siding intended specifically for passing complete trains in the same or opposite direction.

PCC Car—Abbreviation for "President's Conference Committee" streamlined-style streetcars and inter-urbans produced from the mid-1930s through the mid-1940s.

Piggyback—The movement of truck trailers on flat cars. See also, "Intermodal."

Pike—A model railroad layout.

Pilot—Correct nomenclature for the guard structure at the front of a steam locomotive, often called a "cowcatcher."

Pilot Truck—(Also lead or leading truck). The truck located in front of a steam locomotive's drive wheels, which, in addition to providing support, helps guide the engine into curves and turnouts. See also "Pony Truck."

Prototype—The real, life-size object on which a scale model is based.

RDC (Rail Diesel Car)—A lightweight, self-powered commuter and/or mail-carrying car often operated in multiple units; manufactured by the Budd Company.

Right-of-Way—The track, roadbed, and property alongside which is owned by the railroad.

Roadbed—The surface upon which track is laid. This surface is usually raised above ground level by rocks topped with wooden or concrete ties, upon which the tracks are laid and then ballasted.

Rolling Stock—Non-powered freight and passenger cars, which are pulled by a locomotive.

S Scale—Model railroad scale in the proportion of 1:64. Popularized by A. C. Gilbert's American Flyer electric trains in the 1940s through the 1960s. Today, American Flyer trains continue to be produced on a limited basis by Lionel, LLC.

Scale—The ratio in size between a model and its prototype, expressed as a fraction or a proportion (for example: 1/48 or 1:48 for O Scale).

Scenicking—Slang term for the application of scenery materials of various types to a model railroad layout.

Scratch-building—In model railroading, the act of constructing scenery, buildings, rolling stock, or locomotives from raw materials by hand, rather than from a ready-to-assemble kit.

Sectional Track—In model railroading, pieces of track in any scale or gauge manufactured to specific geometric proportions, which can then be joined together in straight lines, curves, and circles.

Sectional Layout—A type of model railroad layout made up of various smaller sections that are joined together to form the larger layout; designed this way so the layout can be disassembled and/or moved without destroying any major components.

Semaphore—A trackside signal, which uses a movable arm to convey track occupancy information to the train crew.

Shay—A gear-driven steam locomotive used extensively in logging and mining operations. It has three cylinders mounted vertically on the right side of the boiler driving a crankshaft geared to all axles—sometimes including the tender's axles, when present.

Siding—A section of track accessed off the mainline by means of a turnout. A dead-end siding connected to the mainline by a turnout at one end only is called a "spur." A siding connected by turnouts at both ends is called a "Passing Siding."

Spur—A divergent track (siding) having only one point of entry; a branch line over which irregular service is offered.

Standard Gauge—In model railroading, toy trains larger than O gauge that operate on track measuring 2-1/8 inches between the running rails. Standard Gauge products were introduced by the Lionel Corporation in 1906 and were commonly produced by Lionel and others up until the start of World War II. In prototype railroading in the U.S. (and in some other countries), track measuring 4 feet, 8-1/2 inches between the inside edges of the running rails.

Switcher (also Shifter)—An engine primarily used to move and position cars on different tracks, such as in a yard.

Third Rail—The center rail on Lionel-type toy train track. On prototype electric, subway, and even some scale model railroads, a third rail for electric current pickup may be located outside one of the running rails.

Throttle—The speed control on a locomotive. In model railroading, a rheostat generally functions as the throttle by controlling the voltage, which reaches the track.

Tie—A supporting cross piece—usually of wood or concrete on prototype railroads—that holds the rails of railroad track the proper distance apart (Gauge) and in proper alignment.

Tin-Litho—Tinplate sheets that have been decorated by a printing process known as lithography. A process commonly used in the construction of toy trains in the period before World War II.

Tinplate—Stamped-steel (usually) surfaces that have been coated with a layer of tin to prevent rust and corrosion. Lionel track is tinplated, and this term has, by extension, commonly been used to refer to all toy trains and their operators ("Tinplaters").

Traction—In the context of rail transportation and associated modeling, a term generally used to connote electric trolley, streetcar, and interurban lines and equipment.

Trailing Switch—A turnout or switch whose points face away from oncoming traffic.

Transition Curve—A section of track with a gradually diminishing radius between the straight track and the circular portion of the curve.

TT Scale—Model railroad scale in the proportion of 1:120. Early competitor to HO scale and still being manufactured in limited numbers, but no longer considered a major force in scale model railroading.

Trolley—Name commonly given to a streetcar, which receives its power from overhead electric lines. Also, the name of the pole-like device used to collect and transfer electricity from the overhead lines into the streetcar itself.

Turnout—Generally regarded as the correct nomenclature for a track switch—a device configured with movable rails, which allow a train to enter an alternate route.

USRA—United States Railway Administration. The federal agency established during World War I to manage and coordinate the nation's railroad industry. Subsequently, most commonly associated with the design of a variety of standardized steam locomotives produced during and after that period.

Whyte Classification System—The numbering system used to describe various types of steam engines by their wheel arrangement. The system uses three numbers: one for the number of wheels on the pilot; one for the number of drive wheels; and one for the number of wheels on the trailing truck. For example: 2-6-4 indicates two pilot wheels; six drive wheels; and four trailing-truck wheels.

Wye—A track system comprised of three switches and three long legs of track, which enables an entire train to turn around as a unit.

Z Scale—Model railroad scale in the proportion of 1:220. Introduced by the German toy and train manufacturer, Märklin. The smallest commercially available model railroading scale.